Citizens of the World

POWER, POLITICS, AND THE WORLD

Series editors: Christopher R. W. Dietrich,
Jennifer Mittelstadt, and Russell Rickford

Power, Politics, and the World showcases new stories
in the fields of the history of U.S. foreign relations,
international history, and transnational history. The
series is motivated by a desire to pose innovative
questions of power and hierarchy to the history of
the United States and the world. Books published in
the series examine a wide range of actors on local,
national, and global scales, exploring how they
imagined, enacted, or resisted political, cultural,
social, economic, legal, and military authority.

A complete list of books in the series
is available from the publisher.

CITIZENS OF THE WORLD

U.S. Women and Global Government

Megan Threlkeld

PENN

UNIVERSITY OF PENNSYLVANIA PRESS

PHILADELPHIA

Copyright © 2022 University of Pennsylvania Press

All rights reserved. Except for brief quotations used for
purposes of review or scholarly citation, none of this
book may be reproduced in any form by any means
without written permission from the publisher.

Published by
University of Pennsylvania Press
Philadelphia, Pennsylvania 19104-4112
www.upenn.edu/pennpress

Printed in the United States of America on acid-free paper
10 9 8 7 6 5 4 3 2 1

ISBN 9780812253986 (hardcover)
ISBN 9780812298574 (ebook)

A catalogue record for this book is available
from the Library of Congress.

For Mom, Dad, and Arnie

CONTENTS

Introduction

"The decade is not far distant," declared Lucia Ames Mead in 1904, "when we shall find that the largest organism to which we owe allegiance is not the United States, but the great World—that we are not, first of all, Frenchmen, Englishmen, Japanese or Americans, but we are first of all citizens of the World; first of all, members of humanity." Florence Guertin Tuttle, as she urged U.S. women in 1931 to support the cause of international disarmament, argued, "If you think locally, you may be a good citizen, but you will not be a world citizen, as is today demanded of you." And from the United Nations' founding conference in 1945, Mary McLeod Bethune noted with pride the presence of women and asserted that their involvement "marks their maturing political vision . . . as well as the growing awareness among women themselves of their contributions as citizens of the world."[1]

References to world citizenship such as these were ubiquitous among internationally minded U.S. women and men throughout the first half of the twentieth century. Yet there was no established definition of the term. Many used it, but few tried to pin it down. This book grew from an investigation into whether "citizen of the world" was just an ornamental phrase or signaled something deeper, particularly for women. Within the context of the early to mid-twentieth century, I suspected the latter. Between 1900 and 1950, debates over what role the United States should play on the world stage and debates over who was and who was not an American went on simultaneously. Amid mass immigration, two world wars, a global depression, and myriad social movements, Americans thought a great deal about what they owed to their country and what their country owed to them. For women, in an era when the rights and duties of citizenship extended only in part to some and not at all to others, the concept was especially salient. Women arguing for suffrage, women struggling against Jim Crow, women immigrating to the United States—they understood the contested nature of citizenship, both its equalizing potential and its false promises. It was not a word they used lightly. What then did it mean for these women to call themselves *world* citizens?

For Mead, Tuttle, Bethune, and others like them, the phrase "citizen of the world" was no mere rhetorical flourish. It signaled an intentional discourse, used not just to convey a sense of an interconnected world but to demand an active and equal place within it. That was what differentiated women's use of the term from men's. White men who called themselves world citizens implicitly assumed their equal standing within the global community. Women did not have that luxury.

To them, world citizenship meant three things. First, and foremost for this book, it represented a determination to participate in shaping the global polity, specifically through the creation of an intergovernmental organization or world federation. These women wanted a geopolitical system in which nations and individuals both would be subject to international law. They did not agree on what that system should look like; some supported the confederation model of the League of Nations and the United Nations (UN), while others sought an actual world state. But whatever form the international government took, they all agreed that women had a right to help inaugurate it.

Second, world citizenship obligated them to work for peace. Citizens bear responsibilities as well as rights, and these women asserted the former as much as the latter, though theirs was a moral rather than a legal compulsion. Some were absolute pacifists; most were not. Some believed safeguarding life was their particular duty as mothers; others rejected essentialist arguments about women's role or nature. However, they all believed the foremost purpose of any international government was to end war, and as world citizens they were responsible for furthering that goal.

Third, women embraced the radical equalizing potential of world citizenship, though they did so in theory more often than in practice. Referring to themselves as citizens of the world was an argument for gender equality because, unlike the white men who tended to dominate the realm of international relations, women could not take any form of citizenship for granted. This book also analyzes, however, the varying degrees to which these women incorporated or ignored demands for racial equality and for decolonization in their schemes for international government. Women like Mead and the others agreed that any world system should be responsible to people as well as nations and should represent all world citizens fairly. They disagreed, though, on which people were *full* citizens and on what constituted fairness. For several of them, implicit in their conception of citizenship was a racialized hierarchy that excluded people of color from equal participation in the world polity.

Citizens of the World excavates the work of a variety of women—white, Black, radical, moderate, liberal, socialist—who asserted both their right and their responsibility to shape and fully participate in efforts to govern the world. Between 1900 and 1950, many politically active women in the United States advocated for greater geopolitical integration in order to end war. They argued that increasing global interdependence demanded both governmental coopeeration and a broader commitment to the international community rather than to nationalist entrenchment, and they believed that ordinary women and men around the world had a responsibility to further that commitment. Over these five decades, some women called for agreements to arbitrate and adjudicate conflicts, others for formal intergovernmental institutions, and still others for a full-fledged world federation. They believed a politically organized world, whatever form it took, was necessary for lasting peace. Despite various differences among them—and there were many—all of these women saw themselves as part of a global effort to end war that required them to act as equal members of an international body politic. In other words, they saw themselves as world citizens.

World Citizenship

The idea of world citizenship is not new, but for centuries it remained illdefined. It dates back at least to ancient Greece, and it reemerged in Western thought at various points, including the Renaissance, the Enlightenment, and the late nineteenth century. One of the few historical surveys of world citizenship describes it vaguely as "an individual's consciousness of belonging to a community of the whole of mankind."[2] To some it represented a kind of moral universalism—a conviction that human beings are fundamentally the same and are all subject to the same natural laws. Others used it more loosely to describe a worldly person, a man—and it was almost always a man—who was a traveler, an ambassador, a global thinker. It has often though not always been linked to the idea of world government, signaling the need to bring the people and nations of the world into one united polity in order to ensure peace.[3]

It was not until the 1990s and 2000s that political theorists and others began to interrogate and try to pin down the concept of world citizenship—or global citizenship, which had become the more popular term by that point. Many of these definitions, however, are rooted in the historical context of the time and thus do not translate readily to the early twentieth century, let alone to the more distant past. They are predicated on circumstances such as the end of the Cold War and the perceived decline of the nation-state; the prominence of non-state entities, such as transnational nongovernmental organizations and multinational corporations; technological advances in travel and communication, especially the internet; and greater global awareness of human rights violations, refugee and migrant crises, and environmental degradation.[4] But many of these circumstances did not exist, or existed in much different form, before 1950. One 2010 study, for instance, defines global citizenship as the obligation of every individual to promote human rights for undocumented immigrants, while other scholars offer examples of global citizens that include businessmen, environmental activists, and individuals like Julian Assange and the artist Banksy.[5]

The other problem with most definitions of world citizenship is that they do not represent women as world citizens or examine how the concept is gendered. Theorists tend to imagine the global citizen as an abstract, universal person without gender, race, religion, class, or other form of real identity. Political scientist Hans Schattle, for example, defines a global citizen loosely as anyone who works for the good of all humanity, and he presents evidence from dozens of interviews with self-identified global citizens around the world to show the common perspectives among them. But he never interrogates potential dissimilarities based on gender, race, or any other category.[6] One important exception to this trend is the work of international relations scholar Kimberly Hutchings, who has argued that maternalist peace activists, such as the British women at Greenham Common or the Argentinian Madres de la Plaza de Mayo, expanded conceptions of global citizenship by protesting war explicitly as women and mothers. They thus offer alternative models for the practice of global citizenship that take into account the lived realities of women's lives.[7] But Hutchings remains an outlier among global citizenship scholars.

Given these shortcomings, I have drawn on a combination of contemporary theories to explain what I see happening in the past. My three-part definition of world citizenship—a demand to participate in shaping the global polity, an obligation to work for peace, and a belief in theoretical equality—emerges from current thinking in a variety of fields. First and most important, I build on the work of political theorists, historians, and scholars who have detached the idea of citizenship from the nation-state and shown that it is neither a stable nor a universal category. It is both a status and a practice, both a formal classification and a subjective identity, and it concerns both rights and obligations. It raises questions about belonging, security, and what we owe to whom.[8] Even in this amorphous context, however, the idea of citizenship has retained its tremendous power to legitimize people and practices alike that might otherwise be ignored or dismissed.[9] When U.S. women referred to themselves as world citizens, they were implicitly demanding recognition both of themselves as political actors and of their ideas as worthy of consideration.

Second, I have borrowed from scholars of global citizenship a definition of the term that captures not just a sense of interconnectedness but also arguments for the validity of a cooperative global order and the equality of all members of the global community. "Cosmopolitan citizenship," as some call it, offers a model in which all human beings are responsible to and engage with each other as equals. Within this model, world politics are conducted not by force and coercion but through negotiation and compromise. It thus takes into account the heterogeneity of the world's population and argues everyone should have a voice in determining the future of the planet.[10] Pacifists Lola Maverick Lloyd and Rosika Schwimmer had something like this in mind as they were designing their plan for a world government. They critiqued the great power politics of the League of Nations and provided instead for the universal membership of all nations on an equal basis.

Third, my definition of world citizenship owes much to countless feminist scholars, particularly U.S. women's historians, who have exposed the gendered nature of national citizenship. In the United States, despite the capacious, equalizing language often used to talk about citizenship, the word's meaning has always been contested. In myriad ways it has been predicated on white, able-bodied maleness. For much of U.S. history, women were recognized as "indirect citizens" only through their husbands—assuming those husbands were eligible for citizenship themselves.[11] Between 1907 and 1922, for instance, and later in some cases, women citizens who married noncitizen men automatically lost their citizenship. Only after decades of argument, debate, popular mobilization, and the slow process of legislative change have U.S. women arrived at a point of what might best be described as near equality with regard to citizenship, though white women are still more equal than women of color.

Other feminist scholars have suggested alternatives to models of citizenship based implicitly on men. Political theorist Mary Dietz has pointed out that traditional conceptions of citizenship are predicated on individualism. They assume all human beings are inherently the same, and they are almost always based on a capitalist system of individual competitors. Her

understanding, by contrast, is fundamentally democratic, based on "the collective and participatory engagement of citizens in the determination of the
affairs of their community." Dietz acknowledges that the community may be
as small as a neighborhood or as large as a nation.[12] For the women in this
book, it encompassed the entire planet. In the late 1910s, for example, educator Fannie Fern Andrews developed a grade-school curriculum in world citizenship based on educating children about their responsibilities in the home,
the city, the nation, and the world.

The women profiled in this book believed in the need for collective engagement, but they were also suffragists and voters. They understood that the
individual components of citizenship mattered too. Historians Kathleen Canning and Sonya Rose, while acknowledging the cooperative nature of feminist citizenship practices, do not discount the importance of the individual.
They define citizenship as subjectivity, signifying its nature as both an identity
and a practice that can be personal as well as communal. Most important for
my purposes, they argue that citizenship is a discourse of *claims-making*. In
other words, women, racial and ethnic minorities, and others excluded from a
given political community invoke the language of citizenship to argue for their
membership in that community and for their rights and duties within it.[13] This
was exactly what hundreds of women—the women Mary McLeod Bethune
praised as citizens of the world—did in 1945 when they traveled to San Francisco to take part in the United Nations founding conference.

It is important to underscore that the women highlighted here would not
have recognized my definition of world citizenship. There was no established
understanding of the term between 1900 and 1950, and despite the frequency
with which they used it, none of these women ever explained what it meant to
her. But, taken together, these insights from contemporary scholarship cap-
ture the ethos of these women. They believed in active rather than passive
citizenship. They felt a sense of responsibility to the global community and
worked to ensure not only its peaceful future but also the adequate representation of all its members. Excluded from full national citizenship, women
saw in the world polity opportunities for engagement and equality as well
as for peace. Claiming world citizenship empowered these women on the
world stage. It gave them a language with which to advocate for international
political cooperation. By positioning themselves as responsible world citizens
advancing global participatory democracy, they implicitly critiqued existing
international systems not just because they perpetuated war but because they
excluded the voices of ordinary women and men around the world. Instead,

these women wanted a global governing system based on the active participation, equal representation, and collective obligation of all the world's people.

Citizenship also matters in a national context, of course. Given the prevailing discourses on citizenship among Progressive reformers in the United States during the late nineteenth and early twentieth centuries, when most of the women of this book came of age, their emphasis on active engagement and participatory democracy is not surprising. The political corruption and financial upheaval of the late nineteenth century convinced thousands of men and women that they needed to do more to protect democracy and regulate business. For women, this meant a renewed campaign for suffrage, but it also meant increased activism at the local and state levels to clean up cities, strengthen public schools, and eradicate vice. Jane Addams is a classic example. Fueled by her faith in democracy and her sense of obligation as a privileged woman, she worked for causes ranging from better sanitation services in her Chicago neighborhood to state laws protecting women workers and prohibiting child labor.[14] The democratic ethos that fueled Addams also fueled the women portrayed in this book. Just as Addams did, they took their practices of active citizenship honed close to home and applied them to the world community.

At the same time, however, Addams, Mead, Tuttle, and others understood that they were not full citizens of their own country. Native-born and naturalized women had neither the same rights nor the same obligations as white male citizens. Such women could not vote or serve on juries in most places, could not serve in the military, and suffered taxation without representation. The Expatriation Act of 1907 made them vulnerable to statelessness when they married noncitizens, because they did not automatically gain citizenship in their husband's country after being expelled from their own. The reverse was not true for men, and in fact, most noncitizen women who married U.S. men immediately became citizens.[15] Campaigning for suffrage, equal nationality, and other civil and political rights for decades made women such as those featured in this book very conscious of their second-class status and fed their desire for full and equal participation on the world stage.

At the same time, most white women evinced much less concern for racialized constraints on U.S. citizenship than for gendered ones. The United States had limited access to naturalization on the basis of race since the 1790s, but beginning with the Chinese Exclusion Act in 1882 and culminating in the Immigration Act of 1924, the boundaries of eligibility for naturalization became narrower and narrower. Over the same period, the federal government restricted citizenship for native-born people of color through such strategies as limiting birthright citizenship for Native Americans and people of Chinese descent and formalizing racial categories of second-class citizenship through Jim Crow and Juan Crow laws.[16] The United States also made access to U.S. citizenship more difficult for the populations of territories it acquired after the War of 1898, such as the Philippines and Puerto Rico, by promulgating deliberately ambiguous constitutional interpretations of citizenship that rendered it almost meaningless as a formal status for those people.[17]

Citizenship is an equalizing term in theory, but it has rarely been implemented that way in practice. Many white women reformers in the early twentieth century saw little contradiction in fighting for equal citizenship for themselves but denying it for women and men of color. Leading white suffragists, for instance, had long positioned themselves as naturally superior to all nonwhite people and argued they deserved the ballot before African Americans and others. Susan B. Anthony in 1866 argued that "if intelligence, justice, and morality are to have precedence in the Government, let the question of woman be brought up first and that of the negro last." Forty years later, the National American Woman Suffrage Association demanded that "the women of the United States . . . no longer suffer the degradation of being held not so competent to exercise the suffrage as a Filipino, a Hawaiian, or a Porto Rican man."[18]

Assumptions of white supremacy such as these informed many women's understandings of what it meant to be a citizen. In addition to being active and engaged, it meant being educated, moral, and "civilized." The discourse of civilization prevalent in the early twentieth century and used by several of the women in this book captured the racialized mindset in which people of northern and western European descent believed themselves more advanced than all others, both within the United States and outside it. Even after use of the discourse declined in the 1920s, some women world citizens followed the lead of many white male leaders in arguing that colonized populations would need a period of "supervision" before they were ready to join the world community on an equal footing. Just as they did with national citizenship, many white women thus discounted the claims of people of color to equal world citizenship.

World Government

World citizenship is the first—and more important—of the two interconnected but distinct concepts at work in this book. The second is world

Figure 1. Edith Wynner, left, and Georgia Lloyd promoting *Searchlight on Peace Plans* (New York: E. P. Dutton, 1944). Photo courtesy of the University of New Hampshire.

government. Few among the myriad activists and scholars who have promoted or studied the idea agree on an exact definition. At the most inclusive end of the spectrum are those who see any effort at cooperation among nations as an example of world government. Those at the other end argue the only entity worthy of the name is a full-fledged world state, within which individual nations no longer exist. Most definitions lie between these extremes. In 1944 two young world government activists, Edith Wynner (the subject of Chapter 8) and Georgia Lloyd, catalogued a wide range of existing models and published *Searchlight on Peace Plans: Choose Your Road to World Government*. The criteria they used included a structured international body with some degree of legislative, administrative, and judicial authority; some method of enforcing decisions; and a plan for bringing the organization to life and securing ratification of its existence. The women profiled in this book, like many male world government proponents, rarely offered concrete

details of what such a body would look like or how it would work in practice, but Wynner and Lloyd's loose criteria accurately reflected their collective
understanding.[19]

This distinguishes the term from global *governance*, the phrase used more
often since the 1950s. That concept is broader and even less concrete. Under
its umbrella falls the work not only of governing bodies like the UN and the
World Court, weak though they are, but also of nongovernmental organizations, multinational corporations, and other private-sector entities. Proponents of global governance recognize that individual states and existing
international bodies like the UN do not have the capacity to solve worldwide
problems such as climate change. Critics, meanwhile, point out that all global
entities, including the UN, lack the power to enforce their authority or ensure
compliance with collective measures.[20] That was precisely the problem world
government advocates in the early twentieth century hoped to solve.

Much like the concept of world citizenship, the idea of world government
has existed for centuries, and the two often go hand in hand. Among the earliest plans charted by Wynner and Lloyd were the leagues of ancient Greece; they
also included, as have scholars more recently, the Roman Empire, the Holy
Roman Empire, the Swiss Confederation, the Hanseatic League of Germany,
and the Iroquois Confederacy. As these examples indicate, an entity did not
need to be universal, representative, or democratic to be considered a world
government. In the early fourteenth century, poet Dante Alighieri envisioned
all of the kingdoms of the world united under a global emperor who would
inaugurate a "universal peace [that] is the most excellent means of securing our happiness." In 1795, German philosopher Immanuel Kant published
Toward Perpetual Peace, in which he offered a charter for a "league of peace":
a confederation of nations that would outlaw secret treaties, abolish standing armies, and settle disputes among member nations. And throughout the
nineteenth century, according to many world government scholars, the idea
developed even further through diplomatic efforts such as the Congress of
Vienna, the development of international bodies such as the Universal Postal
Union, and the creation in 1889 of the Inter-Parliamentary Union, through
which representatives from governments around the world came together to
promote international arbitration and other forms of cooperation.[21]

The first half of the twentieth century witnessed endless debates over
whether and how best to organize the world and what role, if any, the United
States should play in that process. Thousands of globally minded Americans
who supported some form of world government participated in those debates.

Beginning in the 1890s, many of them argued that the only sustainable path to peace lay in permanent mechanisms for world cooperation. Conferences on international arbitration at The Hague in 1899 and 1907 seemed a promising start. Participants established the Permanent Court of Arbitration and agreed to submit certain disputes to the court to be settled by a neutral third party. Reformers supported these early endeavors, but some pressed for more, up to and including a genuine world court and a world legislature. In 1909 the World-Federation League, a group of male journalists, editors, and scholars, drafted a resolution calling on President William Howard Taft to appoint a commission to design a world body with legislative and judicial functions. They met with considerable support in Congress, where the House and Senate both passed the resolution, though Taft never followed through.[22] The outbreak of World War I hindered but did not derail such efforts; most internationalists celebrated the Paris Peace Conference and saw the establishment of the League of Nations as the first step toward a global political community.

Although the United States ultimately rejected both the League of Nations and the World Court, U.S. women and men—the former emboldened by their newly enfranchised status—worked throughout the 1920s and early 1930s to persuade their government that U.S. participation in the international political system was vital for world stability. The League of Nations Association was formed in 1923 to continue pressuring the United States to join the League of Nations and to stimulate general enthusiasm for international cooperation. Other groups focused on such issues as disarmament among nations or "outlawry," the campaign to make war illegal as a means of settling disputes among nations. The latter effort resulted in 1928 in the widely touted but practically ineffective Kellogg-Briand Pact. Disarmament proponents disbanded in the early 1930s in the face of Japanese and fascist aggression. Stymied by both the resurgence of militarism and the Depression, most internationalists retreated during the 1930s, though a few bold voices persisted with even more radical visions of world government. By 1942, with the country fully engulfed in World War II, those voices seemed more prescient than preposterous, as many women and men began formulating plans to institutionalize the postwar peace and rectify the shortcomings of the League of Nations. The thousands of observers who descended on San Francisco for the United Nations' founding conference in June 1945 were a testament to the durability of the notion of world government.[23]

After 1945, some Americans, satisfied with the form of the UN, turned their attention to educating the public about its work and encouraging the

U.S. government to participate fully in it. The American Association for the United Nations, for example, the new iteration of the League of Nations Association, lobbied Congress and the Truman administration to confront the growing Soviet menace through the UN rather than unilaterally. Others, meanwhile, in part because they saw how little the UN could do to corral either the Soviets or the Americans, focused their efforts on implementing a genuine world federation with more power and authority. This group came to represent the most popular and transnational push for world government in U.S. history. Tens of thousands of citizens supported the creation of a strong world government, whether by reforming the UN or scrapping it and starting fresh. By 1950, however, rampant infighting and the entrenchment of the Cold War had frustrated many of their efforts.[24]

Between 1900 and 1950, thousands of Americans were engrossed in the problem of creating a global governing body and convincing both the people and the government of the United States to participate in it. But while many scholars have examined this phenomenon, few have recognized that women were just as engrossed as men. Studies of male-dominated organizations such as the League of Nations Association have marginalized the contributions of women to those and other groups.[25] More broadly, numerous recent histories of the League of Nations, the UN, the world government movement, and international law and politics in general have been written as if women were only bit players on the global stage.[26] Examining U.S. women's particular arguments for world government and their assertion of world citizenship provides a more complete understanding of the kind of world these women envisioned and the ways in which they claimed membership in the global community. It also draws attention to the ways in which they were excluded from international institution-building and to the critiques many of them leveled at those institutions.

That exclusion did not discourage women's international activism, of course. As far back as the 1830s, U.S. women had been corresponding and exchanging visits with their activist counterparts in Britain and parts of Europe. Their transnational work for abolition, suffrage, temperance, and other causes culminated in the formation of such groups as the International Council of Women, the International Woman Suffrage Alliance, and the Women's International League for Peace and Freedom (WILPF). Both before and especially after the outbreak of World War I, global peace was a high—if not the highest—priority for internationalist U.S. women. Throughout the 1920s they joined these and other organizations, such as Carrie Chapman

Catt's National Committee on the Cause and Cure of War; they campaigned for disarmament and outlawry; and they pressured the U.S. government to pursue negotiation and compromise rather than the use of force in its foreign policies.[27]

These organizations were dedicated to peace and international cooperation, but they did not prioritize world government for its own sake. Addams, Catt, and others were more likely to see a body such as the League of Nations as an arena in which they could advance other causes than they were to support it as an end in itself. For example, in the late 1920s, members of the International Council of Women, the International Woman Suffrage Alliance, the U.S. National Woman's Party, and other groups launched an extended campaign at the League of Nations to secure equal nationality rights for married women, so that they would no longer lose their citizenship when they married foreigners. The league was thus the site of their activism rather than the purpose of it. Many of the women highlighted here belonged to these and other organizations and worked for similar causes. But they believed a politically organized world was a prerequisite for peace and social advancement and thus devoted more of their time to world government. At times this even set them at odds with their organizations. Lola Maverick Lloyd, for example, was a founding member of WILPF and a faithful volunteer for over thirty years. But she cut ties with the organization in 1942 when the national board failed to endorse her world government plank in its platform.

By 1950, none of these women's visions of world government, whether in the form of a strong UN or a genuine world federation, had been realized. But success is not the sole measure of significance. Women's arguments for world government and their practices of world citizenship represented an alternative reaction to the crises of the first half of the twentieth century, one predicated on cooperation and equality rather than competition and force. At crucial moments between 1900 and 1950, they forced policy makers to contend with their ideas. Rediscovering the activism of these women illuminates the engagement of ordinary people with world affairs and calls our attention to the marginalization of women in the realm of international relations. This book is part of a larger effort not only to recover women's international thought but also to demonstrate how their ideas challenge the perceived inevitability of U.S. military supremacy in the post-1945 world and the presumed superiority of "realist" interpretations of international relations.[28] These women proposed solutions they believed would lead not to decades of armed interventions, proxy wars, and humanitarian crises but to a stable global community characterized by the peaceful settlement of disputes and the equal participation of women.

On a similar note, dismissing these women's ideas for world government as utopian and therefore irrelevant obscures the ways in which women internationalists sought state-sponsored, as opposed to non-state, paths to global community.[29] By the late twentieth century, many Americans had lost faith in the ability of their government to make their lives and their country—let alone the world—better. The rise of global governance in the same period was not a coincidence. International activists for peace, human rights, and other causes turned increasingly to such nongovernmental organizations as Doctors Without Borders and Amnesty International to advance their causes. The women in this book, by contrast, believed that only a genuine government could bring about the changes they sought. What world leaders needed in order to form one, they argued, was public pressure. Mobilizing that pressure was their task as world citizens.

Nine Citizens of the World

The women whose work and ideas provide the foundation for this book came from different generations and were active at different times between 1900 and 1950. They invoked world citizenship in myriad ways and had various perspectives on world government. But they all fit my definition of a world citizen, and their ideas fit under Wynner and Lloyd's definition of world government. Each of the eight chapters centers on one U.S. woman (or a pair of women, in one case) whose life provides a lens through which to examine specific eras and ideas. Chapter 1 focuses on Mead, who synthesized prevailing arguments from women reformers and leading male pacifists into her "practical program for world organization." Chapters 2 and 3 turn to women's views on the League of Nations. The former examines Andrews's efforts in 1919 to strengthen the league's authority and to involve women in its administration; the latter focuses on Tuttle, whose Woman's Pro-League Council advocated for U.S. membership in the League of Nations throughout the 1920s. Shifting forward to the 1930s, Chapter 4 examines Rosika Schwimmer and Lola Maverick Lloyd's radical Campaign for World Government, while Chapter 5 uses Esther Caukin Brunauer as a lens to explore advocacy for collective security among women's groups.[30] Chapter 6 considers women's efforts, especially those of Bethune and the National Council of Negro Women, to influence the formation of the UN. Chapters 7 and 8, finally, turn to the immediate post–World War II era, examining, respectively, Dorothy Kenyon's advocacy for the UN and her work for the Commission on the Status of Women and Wynner's rejection of the UN and promotion of a federal world government.

Why these women? They were not the only ones who used the rhetoric of world citizenship or expressed a sense of belonging to the world community. But their desire for some form of intergovernmental organization was a key component, I argue, of world citizenship in this period. These nine women were not simply promoting an abstract sense of unity among all humankind. They were demanding to participate in shaping a real, tangible global polity in the form of a world government. A structured international body with authority and power was a prerequisite, they believed, for lasting peace among nations and greater equality among human beings. In a different time frame— the mid-nineteenth century, perhaps, or the late twentieth—it would likely not make sense to tie a definition of women's world citizenship so closely to a desire for world government. That desire simply was not as prevalent within American society as a whole, and thus it would not be a good measure for any-one's status as a world citizen. But between 1900 and 1950, world citizenship and world government were closely intertwined. These women practiced the former by working toward the latter.

These nine women, I want to emphasize, agreed on very little beyond their commitment to a politically organized world. Most notably, they dis-agreed on the form and functions of a world government. Many supported the League of Nations and the United Nations as necessary first steps toward a genuine world government, but Schwimmer, Lloyd, and Wynner were out-spoken critics of both bodies. Andrews believed the United States had to lead the world toward greater integration; others contended that any world system would fail if it were dominated by one or more of the great powers. These women also disagreed on the role of force in a world government. Brunauer believed any world government would have to enforce its authority, likely through some sort of international military, while others believed member nations had to renounce the use of force.

They also had different definitions of peace and different ideas on how to achieve it. Schwimmer and Lloyd were absolute pacifists who argued that all forms of war and violence were immoral. Others accepted the necessity of war to secure long-term global peace. Mead, Andrews, Tuttle, Schwimmer, and Lloyd were all founding members of the Woman's Peace Party, the U.S.

precursor to WILPF. They supported women's efforts in 1915 to mediate a neutral end to World War I. When the United States entered the war in 1917, however, Andrews and Tuttle threw their personal support behind the war effort, agreeing with President Woodrow Wilson that it was the "war to end all wars," while Mead, Schwimmer, and Lloyd opposed U.S. intervention. A similar split emerged in the 1930s. As global tensions increased in Europe and Asia, Schwimmer, Lloyd, and Wynner advocated strict U.S. neutrality. They were not isolationists, but they did not support the United States engaging in state-sponsored violence in any form, for any reason. Brunauer, Bethune, and Kenyon, by contrast, joined the growing chorus of Americans who believed the United States could not stand by in the face of atrocities. They endorsed U.S. support for the Allies between 1939 and 1941 and supported U.S. entry into the war after Pearl Harbor.

While they did not all call themselves feminists, they did support women's rights in their own ways. They all were suffragists—or would have been, had they been old enough. Mead and Andrews were typical Progressive-era advocates for women's rights, much like Jane Addams. Women had just as much right to engage in civic and political activity as men, they argued, but their efforts were best directed toward women's "traditional" concerns, including temperance, education, public health, and care for children and the elderly. Tuttle's feminism—she did use the word—was even more maternalist; it was also eugenicist. She believed that as the creators of life, women were responsible for its preservation. For her that meant women, especially mothers, needed not only to nurture their children but also to rid society of such evils as prostitution and child labor and to promote the "spiritual advancement" of the race. None of these three women supported the egalitarian feminism of the National Woman's Party or Alice Paul's Equal Rights Amendment (ERA). Schwimmer and Lloyd—both of whom also called themselves feminists—were the only ones who supported the ERA in the 1920s. Brunauer and Kenyon were what historians usually call social feminists; they opposed the ERA because they feared it would erode women's protective labor legislation. Kenyon in particular, though, was an outspoken supporter of women's rights, including suffrage, equal nationality for married women, and labor protections. Bethune, like many Black women of her generation, did not describe herself as a feminist because she did not believe in fighting for gender equality separately from racial equality.[31] But all of these women supported and worked for various measures to advance women's political, legal, and economic status.

And they all believed women had a right and a responsibility to participate on the world stage equally with men.

Like their understandings of feminism, however, their definitions of equality were neither uniform nor absolute. Mead, Andrews, and Tuttle subscribed to that civilizationist mindset common among Progressive reformers, in which white people had a moral duty to care for and uplift nonwhite people around the world, particularly the colonial populations controlled by the United States after the War of 1898. But these women rarely, if ever, mentioned the status of Black people within the United States. Along with many of their white contemporaries it is likely they saw African Americans as a group to be segregated and excluded rather than educated and assimilated.[32] Schwimmer, Lloyd, and Wynner, by contrast, professed commitments to racial equality, though in fact theirs was simply a milder civilizationist discourse. Schwimmer and Lloyd incorporated into their plan a system of colonial supervision, administered by the world government, that would ensure the development and eventual independence of colonial territories. They assumed colonial populations would have to progress through a period of vicarious representation before they could become equal participants in the world polity. Only Bethune demanded immediate and absolute racial equality within the world community. But her definition of equality was not uncomplicated either; as a womanist she believed in expanding women's rights and autonomy as part of racial advancement rather than in gender equality for its own sake.[33]

They all came with their own priorities and prejudices, but what these women had in common was that they saw the world as an integrated whole and saw themselves as equal members of it. They practiced active membership in the world community by calling for political integration. Unlike many of today's "global citizens," who often operate outside of governmental structures, these women believed that their collective endeavor necessitated intergovernmental cooperation—at the least, treaties and agreements and international laws and, at most, a world federation. They felt a responsibility to the people of the world and to future generations to inaugurate mechanisms that would end war. As Andrews put it, "Citizenship involves obligations beyond our borders."[34]

CHAPTER 1

Lucia Ames Mead's Practical Program for World Organization

At the dawn of the twentieth century, forty-four-year-old Lucia Ames Mead could already look back on two decades of public service. Having grown up steeped in the reform traditions of late nineteenth-century New England, she advocated for causes ranging from housing reform for the urban poor to education for immigrants to women's suffrage. Even as she supported herself throughout her twenties and thirties by teaching music, she dedicated every spare moment to improving her community and furthering her own education. It was not until the late 1890s that she discovered the cause to which she would devote the rest of her life. In 1897, Quaker philanthropist Albert K. Smiley invited her to address the third annual meeting of the Lake Mohonk Conference on International Arbitration. There Mead met a variety of peace activists and learned more about the goals and processes of international cooperation. Though she continued to support myriad social reform movements, the most important issue to her mind from then on was how to organize the world to ensure lasting peace.

She was hardly alone in this conviction. By 1900 peace had become a widely recognized cause in the United States, fed by opposition to the militarism of the 1890s, the anti-imperialist movement that arose in the wake of the War of 1898, and the growing popularity of international arbitration (the use of a neutral third party to settle disputes among nations). Many ordinary citizens argued the United States should not be in the business of using force to resolve conflicts abroad or to subjugate foreign populations. Enthusiasm for arbitration accelerated after the first Hague Conference on International Arbitration in 1899. It represented the first modern effort to create institutional mechanisms for cooperation among nations, and it resulted in the formation of the Permanent Court of Arbitration.[1] Although women's participation in the peace movement was not as widespread before 1914 as it would become during World War I, peace and international arbitration were on the agendas of several major women's organizations, including the Woman's Christian Temperance Union (WCTU), the International Council of Women (ICW), and the National American Woman Suffrage Association (NAWSA). Mead was a member of many of those groups and was especially active in the U.S. National Council of Women (NCW). But unlike other women advocates of arbitration, including Frances Willard of the WCTU and May Wright Sewall of the ICW, she did not confine her activism within such groups' bounds. She attended any meeting, spoke to any audience, and wrote for any outlet where she could promote her cause.

Mead was also one of the only women in the pre–World War I era who pushed her ideas beyond a system of arbitration and developed a gradual plan for world government. When she told her audiences she wanted to "organize the world," she had in mind political cooperation, not just dispute resolution. More than diplomacy, more than treaties or other agreements, she wanted to see a permanent institution where representatives could gather, debate, and even legislate. In the summer of 1903 Mead announced her "practical program for world organization." In speeches to the American Peace Society, the Lake Mohonk Conference, and NAWSA, as well as in the pages of the *Outlook*, the *Club Worker*, the *Advance*, the *Union Signal*, and other outlets, Mead promised that permanent peace was within reach through international cooperation. "'Organize the world' should be our motto," she told NAWSA. "It is not too much to say that the organization of the world is the most important subject for Americans to consider today."[2]

For Mead, being a citizen of the world meant recognizing that she belonged to a global community, an international body politic made up of women and men who believed "civilized" nations had evolved beyond war and now needed to create machinery to govern the world. Her program, she believed, harnessed existing sentiments and channeled them into practical measures to achieve that goal. She also embodied the prevailing conceptions of citizenship in the Progressive-era United States and brought those to bear on her philosophies. She promoted participatory democracy and civic engagement and was an active suffragist. While she would not have called herself a feminist (it is doubtful she even heard the word before the late 1910s), she believed she had just as much right as any man to speak and organize for peace. At the same time, however, Mead adhered to the paternalistic, racialized thinking common in this period. She believed that all people had the potential to become full participants in the global community but also that it was the responsibility of those higher on the civilizational ladder to educate those below them. While this worldview highlights the limits of Mead's global thinking, the programs she proposed laid the groundwork for the dramatic expansion of women's peace activism during and after World War I.

Women's Responsibility for Peace

Mead's commitment to peace and social reform reflected the prevailing attitudes both of late nineteenth-century Boston and of her own family. Lucy Jane Ames was born in Boscawen, New Hampshire, in 1856. Her mother died when she was five, and her father moved the family to Chicago. At fourteen she moved back east to live with her older brother; she graduated from Salem High School in Massachusetts in 1874. She did not attend college, but her maternal uncle, Charles Carleton Coffin, tutored her privately and encouraged her to read widely. Between 1875 and 1886, she supported herself by teaching music; by the late 1880s she had become a full-time writer and lecturer. In 1889, she published *Memoirs of a Millionaire*, a (rather mediocre) novel about a young woman who inherits a large fortune and dedicates herself to various causes, including urban overcrowding and public education. Lucia Ames did not marry Edwin Doak Mead until she was forty-two, by which time she was an established member of the social reform culture of the 1890s.[3]

Mead's philosophies reflected many aspects of early twentieth-century Progressivism that would have been familiar to her contemporaries. She condemned political corruption and the evils of big business, especially after witnessing firsthand the effects of the mid-1890s financial crises on the poor and unemployed in Boston. Raised a staunch Congregationalist, she believed in the Social Gospel and felt a personal calling to help the less fortunate. A self-described "quasi-socialist," she advocated for industrial reform, public works programs, a graduated income tax, and a prohibition against child labor. She was also a suffragist, though for her the vote was just one of many changes needed to transform society. And, as it was for many Progressives, education was key to her program. Not only would it enlighten Americans to the dangers of unregulated capitalism, it would also serve to assimilate and "uplift" immigrants and nonwhite people. Like many women of her generation, she pursued these aims through a variety of organizations, including

Figure 2. Lucia Ames
Mead. Photo cour-
tesy of the Swarth-
more College Peace
Collection.

the Women's Municipal League, the National Consumers' League, and the
Twentieth Century Club.[4]

Mead believed that privileged women bore a particular responsibility for
social reform and had little patience for those who squandered opportunities
to better society. In her 1899 book, *To Whom Much Is Given*, she echoed
Thorstein Veblen's critique of conspicuous consumption, condemning excess
and ostentation, especially at the expense of capability and "noble happiness."[5]
She castigated women who wasted their efforts on leisure and intellectual
dilettantism, reading books just to be able to say they had read them rather
than considering what action they might take as a result. "It is a question,"
she argued, "whether the otherwise praiseworthy book club, magazine club,
and the miscellaneous programs of the average woman's club have not greatly

increased the mental dyspepsia which is undermining a healthy American culture."[6] In combating the evils of the industrial age, Mead believed, privileged women—like herself—had a special part to play.

These were the attitudes Mead brought with her to Lake Mohonk. The Lake Mohonk Conference was emblematic of Americans' growing interest in arbitration as the best method for preventing war. Most conference attendees argued that instead of using an individual or another government as the neutral third party to settle disputes, there should be some kind of body created by participating nations to act as an arbitral court. That court, many believed, would be the germ of a global assembly of nations. The "Hague movement," in fact, invigorated the campaign for a political world organization that had been growing since the nineteenth century and culminated twenty years later in the League of Nations. In the interim, the mantle was born by groups including the long-standing American Peace Society (APS), the Universal Peace Union, and the World Federation League. Most such groups were dominated by men, although Mead served on the executive board of the APS for several years.

The fact that Mead worked with the APS in addition to an organization like the NCW reflected her conviction that privileged women's obligation to work for peace arose more from their status than their gender. Unlike many of her contemporaries, Mead did not think women were any more naturally suited for peace work than men. "We have heard something said about the work for women for peace as being of great importance," she told an audience at Lake Mohonk in May 1902. "I wish it were, but up to-date women have been as ill-informed as men on this great question, and they are as likely to be misled by specious arguments." Women could be just as fascinated as men by "brass buttons" and often subscribed to popular slogans, such as "In time of peace, prepare for war."[7] Mead did not hold *all* women responsible for furthering peace; she targeted the ones who enjoyed the "peculiar privileges of leisure and influence in home and school." On these women, she came down hard: "The work of spiritualizing the nation, of changing its mind, is the special work for its fortunate women, who, protected, respected, and independent in the control of part of their time, are *more than any other citizens to be held accountable if that task is left undone.*"[8]

It was not just in organizational work that women could fulfill this obligation. In some instances, Mead believed, personal interactions were even more important. Privileged women had access to social spaces where they could advocate for peace causes in informal ways, such as cultural exhibits or afternoon teas. "When you ladies sit on the hotel piazza this summer over your embroidery," she told one audience, "you might, with genial, tactful words, accomplish more than many an orator. It is the personal word that counts. Some old lady peering over the [newspaper], thinking to what object she shall leave her money, may, all unknown to you, heed your word."[9] Mead thus encouraged women to use their leisure-class status to their advantage, incorporating subtle efforts toward reform into their everyday social activities.

Other women peace activists took much more maternalist approaches to arbitration. Frances Willard of the WCTU, for example, did invoke women's natural inclinations toward peace. She justified the union's work on behalf of arbitration by setting it within the framework of domesticity. Women were experts on the subject, she argued, because for centuries they had been the "chief member of a board of conciliation in the home, hearing complaints, adjusting differences, forming treaties of peace, administering justice, and anointing the machinery with patience and goodwill."[10] May Wright Sewall, president of both the NCW and ICW, cited the effect of the War of 1898 on women's commitment to arbitration, arguing that "mothers whose sons had been buried in distant islands" had been "roused" to support the cause.[11]

Mead and her contemporaries tied their arguments for peace and arbitration to the battle for women's suffrage. She urged women in suffrage states to vote for representatives who would support arbitration treaties and oppose naval expenditures. She encouraged suffragists to educate themselves on peace causes in order to bolster their arguments about the potential impact of their votes. Once women—even antisuffragists, she claimed—learned "both the appalling and hopeful facts" about the connections between municipal corruption, race prejudice, and labor exploitation, "it will be clear to all women—the givers and nurturers of life—that their first task must be to overthrow that hoary system which involves the grossest injustice to life which still survives from the barbaric past." She also pointed out that Americans who supported militarism and high defense spending in the belief that "government is based on force" were the same ones who opposed woman suffrage.[12]

Others argued that because women bore the brunt of the emotional costs of war, they had more at stake in ensuring its elimination, and they should be able to vote for representatives and measures that would achieve that. An editorial in the *Woman's Tribune* protested the lack of women at the National Conference on International Arbitration, held in Washington, D.C., in April 1896, citing the need for suffrage in order to make women's voices heard on international affairs: "The incident should serve to show women of how little weight they are in movements which are to shape National policy as long as they are disfranchised. If women had been a recognized factor in government, the President of Wellesley College would have been invited as urgently as the President of Harvard."[13] Women activists felt they had a responsibility to work for peace, and they called on their government to let them exercise it.

That responsibility had one further dimension. Mead and her colleagues wanted to reshape Americans' conception of patriotism. Dedication to one's country, they asserted, was not the sole measure of loyalty. "True" patriotism required dedication to all humankind and a respect for other nations. Sewall, in an address to the Lake Mohonk Conference in 1903, articulated her desire for a more globally minded patriotism in which individuals saw themselves as members of humanity, and their nations as part of a global community. "We need that kind of patriotism," she proclaimed, "which shall be neither arrogance nor a maudlin sentimentalism, but which shall be a love of one's country larger than the love for one's self."[14] Mead agreed, contending that a new approach to patriotism was especially needed among schoolchildren. Schools, she argued, in the interest of assimilating immigrants, increasingly emphasized celebration of national holidays, many of them centered on "bragging and bunting and relic-hunting" as well as militarism, guns, and violence. She recounted an illustrative exchange: "What is patriotism?" asked a teacher in Washington, D.C. "Killing Spaniards," replied a student.[15]

Such an attitude proved to Mead the need for a new approach to education, not just in the classroom but in the family and society. That education, she maintained, was largely the responsibility of women. In her 1897 Lake Mohonk address, she spoke extensively on the need for schoolchildren to be educated on the subject of arbitration and "true patriotism." Women, she emphasized, had a special role to play as teachers, both formally within the classroom and informally within the family and society. "Part of the work for arbitration which we, as women, have to do is to begin by teaching in our own circles the fundamental principles of law and order and justice," she told her listeners.[16] Over the next decade, Mead's focus on education to promote peace and arbitration would grow more and more pronounced.

In her organizational work, her writing, and her lectures, Mead did everything she could to publicize the cause of international arbitration, rally support for the first Hague Conference, and encourage discussions of the issue. But while for many women at the turn of the century a system of international arbitration was itself the goal, for Mead it was only the beginning. During these years she began studying theories of world government and formulating her own. She read *The Federation of the World* by Benjamin True-blood, executive secretary of the APS, which declared, "The human race is one race," and posited the "natural" development of global political unity.[17] Through her work with the APS, Mead also encountered the work of Ray-mond Bridgman, a Boston journalist who petitioned the Massachusetts legis-lature in 1902 to ask Congress to "empower and request" President Theodore Roosevelt to convene an international gathering to establish a world legis-lature. Bridgman later published his larger plan for world organization. He envisioned an international system, based on the American federal model, made up of legislative, executive, and judicial branches. Like Trueblood, Bridgman believed that natural impulses were "forcing" the nations of the world "into a formal union, and the consummation is as sure to be reached in the case of the world as it has been reached in the case of the United States."[18]

Mead, however, had little patience for "natural" impulses. In order to har-ness the enthusiasm for international cooperation stirred up by the Hague Conference and the establishment of the Permanent Court of Arbitration, she presented to the American public a concrete agenda for furthering geopolit-ical integration. "Arguments alone will fail to quench the fire" of militarism, she argued. "We must lose no time in building a back fire . . . those definite measures that we must undertake today if we are to circumvent the ambitious or fallacious, who hoodwink press, pulpit and people, in the name of peace."[19] She took it upon herself, therefore, to lay out such measures. As a privileged woman and a patriotic citizen—both of her nation and of the world—it was her responsibility to chart a course by which humanity might end war per-manently. In doing so, and especially in promoting her practical program, she brought together many of the prevailing ideas of the early twentieth century peace movement.

The Practical Program for World Organization

Mead's "practical program for world organization" was her effort to help shape the global polity. In it she synthesized the myriad ideas she had studied for so many years and added a staunch antimilitarism and a few original ideas on how the new world government would work in practice. The program drew on several existing concepts, including Immanuel Kant's faith in rep-resentative government, the Hague model of international arbitration, and Bridgman's vision of a world legislature. Mead melded these approaches and added layers based on her own convictions, particularly the need to combat militarism through disarmament. Finally, she incorporated a plan for an international police force to ensure that violators of international laws would be brought to court. In her speeches and articles publicizing her program, she continued to emphasize the importance of education and women's special responsibility for promoting world organization.

The program itself was simple and straightforward, made up of just six steps. The first two had already been accomplished: (1) the establishment of representative government "in all Christendom except Russia" and the consolidation of countries such as Italy and Germany, and (2) the founding of the Permanent Court of Arbitration in 1901.[20] The first step was important, Mead contended, because in order for a world organization to ensure peace it had to represent the will of the people. She agreed with Kant that pacts among hereditary monarchs would only perpetuate domination of the mighty over the weak.[21] In Italy and Germany, meanwhile, Mead saw proof of the idea that disparate groups could come together and form a national entity that would mitigate war: "Every such voluntary union of small entities to form a larger union means a broader area in which a common coinage and free trade promote neighborliness and peace."[22]

Step two stemmed from Mead's admiration for the first Hague Conference in 1899 and her belief that the Permanent Court of Arbitration represented the seed of a new world government. She referred to the former as "the most momentous conference the world ever saw between sovereign states," comparing it in significance only to the U.S. Constitutional Convention.[23] To her audiences, Mead often cited the number of cases resolved by the court as evidence of its effectiveness, but she understood its limits. It was not actually a court; it was a list of arbiters that nations could select to settle their disputes. Further, no country was obligated to submit any dispute to The Hague. The process was entirely voluntary.[24] But for Mead and her colleagues in the peace movement, the Hague court represented a significant step toward greater geopolitical cooperation. Mead was determined to see the process continue.

Hence came steps three through six. Step three followed logically on step two; Mead called for arbitration treaties between all nations that included promises to submit disputes to the Hague court. She often encouraged her audiences to pressure their senators for such treaties, arguing that those arrangements would "be vastly more efficient than battleships to keep the peace." This ability to pressure policy makers was one of the reasons women needed the vote. "Ballots," Mead pointed out, "can elect the President and the Senate who have sole power to make arbitration treaties."[25]

Step four signaled Mead's ultimate desire for a genuine world government. She called for "the establishment of a Stated World Congress, at first only advisory, but gradually increasing its powers and evolving a code of international law." This would be a permanent body, made up of representatives from individual nations and scheduled to meet at regular intervals. Mead did not take credit for this idea, tracing it back to various proposals of the American Peace Society throughout the nineteenth century and tying it to more recent ones such as Bridgman's. According to Mead, such a congress would have little authority at the outset. Its initial purpose would be to study "increasingly complex international interests" and make recommendations concerning them. At this stage, the real value of the assembly would lie in its ability to "forestall evils, remove friction, develop international law, and lessen the likelihood of war." Eventually, the congress would evolve into a legislature capable of passing international laws. However, Mead assured her audiences that states would not be compelled to submit to those laws until they had been ratified at the national level. She acknowledged that such a process was far from that of a legislative body like the U.S. Congress but argued "it would be an immense step toward such a Congress which must someday come, when we begin to realize the frightful waste and friction that occur when nations are unorganized."[26]

This was the key point at which Mead diverged from her women contemporaries. Willard, Sewall, and other advocates of arbitration did not envision, as Mead did, a progression from treaties and methods for settling disputes to the creation and implementation of international law. While they supported the Hague Conferences and occasionally floated the idea that other international conferences on different topics might be desirable, Mead's colleagues in such organizations as NAWSA or the NCW did not imagine that any world body would have the authority of an actual government.

Mead's fifth step, "gradual proportionate disarmament," was the one nearest to her own heart. Throughout the latter half of her life, Mead's primary motivation was the tremendous waste she saw in pursuit of war—in money as well as in lives. Over and over again she emphasized how much money the United States and other nations of the world were spending on militarism, and she was convinced that if ordinary men and women understood the scale of these expenditures, they would support any measures available to reduce them. "Not one man in a thousand, not one woman in ten thousand," she argued, "has any conception of how the hard earned money of the world is being wasted in the multiplication of armaments." One of Mead's favorite selling points was that one warship cost as much as all the land and buildings of Harvard University, the Hampton Institute, and the Tuskegee Institute combined.[27]

She particularly targeted naval expansion. "An insane ambition has seized a part of the American nation to have a navy proportionate to our size and wealth and importance," she argued to the American Peace Society. She attributed that insanity in large part to Alfred Thayer Mahan, the naval strategist whose *Influence of Sea Power upon History* led to dramatic buildups not only in the United States but around the world. In reality, Mead argued, the United States did not need an enormous navy, given that it was protected on both sides by vast oceans and had no enemies on its own continent. "The devil has never done a cleverer stroke of work," she told the APS, "than to nail the white flag of peace and the symbol of the cross to the masts of the costly, steel-clad destroyers which each nation is taxing itself to build to terrorize its neighbors."[28] As a countermeasure she proposed arms limitation treaties, such as the one signed in 1902 between Chile and Argentina. In that arrangement both countries agreed not to increase their navies for a period of five years without notifying the other and not to sell any naval armaments to any country that had a dispute with the other.[29]

The sixth and final step in Mead's practical program was the creation of "a small armed international police force." She was very clear that she did not want any kind of international military that would be used to enforce international law. Her system relied on negotiation and on sanctions when necessary. But she did see the need for police. "Today," Mead noted, "in thoroughly civilized communities, he who avenges his own wrong becomes a criminal. The State has established a disinterested method of settling disputes according to evidence and justice. Force is employed, but not to settle the dispute. The policeman brings the contestants to a court." This was controlled force, the kind Mead envisioned for the new world organization. A small police force, created by the world legislature and overseen by an executive, would be responsible for bringing to court those charged with violating international law.[30]

Mead's program was well received. The American Peace Society published it as a pamphlet, *A Primer of the Peace Movement*, in 1904. Within three months it had sold more than twelve thousand copies, and it eventually went through several editions and was translated into multiple languages. It was by far the society's most popular publication that year, outselling the runner-up, Tolstoy's "Letter on the Russo-Japanese War," almost two to one. The *Woman's Journal* called it "the most telling arraignment of the war system." W. P. Byles, a Liberal member of Parliament from Yorkshire, recommended it to every attendee of the Universal Peace Congress. And prominent Presbyterian minister Robert Erskine Ely sent a copy to Woodrow Wilson to help him prepare an address to the National Arbitration Congress.[31]

It was popular, but was it in fact practical? It certainly was not radical; it incorporated and built on many existing ideas about world organization. Many internationalists, pacifists and nonpacifists alike, believed nations were trending toward greater political integration. In that regard, a world parliament was not terribly far-fetched, and the idea that such a body could evolve from the international congresses of the late nineteenth century seemed reasonable. Mead did not spell out the exact steps by which that might happen, but then, neither did any of her contemporaries, such as Trueblood or Bridgman. Comparing Mead's program to others offered at the time shows that much of her thinking would indeed have been considered practical—with one important exception.

The Hague Conferences inspired a multitude of plans for world organization. Trueblood's and Bridgman's were among the best known. Hayne Davis, a lawyer from North Carolina, published in the *Independent* essays on a world government based on the model of the United States. He later converted the magazine's editor, Hamilton Holt, to the cause. Holt proposed his own "Constitution of the World" in 1907 and three years later helped organized the World Federation League. Richard Bartholdt, a German immigrant and Republican congressman from St. Louis, was a member of the Interparliamentary Union and brought that group to the United States for the first time in 1904. His goal was to develop the union into an international legislature.[32]

Among world organization proponents, by far the most widely accepted aspects of Mead's program were steps three and four: her demands for the expansion of arbitration, both through greater use of the Permanent Court of Arbitration and the extension of bilateral treaties, and her belief that periodic international congresses, like the first Hague Conference, would slowly develop into a world parliament. With the exception of Trueblood and the APS, which advocated for periodic congresses as opportunities for exchange rather than for lawmaking, every major proponent of world organization in the 1900s included some kind of legislative world body in their plan. Holt's

"Constitution of the World" provided for a general assembly of nations that would meet regularly to debate and adopt international laws. Others were more explicit. Davis laid out a system much like that of the U.S. Congress. Bridgman outlined not only a working legislature but also a world executive to oversee the implementation of international law.[33]

There was less agreement on the issue of enforcement. Early theorists like Trueblood and Bridgman did not believe force would be necessary within a world organization because the moral weight of mankind would ensure compliance. But later thinkers made provisions for a greater use of force. In 1907 Andrew Carnegie proposed a "League of Nations" that would include an international police force to "protect nations from attack" and "enforce the decisions" of the world legislature. Mead's police force, on the other hand, would be employed only to bring violators of international law to court. It would not be used to ensure compliance in the first place. For that, Mead supported the use of economic sanctions. Davis and Holt also later added sanctions to their plans.[34]

This issue of force spoke to the least practical aspect of Mead's plan: disarmament. Mead's most cherished cause was impractical not because it was unpopular but because at the time there was no chance it would ever be implemented. Antimilitarism was widespread in the two decades before 1914, largely in response to U.S. naval expansion. The growth of international arbitration seemed to many peace activists an ideal opportunity to propose arms limitation measures, since disputes could now be settled by nonviolent means. But while some U.S. policy makers were willing to entertain the ideas of arbitration and international law, none was willing to seriously consider disarmament.[35] The United States paid lip service to the idea of international cooperation in this period but would never have relinquished its ability to settle conflicts by force when necessary. Theodore Roosevelt, for example, won the Nobel Peace Prize in 1906 for negotiating an end to the Russo-Japanese War and championed the second Hague Conference the following year. Then he sent the U.S. Navy around the world just a few months later to display American military power.

Other world government proponents, in contrast to Mead, kept any mention of disarmament vague or avoided the topic entirely. Bridgman promised vaguely that with a world court, "the problem of disarmament would be solved." Bartholdt helped pass a congressional resolution calling on President Roosevelt to negotiate more arbitration treaties and "discuss the advisability" of arms reduction. Those discussions never materialized. Davis, on the other

hand, argued every nation should be able to judge for itself the level of armaments necessary to its safety. Holt's constitution was very similar, though it
encouraged nations to negotiate arms reduction as part of arbitration treaties.
By the time of the second Hague Conference in 1907, skepticism on disarmament was widespread, even among internationalists. That year Nicholas Murray Butler, president of the Lake Mohonk Conference, convinced the group
not to include it in their annual platform. It would take a world war for the
issue to gain traction again.[36]

They may have disagreed on disarmament, but Mead and her contemporaries all believed a world organization was inevitable. "A World Legislature,"
Mead proclaimed, "is as definitely bound to come as the Isthmian canal or
the Cape to Cairo railroad."[37] Her comparison to technological progress was
common. Both Trueblood and Bridgman frequently cited the growth of such
bodies as the International Postal Union and such advancements as the inter-
continental railroad and the telegraph as proof that the nations of the world
were drawing closer together. Mead agreed: "International relationships are
increasing with such enormous rapidity, and steam and electricity have made
the globe so shrunk in proportions, that unregulated, haphazard methods are
becoming more and more wasteful and dangerous. Nations must needs [sic]
unite for the common weal in regulating common interests."[38] Her conviction only strengthened after the outbreak of World War I. To Mead, the war
proved not the futility of her program but its necessity.

As a woman, Mead was in a very small minority among world government theorists before World War I. She was routinely the only woman on
bibliographies and study lists related to international government, and
she was one of only a handful of women who held leadership positions in
mixed-sex peace societies. While she rarely discussed these circumstances,
she was undoubtedly aware of them.[39] But women's status in relation to men
was less important to Mead than whether their ideas were heard and taken
seriously. When she proclaimed in 1904 that it would not be long before all
women and men recognized "we are first of all citizens of the world," she
issued a rallying cry for all people to take a more active interest in shaping
the global polity.[40] Her responsibility as a world citizen was to further peace
by promoting her practical program. But writing pamphlets and speaking to
audiences of adults was only one way to do that. In order to ensure the long-
term success of a world government, Mead had to educate younger generations about the necessary steps toward peace and about their obligations as
world citizens.

The Civilizing Power of Education

From the earliest days of her peace activism, Mead stressed the importance of education, both for the general population and for schoolchildren in particular. For her, the way to peace lay not only through governments; it also lay with people, who could be brought to understand the full costs of war and then mobilized to demand change. Educating the next generation of political leaders seemed an obvious way to do that. Boston publisher Edwin Ginn established the World Peace Foundation in 1910 to study the cause of international peace and distribute information to colleges and secondary schools. The Carnegie Endowment for International Peace was established in the same year to promote educational campaigns for peace. Prominent Progressives like David Starr Jordan, president of Stanford University, and Nicholas Murray Butler, president of Columbia University, lectured and wrote widely on the need to educate Americans on the benefits of arbitration and international law. Mead knew Butler in his capacity as president of the Lake Mohonk Conference, and her husband regularly corresponded with Carnegie. She was well aware that when these men promoted peace education, their targets were college students and young adults.

Mead, by contrast, focused on children. Throughout the decade before World War I, she wrote articles, pamphlets, and lesson plans aimed at helping educators integrate peace topics into their curricula. Students should learn, for instance, that patriotism meant "gratitude, unselfishness, and responsibility" rather than aggression or blind allegiance. She suggested the annual observance of Peace Day on May 18, which marked the anniversary of the first Hague Conference. Children could reenact the proceedings, with each child representing a different country, and discuss how arbitration would benefit all nations.[41]

Above all, Mead emphasized teaching children not about the thrill and glory of war but about its costs. This should begin, ideally, even before they attended school. "Begin in your nurseries," she told a NAWSA audience in 1904. "If you want to bring up your children as peace men, do not let them play at killing things." Children should be taught to be statesmen, Mead argued, not warmongers: "Let our youth be taught that it is the weakling and the craven, not the valiant and courageous, who never trusts himself in the world's thoroughfare without a bull-dog and revolver and bowie-knife." She did not seek to banish all mention of war from children's books or school textbooks, but war stories should teach very particular lessons. She recommended, for instance, having students read Émile Zola's *Le Débâcle*, a gruesome account of the Franco-Prussian War. "We need not fear to let children read of war," she believed, "provided they are taught that it is the most savage and most foolish method ever discovered for settling disputes."[42]

In her work for peace education, Mead had no greater ally than Fannie Fern Andrews. Andrews founded the American School Peace League (ASPL) in Boston in 1908 in order to educate children in the principles of world citizenship. Heavily influenced by Mead's ideas, the ASPL in its early years not only distributed her publications but also based much of its peace curricula for teachers on her theories of internationalism. Like Mead, Andrews was an advocate of arbitration and a great admirer of the Hague Conferences. Also like Mead, Andrews believed arbitration was merely the first step in the process of greater world integration. Educating children for world citizenship, both women believed, ensured the future development of the Hague system into a world federation. A generation raised to understand the interconnectedness of the United States with the rest of the world, to respect not only other Americans but all peoples around the world, and to renounce war and embrace arbitration and peace would guarantee the success of a world court and a world legislature. "One generation of teaching the principles of justice, peace, and international unity," Andrews declared to the National Education Association in 1907, "would revolutionize the world."[43]

But it was not just schoolchildren in the United States who had to be taught the responsibilities of world citizenship and the benefits of world government. Despite the universalizing rhetoric of women like Mead, Andrews, and others, their visions of an international community did not, in fact, extend automatically to every human being on the planet. Like many of their white, educated, middle-class contemporaries, these women believed in the racial and cultural superiority of white "Anglo-Saxons," and they often used the language of civilization to elucidate the prerequisites for participation on the global stage. In order to join the world community—including, of course, any sort of political world organization—nations had to learn its principles. They had to demonstrate a capacity for self-government, renounce war and accept arbitration, and embrace and abide by international law. These women's definitions of civilization made clear not only what they expected the new global political order to look like but also who they assumed would belong to it.

Fortunately, to their minds, progress was possible. Many white women reformers emphasized that civilization could be taught. Andrews's curriculum, for example, taught children that U.S. commercial investments went to "South America, Asia, Africa, and Europe itself to do useful work and help bring the standards of civilized endeavor up to the best examples of America and Europe."[44] Hannah Johnston Bailey, chair of the WCTU committee on peace and arbitration, told the Lake Mohonk Conference that "the eyes of the people of all civilized nations are surely opening to the sinfulness of warfare and the righteousness of peace." She pointed to the growth of international law as a discipline in colleges and universities as a sign of progress.[45]

Much of Mead's civilizationalist worldview would have been informed by the War of 1898. In the years both before and after the war, the United States positioned itself as the guardian of "backward" nations and territories, such as the Philippines, Cuba, and Puerto Rico. Between 1898 and 1902, the United States waged a bloody war of pacification against Filipinos in the name of restoring order and bringing civilization to the islands. Over the next twenty years, the United States further imposed its authority on various countries in Central America and the Caribbean. In this period the United States believed it could shepherd foreign peoples toward modernity by imposing U.S. forms of governance, law, economics, education, and social behavior.[46]

This racialized paternalism was built into Mead's vision of a world government. Within the federation of nations that would grow out of her practical program, countries like the United States and Britain would assume authority over nonwhite populations from the Caribbean to Africa to Asia. It would be their responsibility to guide and teach the uncivilized how to participate in the world community. "The inevitable result of forces now at work," she wrote, "will be a federation that must provide control and guidance of the savage races while it would deprive any one nation of the right to dictate or assume authority; it would, therefore, be a world protectorate under which these races would be brought gradually into the family of nations."[47] Mead thus delineated who was and who was not qualified for full membership in a world government. Even as she wrote and spoke on behalf of her own practical program—as she demanded to participate in shaping the world polity—she made clear that her idea of equality had limits.

Mead was a staunch anti-imperialist, but that term had varied meanings in the early twentieth century. She did not believe the United States should be involved in the forcible conquest of other nations and peoples for its own aggrandizement, nor did she want her government wasting its resources on pacifying and annexing Cuba and the Philippines. But many anti-imperialists, Mead included, did support what some Americans thought of at the time as more "benevolent" forms of intervention. She believed Cubans and Filipinos should be educated in some fashion toward eventual self-government and involvement in the world community. For Mead, the problem in the Philippines was that the United States never planned to grant the country independence. But she took no issue with the United States' control of the archipelago. Given that not all populations were equally advanced or prepared for self-government, it was only natural that "a period of tutelage" would sometimes be necessary. Mead championed the "true parental attitude, which always recognizes the potential and ultimate political equality of the weak with the strong," and she contrasted that with "the imperialistic view, which recognizes nothing of the kind."[48] In other words, she would have supported U.S. authority over the Philippines within the context of a world government but not in a colonial context marked by violence.

Mead professed—and was no doubt sincere in—her opposition to militarism, imperialism, and territorial aggrandizement, but that did not mean she was immune to the civilizationalist thinking of her time. The combination of industrialization, mass immigration, and U.S. territorial expansion in the late nineteenth century resulted in a potent American nationalism that shaped much of the United States' engagement with the world in the early twentieth century and, consciously or not, shaped much of the thinking of white, middle-class reformers like Mead and her contemporaries. Many peace activists in this period adhered to racialized ideas about progress that positioned white Euro-Americans as the standard to which all others should aspire. Whether a nation settled disputes through negotiation and compromise or through violence was one way these activists measured that progress. Both before and after 1914, this view made it easy for advocates of world government to distinguish between those who belonged in the global community as equals and those who did not.

The American Peace Society reissued Mead's *Primer of the Peace Movement*, in which she first published her practical program, five times before 1914. For the sixth edition, which appeared in early 1915, Mead wrote a new preface. "The world now stands at the turning point of human history," she declared, "and the fate of civilization hangs in the balance." Among the world's great powers, "the United States, alone free and unmenaced, bears a stupendous responsibility to help the nations at the war's end to attain a permanent peace. Its peculiar privilege is to show the way to a United World." As the leading neutral nation, the United States would have to take the lead in the postwar peace process. The most important step in that process, according to Mead, was the implementation of "World Organization—as sound and healing a remedy for world anarchy as it has been for three-quarters of a century while the physicians of peace have offered it to blind and stubborn governments who now cry out in anguish because they had not taken it."[49] Mead's anger at world leaders for not having taken steps to prevent the war was shared by Jane Addams and others who organized the International Congress of Women at The Hague in May 1915. There they took up Mead's mantle and laid the groundwork for women's involvement in the post–World War I peace process.

That so many women, Addams included, knew so much about peace by 1915 was due in no small part to Mead. Her speeches, pamphlets, books, and articles reached audiences across the country and publicized her practical program as well as her suggestions for educators and her belief in the responsibilities of privileged women to improve society. Not content to stop at arbitration, Mead pushed her internationalist ideas further than many of her contemporaries and developed a gradual plan for world government. Her ability to synthesize the most popular plans for world organization, layer them with antimilitarism in ways that would resonate strongly with Addams and others during the war, and circulate them among popular audiences was unique among prewar world government theorists. Many of her ideas laid the groundwork for the women's peace movement that emerged during and after World War I.

Mead's world citizenship thus manifested itself as a demand to shape the global polity through her practical program, a strong sense of responsibility to work for peace, and a civilizationist definition of equality that was in fact racialized and hierarchical. Like many of her contemporaries before 1914, both women and men, she believed the advanced nations of the world were progressing steadily toward permanent peace, and she felt certain her program could play a key role in that process. Through her arguments for suffrage as well as for world government, she implicitly asserted women's equal right to participate on the world stage and their equal responsibility for the welfare of the global community. For Mead equality was not absolute; it was limited by race and nationality. But safeguarding the welfare of the global community encompassed the obligation of privileged women to educate others in the principles of world citizenship. That obligation was what motivated Fannie Fern Andrews.

CHAPTER 2

Fannie Fern Andrews and
an American-Led World Order

At Lucia Ames Mead's memorial service in 1937, Fannie Fern Andrews paid tribute to a woman she considered both a colleague and a mentor. She described their first meeting. Mead called at Andrews's home on December 24, 1907, at about eleven o'clock in the morning. "Almost immediately," Andrews related, "she said, 'Are you interested in the Peace Movement?' 'I don't know,' said I. 'Do you know,' said she, 'how many school buildings could be built with a million dollars, the cost of one battleship?' I said, 'No.' 'Well,' she said, 'do you believe in war?' 'Of course not,' I exclaimed. Thereupon, Mrs. Mead talked to me about an hour and a half, and I suppose she gave me all the arguments against war that she was accustomed to give a new recruit. At any rate, I listened with the closest attention and wondered why war should still go on." Mead left several books and pamphlets with Andrews, which the latter shared with her husband. The couple stayed up almost until midnight reading them aloud. "Mrs. Mead's Christmas present had clinched the interest," Andrews recalled, "not only of one person, but of two, in the movement against war."[1]

Given that by this time Andrews had already lectured and published on the peace movement and had set in motion the creation of the American School Peace League, Mead's visit could not have been Andrews's *first* introduction to the cause. But the story conveys the appreciation Andrews felt for Mead's guidance. Over the next several years Andrews, like Mead, developed her ideas on educating children for world citizenship. The ASPL produced curricula and other programs for use in classrooms, all of which were heavily informed by Andrews's philosophies on world citizenship and government. She believed American federalism represented the highest form of democratic civilization and should be used as a model not only for other countries but for a world federation itself.

As it did for many Americans, World War I drove home for Andrews the need for a permanent world organization. Much like Woodrow Wilson, she believed the United States had an opportunity to lead the new world order she was sure would emerge after the fighting ceased. During the war she helped found the Central Organization for a Durable Peace and recruited support for its "Minimum Program" for peace. The cornerstones of that program were popular among many internationalists; they included a "society of nations," a permanent world court, provisions for the peaceful settlement of disputes, and the gradual reduction of armaments. While never as well known in the United States as the more conservative League to Enforce Peace, Andrews's Central Organization reflected the thinking of many of her contemporaries—not least because of her beliefs that Americans were best positioned to lead the new world order.

In Andrews's mind, as world citizens, Americans were first among equals. Her school curricula taught children that the United States enjoyed a strong tradition of federalism and tolerance, both of which could be brought to bear on the problem of ending war. But any postwar order would fail, she was sure, without strong American leadership. After the war, Andrews attended the Paris Peace Conference and argued that the United States had to join the League of Nations to ensure that the new world organization would be both American-style and American-led. She was also determined, however, to see women play a significant part in the new league. Along with other colleagues from the United States and Europe, she pressured Wilson to build women's rights into the League of Nations program and make provisions to ensure women's participation. Unsurprisingly, those requests fell on deaf ears.

Other U.S. women internationalists in this period agreed with Andrews's arguments that the league should advance gender equality, though many of them also subscribed to her particular brand of nationalistic internationalism. Members of the newly formed Woman's Peace Party, led by Jane Addams, and members of international suffrage organizations not only echoed popular calls for a league of nations but also demanded greater world citizenship as part of the peace process. They wanted the extension of women's suffrage around the world, equal representation in the League of Nations, and political processes to ensure that control of international relations would remain in the hands of parliaments, the people's representatives, rather than presidents and prime ministers. Andrews supported and participated in much of this work. However, while by the spring of 1920 she could rejoice in the existence of the League of Nations, her hopes that the United States would lead the new world order, like the hopes of her colleagues that women would become full world citizens, were not yet realized.

Education for World Citizenship

Andrews's faith in education stemmed from her own background as well as from prevailing trends of the Progressive era. Born in Nova Scotia in 1867, Fannie Fern Phillips grew up as one of seven children in a working-class family in Lynn, Massachusetts. Her parents encouraged her to pursue her education; she attended public schools and eventually graduated from the Salem Normal School in 1884. She taught for six years before marrying Edwin Andrews, a prosperous local businessman, and moving with him to Boston's Back Bay. Andrews's marriage brought upward social mobility. She now had greater access to intellectual and reform circles in Boston as well as the means to continue her own education; she graduated from Radcliffe College in 1902 with degrees in education and psychology. With a supportive husband, financial security, and no children, she was able to devote her time and energy to her chosen cause. Education was her life's work. Before founding the ASPL, she gave most of her time to the Boston Home and School Association, which she founded as a kind of early parent-teacher association, despite not being a parent herself.[2]

The growth of the international peace movement in the early twentieth century, especially in the wake of the first Hague Conference, awoke in Andrews the "Hague spirit," as she called it, and she wondered how she could contribute her own expertise. Education, she was sure, was key to the movement's success; the question was how to deploy it. "Nothing had ever entrapped my imagination like this engaging problem," she later recalled.[3] In an address to the American Social Science Association in September 1907—the same time the second Hague Conference was meeting in the Netherlands—Andrews argued that "the phenomenal growth of a world consciousness is the distinctive feature of the twentieth century."[4] Teachers, she believed, had to embrace a new responsibility to instill that consciousness in their pupils. In 1908 she convinced a group of like-minded educators, first in Boston and eventually across the country, to form the American School Peace League "to promote, through the schools and the educational public of America, the interests of international justice and fraternity."[5]

Figure 3. Fannie Fern
Andrews. Photo cour-
tesy of the Library of
Congress, Prints and
Photographs Division.

Andrews belonged to a breed of Progressive reformers who believed
rational, scientific study could be applied to a wide range of social problems,
including militarism and war. In many ways the "Hague movement" encap-
sulated the pre–World War I blending of peace activism and Progressivism.
It was led by men who sought to regulate conflict through the application
of international principles and international law.[6] In that regard the movement relied on the practical application of expertise. Andrews adhered to
this approach; in her mind, peace education should be devised by specialists
and carried out by teachers. To enhance her organization's prestige, Andrews
recruited school principals, district superintendents, and university faculty
members to serve on the ASPL board and to staff its executive committee.
Most were men. While teachers, most of whom were women, were her primary audience, they were rarely involved in the league's leadership. To a large
extent this reflected Andrews's own elitism; she believed in top-down leadership rather than any kind of grassroots activism. Throughout her career
Andrews favored associations with prominent men and male-dominated

organizations rather than with women, believing she could be more effective through traditional power channels.[7]

More conservative in her political outlook than either Mead or their more leftist contemporary Jane Addams, Andrews was a peace reformer rather than a pacifist: in other words, she did not oppose war on principle. Unlike later activists who would reshape the movement after World War I, Andrews did not link the cause of peace with other reforms or with broader campaigns for social justice. She was a suffragist—she maintained a membership in the Boston Equal Suffrage Association for Good Government—but did not actively participate in campaigns for the vote or make connections between suffrage and peace activism.[8] Unlike others such as Frances Willard, Andrews never offered gendered rationales for women's involvement in the peace movement. She did point out that as mothers and teachers, women had particular opportunities to educate children about peace, but she did not suggest that their feminine nature made them more suited to do so.

Concerned with keeping the ASPL in touch with established, mainstream peace and education organizations, Andrews maintained close ties with such groups as the National Education Association and the American Peace Society, but the league's primary source of funding in its early years was Edwin Ginn's World Peace Foundation. Ginn was a Boston businessman and philanthropist who made his fortune publishing textbooks. Like Mead, Ginn's commitment to peace and international organization grew out of his attendance at the Lake Mohonk Conferences in the late 1890s. His primary concern was educating the broader public on the necessity of world organization, and he was enthusiastic about Andrews's plans to develop curricula for schoolchildren.[9]

One of the ASPL's central tasks was to distribute material for teachers to use in classrooms. Andrews's thinking on world citizenship and government can be gleaned from much of this material, particularly regarding the obligation of world citizens to work for peace. The ASPL's core curriculum, *A Course in Citizenship*, focused on educating children for world citizenship. Published in 1914 and coauthored by Andrews and four other women educators, *A Course in Citizenship* presented teachers with monthly lessons for children in first through eighth grades. The idea of the curriculum's designers was that students would learn the basic principles of fairness, cooperation, and goodwill toward others in familiar settings, and then as they grew older, they would be encouraged to apply those principles to broader contexts. Grades one through six centered on the family, the playground, the neighborhood, the town, and the nation. Students learned lessons about friendship, civic responsibility, and other values whose larger role became apparent as they approached grades seven and eight. In these culminating years, students examined the international origins of the United States and the current role of the United States in the "world family." Through these lessons, according to Andrews, children learned how to become citizens of the world: "The child will readily see that being a member of a family, a school, a town, state, nation, and the world, he is a citizen, and therefore has functions to perform in all these relations."[10]

Andrews agreed with Mead and other pre–World War I internationalists that the Euro-American nations were moving slowly but surely toward greater cooperation and that the interconnectedness of the world demanded a system to govern it. *A Course in Citizenship* told the story of the United States as one of relationships with the rest of the world, particularly Europe. Reflecting her own Progressive beliefs, Andrews laid out a plan by which teachers could show students that the growth of international law and of arbitration treaties in the late nineteenth and early twentieth centuries was the foundation of a world federation. Laws had been the means of ending the slave trade, of providing for religious freedom, and of regulating international trade; their next logical application was to end war. She outlined lessons on the Hague Conference and the Permanent Court of Arbitration. Teachers would show students how arbitration worked, how the court functioned, and how a world legislature could grow from these beginnings. "The holding of such periodic conferences," she proclaimed, "has laid the foundation for a Parliament of Nations, which will stand side by side with the International Court, the dream of poets and statesmen for the past three centuries."[11]

For Andrews, there was one clear model for what that parliamentary system should look like: the United States. As a federation of individual states, with a legislature to make laws and a judiciary to settle disputes, the United States served for Andrews as the model of a cooperative association. In this belief she echoed other world government advocates of the day, including Boston clergyman Edward Everett Hale, Tennessee lawyer Hayne Davis, and even Theodore Roosevelt.[12] Many proponents saw the United States as an archetype, with its federal structure, its representative government, and its balance of legislative, executive, and judicial power. "Founded on the idea of democracy," Andrews wrote, "which makes every person responsible for the common good, the United States is distinctly the nation which can extend the idea of human brotherhood throughout the world. . . . The principle of federalism implies a desire to live together peacefully; in it we see the seeds of permanent peace between nations."[13] The historical success of the United States proved to Andrews not only that world federation was possible but also that her country represented the apex of civilization to which the rest of the world could aspire.

That civilization, in her mind, was white. Like Mead and many other U.S. Progressives, Andrews believed both in social progress and in racialized hierarchies. Equality for her meant social and political equality for elite white women. It did not mean racial equality, either for people of color within the United States or for nonwhite populations outside it. *A Course in Citizenship* painted a picture of a nation built by immigrants from Europe, in which people of color were rarely mentioned and always marked as foreign. For instance, there was no discussion at all of Asians or Asian Americans, which is notable but not surprising given the restrictions on immigration from China and Japan and the widespread prejudice against anyone of Asian descent. Nor was there much discussion of African Americans. Slavery was mentioned only in the context of white benevolence: Lincoln served as an example of pity toward slaves and of kindness in emancipating them; European Christians became a model of bravery by outlawing slavery in "civilized" nations. Perhaps the most telling passage was a short one. Toward the end of grade five's lesson on "The Contribution of Each Race to American Life," as suggestions for further reading, coauthor Ella Lyman Cabot listed chapter 2 of Booker T. Washington's memoir *Up from Slavery* and Phoebe Cary's poem "Ready," about a black sailor during the Civil War who sacrificed his life for his (largely white) crew. Immediately following these two entries Cabot wrote, "Through the appeal of these stories the children themselves will be led to honor, understand, and treat kindly any foreigners they may meet."[14] She thus designated all Black people as foreign.

Even Native Americans were foreign. This is striking but also not surprising, again given widespread prejudice as well as the fact their U.S. citizenship status was ambiguous before 1924. Grade two's introduction to "foreign cultures" included a story about "The Forgiving Indian," who took pity on a lost white hunter, sheltered him for the night, and escorted him home. The Indian then revealed to the hunter that he had been to the hunter's house before and chided him, "When an Indian calls on you again, hungry and thirsty, do not say, 'Begone, you Indian dog!'" This lesson fit with the chapter's emphasis on treating foreigners kindly. Several chapters included references to stereotyp-ical stories about how Indians helped the Pilgrims celebrate the first Thanks-giving or how Sacagawea and others guided Lewis and Clark. But they were always treated as a group separate from white Euro-Americans.

Andrews applied these racialized distinctions to people outside the United States as well. For her, as for many U.S. policy makers at the turn of the century, one key marker of civilization was not resorting to violence to settle disputes. A nation's commitment to negotiation and arbitration—the ideals of the Hague movement—signaled its readiness to participate in the world system. Just as individuals used courts rather than duels or street fights to demand justice, nations should turn to international tribunals instead of armed conflict. Efforts to further the growth of world peace and the use of international arbitration were thus integral to Andrews's definition of civiliza-tion and progress.[15] By this measure, such nations as the Philippines and Cuba marked themselves as uncivilized simply by resisting U.S. imperialism. The fact that they not only rejected benevolent American assistance but also used force to do so violated all the standards the United States had erected to mea-sure their capacity for independence. As the *New York Times* noted shortly after the outbreak of the U.S.-Philippine war in 1899, "The Filipinos have chosen a bloody way to demonstrate their incapacity for self-government, but it has been effectual."[16]

Andrews's materials for the ASPL demonstrated both her belief that world citizenship could be a powerful tool for ensuring international cooperation and that "uncivilized" people would, like schoolchildren, need to be educated in its precepts before they could be full participants in the world polity. For her, these were the responsibilities of world citizenship: to promote peace and to civilize. Individual Americans as well as the United States as a whole had their parts to play. "The child should be shown," she wrote near the end of *A Course in Citizenship*, "that just as he has duties in the smaller community, his nation has duties and privileges and responsibilities in the family of nations." In performing those duties, young Americans were strengthening not only their own country but also the world and everyone in it: "By his doing what he can toward bringing the world into a closer community of interest he is not only working to the great advantage of his own nation, but also to the advan-tage of the family of nations and of the people of the world themselves."[17] The global responsibilities of the United States had to be carried out by its citizens. Through the ASPL and its curricula, Andrews was doing her part to shoulder that obligation.

World War I and the "Minimum Program" for Peace

Andrews's sense of responsibility shifted with the onset of World War I. She remained committed to educating schoolchildren for world citizenship, but the work of the ASPL took a back seat during the war to the necessity of educating the American public about the need for a permanent world organization. She sensed "the general revulsion of feeling against this war," she told a colleague, and believed the time was ripe to discuss long-term peace.[18] But Andrews was no pacifist. She refused to sign a petition sent to her by an ASPL member calling for an immediate cessation of hostilities. "Although an immediate armistice might seem to be the best thing to work for," Andrews wrote, "I believe if barbarism predominates sufficiently to compel nations to resort to brute force, then brute force must be the arbiter. . . . The appeal to the nations will come when the battles have ceased."[19] Once the war had started, Andrews believed it needed to be fought to the end; only then would the time be right for a solution that would end war permanently. This perspective put her at odds not only with members of her own organization but also with the majority of U.S. peace activists, most of whom sought a mediated end to the conflict throughout the first three years of the war.[20]

Andrews focused her efforts on the Central Organization for a Durable Peace (CODP), formed by emissaries from both belligerent and neutral nations at The Hague in April 1915. Members of the Netherlands Anti-War Council, who initiated the meeting, sought to coordinate a close study of what had led to the current war and formulate methods for avoiding future ones.[21] Andrews was invited because she knew many of the Dutch men who planned the gathering through her correspondence with experts in peace education throughout Europe. She was the only U.S. representative and one of the only women in attendance. Nonetheless she took a lead role, helping to craft what the group called a "Minimum Program" for lasting peace.[22]

The nine-point program reflected the influence of the liberal internationalist ideals—peaceful settlement of disputes, equality of large and small nations, national self-determination, free trade, and reduction of armaments—that had increased in popularity throughout the United States and Western Europe since the 1890s. Many of the points thus also foreshadowed the fourteen Woodrow Wilson proposed in 1918. Point one targeted the Central Powers, especially Germany, declaring "no annexation or transfer of territory shall be made contrary to the interests and wishes of the population concerned," while point two recognized the nationalist sentiments that had sparked the war, particularly within the Austro-Hungarian Empire: "The states shall guarantee to the various nationalities, included in their boundaries, equality before the law, religious liberty and the free use of their native languages." Like Wilson and many other liberal internationalists, however, the CODP did not intend that guarantee to extend automatically to colonial territories outside Europe. Their primary concern regarding those territories was to end mercantilism and ensure a greater degree of free trade for the world's commercial powers. Point three, for example, read, "The states shall agree to introduce in their colonies, protectorates and spheres of influence, liberty of commerce, or at least equal treatment for all nations." Point nine, meanwhile, reflected a different strand of contemporary thinking. It declared "foreign policy shall be under the effective control of the parliaments of the respective nations. Secret treaties shall be void."[23] The idea that foreign policy should come under democratic control was popular among internationalists during this period, who believed that secret alliances among old world powers had dragged the whole of Europe into World War I.[24]

Andrews, though, was most interested in points four through eight, which concerned the "society of nations" to be developed once the war was over. The Hague Conferences would continue and become the germ of that society, although the degree to which states might eventually federate was not clear from the Minimum Program. In addition to the existing Hague Court of Arbitration, point five called for a permanent Court of International Justice and an International Council of Investigation and Conciliation. These three bodies would have the capacity to resolve any dispute brought before them. Point six provided for the imposition of sanctions; in the event that "any state should resort to military measures" rather than submit a dispute to the Hague system, "the states shall bind themselves to take concerted action, diplomatic, economic or military." Points seven and eight concerned the reduction of armaments. The former simply said "the states shall agree to reduce their armaments," while the latter proclaimed the freedom of the seas "in order to facilitate the reduction of naval armaments."[25] Taken together, these points did not go so far as to call for a world legislature, but they did provide for an international judiciary as well as the means to enforce collective security among member nations.

In May 1915 Andrews returned to the United States, where she quickly assembled an American branch of the Central Organization and focused on publicizing the Minimum Program. She recruited several prominent internationalists, including Jane Addams, Emily Greene Balch, David Starr Jordan,

Louis Lochner, Edwin Mead, and Anna Garlin Spencer, and encouraged them to educate the public about the need for a permanent international organization. The peace settlement itself, she predicted, would involve only the belligerents; without strong public interest Andrews feared a punitive and unjust peace. "It is evident," she wrote to Jordan in May 1916, "that people do not understand how important the peace settlement conference is. . . . If the public sentiment of the world were against . . . measures which involve permanent injustice, the peace settlement conference would be made on a peace basis and not on a war basis."[26] Andrews was confident that a "world congress," held separately from the main peace conference, could establish the new world order. This congress, involving not just the belligerents but "the whole body of civilized states," would lay the foundation for the system of international law outlined in the Minimum Program and set in motion a permanent "League of Peace."[27]

Though she never reflected on it, the Minimum Program undoubtedly appealed to Andrews because she, like Woodrow Wilson himself, sought to remake the world order in the image of the United States. Wilsonianism carried with it the seeds of a messianic nationalism, in the form of a belief that Americans had a God-given mission to redeem the world.[28] "Making the world safe for democracy" required active intervention and leadership on the part of the United States to ensure a world order free from war and to protect the territorial integrity and independence of all nations. Andrews was fully on board with this idea. In the revised edition of A Course in Citizenship, published in 1918, she wrote, "The United States is peculiarly fitted at the present time, the greatest crisis of the world's history, to take a leading part in the struggle for liberty and justice. World democracy is but the expansion of American faith."[29] As she toured the country gathering support for the Minimum Program, she tried to convince her listeners that the United States had no choice but to accept its new responsibilities.

Compared to other visions for a postwar organization, the Minimum Program is best described as centrist. It was more extensive and demanded a greater relinquishment of U.S. sovereignty than some plans, and it was less concerned with justice and equality for the world's people than others. The best-known plan was that of the League to Enforce Peace (LEP), which emerged in 1915 among a conservative group of internationalists, including former U.S. president William Howard Taft. The league endorsed a series of resolutions to form "a League of all the great nations" in which all members would create and abide by international laws, all disputes among members would be settled peacefully, and all members would jointly use "both their economic and military forces against any of one their number that goes to war, or commits acts of hostility against another of the signatories" before the matter had been submitted to a judicial tribunal.[30] But there was no mention in the league's platform of any of the other points raised in the Minimum Program—free trade, freedom of the seas, reduction of armaments, or democratic control of foreign policy. Perhaps because of its limited program, and certainly because of the prominent men like Taft at its helm, the LEP became the most popular internationalist organization in the country during the war, encompassing more than four thousand branches in nearly every state by January 1917.[31]

By contrast, one of the most progressive peace programs came from the Woman's Peace Party (WPP), formed in New York in January 1915, and its international counterpart, the International Council of Women for Permanent Peace (precursor to the Women's International League for Peace and Freedom). Initially organized by English suffragist Emmeline Pethick-Lawrence and Hungarian feminist and pacifist Rosika Schwimmer, the WPP quickly enlisted the support of prominent U.S. reformers, including Jane Addams, Carrie Chapman Catt, and Lucia Ames Mead, as well as Andrews. The party's official platform represented U.S. women's first organized demand for peace. Members of the new organization argued that as "the mother half of humanity," women had not only the right but the responsibility to participate in international relations. Their declared purpose was "to enlist all American women in arousing the nations to respect the sacredness of human life and to abolish war." Among their platform issues were the limitation of armaments, opposition to militarism, more widespread peace education, democratic control of foreign policies, women's suffrage, and "action toward the gradual organization of the world to substitute Law for War."[32] In addition to this broader range of demands, a key difference between the women's party and other organizations was the call for a negotiated end to the war. WPP members were not content to wait until the world exhausted itself in battle to seek a permanent settlement. Within a year the party had forty thousand members, although many would drop out when the United States entered the war.[33]

In April 1915, more than 1,100 women from 12 different countries, including Addams, Andrews, and other representatives of the WPP, gathered at The Hague for the first international women's peace conference. The resolutions adopted by the delegates centered on two demands: an end to the war and equality with men. In their "principles of a permanent peace," they expanded on the measures they saw as necessary to achieving those ends. These included respect for nationality; a permanent system of arbitration and conciliation, including a general approval of the use of sanctions; and democratic control of foreign policy around the world, with the stipulation that only systems that included women's suffrage and were based on "the equal representation of men and women" would be recognized as democratic.[34] The delegates also urged the organization of a "Society of Nations," including a permanent international court, a permanent conference with regular meetings, and a permanent Council of Conciliation and Investigation.[35] Such a society, however, to their minds, would not go so far as to constitute a world parliament with legislative authority—showing again that not many women went as far as Mead in that respect.

Several resolutions represented demands for world citizenship. Their resolution calling for women's suffrage emphasized what they could contribute to permanent peace: "Since the combined influence of the women of all countries is one of the strongest forces for the prevention of war, and since women can only have full responsibility and effective influence when they have equal political rights with men, this International Congress of Women demands their political enfranchisement."[36] And it was not just on the national level that women's political participation was essential. The delegates called on the governments of the world "both nationally *and internationally* to put into practice the principle that women should share all civil and political rights and responsibilities on the same terms as men."[37] In other words, in order to guarantee both peace and equality, women had to be full participants in the world polity.

Andrews's membership in all three organizations—the conservative League to Enforce Peace, the moderate Central Organization, and the more radical Woman's Peace Party—reflected both her pragmatism and her real though unstated demand to be taken seriously as a woman. Her primary concern was for a postwar international organization; thus she was willing to support the LEP's platform even though it did not include several points from the Minimum Program or the demands for gender equality from the Woman's Peace Party. Andrews served as platform secretary at the women's conference, which means she would have helped craft the language of the resolutions. Despite that, she never made any suggestion that the program of the Central Organization should include a demand for gender equality, nor did she ever mention during the war the need for women to participate directly in the peace process. Yet she clearly believed they should. In her advocacy for the

Minimum Program during the war and in her work first to shape and then to participate in the peace conference, Andrews took for granted her right to contribute to the establishment of a postwar world order. She never offered gendered rationales for her activism; she never suggested that women's nature or their social roles as mothers gave them special authority as peacemakers. She simply went about her business as though she had as much right to be there as any man.

Once the United States entered the war in April 1917, Andrews and other internationalists concentrated on trying to influence the peace conference that would follow it. As Wilson began to discuss publicly his support for a league of nations, she kept a close watch on both domestic and international progress toward that goal. When Republican opposition to the idea began to emerge, Andrews wrote to her own senator from Massachusetts, Henry Cabot Lodge. "I was born a Republican and have always been one," she told him, "and I therefore feel very much disturbed to think that the Republican Party of the United States should place itself in the awkward position of opposing a constructive measure that has been accepted by all liberal-minded thinkers throughout the world."[38] Despite her party affiliation, Andrews greatly admired Wilson, and she no doubt watched with pleasure as he outlined his hopes for the peace settlement in early 1918. His "Fourteen Points" dovetailed in many ways with the CODP's Minimum Program, though none of them went quite so far as Andrews likely hoped. Wilson called for "open covenants of peace, openly arrived at," but not for full democratic control of foreign policy. He supported "absolute freedom" of the seas and "adequate guarantees . . . that national armaments will be reduced to the lowest point consistent with domestic safety." He also included the removal of trade barriers "among all nations consenting to the peace," though he made no mention of a broader "liberty of commerce." Wilson called for the "free, open-minded, and absolutely impartial adjustment of all colonial claims," based on the principle that "the interests of the populations concerned must have equal weight with the equitable claims of the government whose title is to be determined." Such "adjustment" went further—potentially—than the Minimum Program, which included nothing resembling colonial autonomy. On the other hand, the CODP provided for legal and civil protections for national minorities, which Wilson did not mention. Wilson's proposals for territorial adjustments in and around Europe—Russia, Belgium, France, Italy, Austria-Hungary, the Balkans, Turkey, and Poland—generally conformed to the CODP's principle of respect for nationality, but he did not include any points related to the establishment of a permanent international system for justice and arbitration.[39]

Most famously, of course, Wilson called for a "general association of nations ... for the purpose of affording mutual guarantees of political independence and territorial integrity to great and small states alike."[40] His determination to inaugurate such a league was the key factor in Andrews's continued support for him throughout the closing year of the war. As world leaders prepared to gather in Paris to negotiate the peace, Andrews was optimistic that her vision of a postwar international organization, led by the United States, would soon be a reality.

Women Respond to the League of Nations Covenant

Andrews was in attendance when Wilson read the first public draft the Covenant of the League of Nations to a plenary session of the Paris Peace Conference on February 14, 1919.[41] Thanks to the help of the U.S. commissioner for education, whom she knew through the ASPL, she traveled to Paris as an official representative of the U.S. Bureau of Education. The experience had a profound effect on her. "There was not a person in that vast hall," she later wrote, "who did not feel that something new had transpired in the life of the world."[42]

The first public draft of the covenant outlined the structure of the proposed league. It reflected many of the principles advocated by WILPF and Andrews's Central Organization, though not some of the key ones. The long-sought society of nations would take the form of a general assembly, to which all members would belong, and an administrative secretariat. The main power of the league rested in the smaller Executive Council, made up of nine members, including the "Big Five"—Britain, France, Italy, the United States, and Japan. But neither the assembly nor the council would have any legislative authority, and they were not judicial or arbitral bodies. The draft merely said the council would "formulate plans for the establishment of a permanent court of international justice." Likewise vague was the language on disarmament. Article 8 acknowledged that "the maintenance of peace will require the reduction of national armaments to the lowest point consistent with national safety," but said only that the council would "formulate plans for effecting such reduction." There was no provision in the draft for the democratic control of foreign policy, nor was there any mention of protecting the rights of national minorities. It did include the article most important to Wilson, in the same language later adopted in the final version: all members of the league would pledge themselves to respect and to guarantee one another's territorial integrity in the face of "external aggression."[43]

Reaction in the United States was swift and, at least initially, favorable. In the days before public opinion polls, observers relied on newspaper surveys and other measures to gauge popular sentiments. Their best estimates were that in the spring of 1919 around half the population supported joining the League of Nations, with another 20 to 30 percent in favor of joining with reservations. The other quarter of the population rejected the idea of the league outright.[44] Members of the League to Enforce Peace were largely supportive, despite the covenant's lack of clear provisions for an international court, although many favored amendments to protect U.S. interests, particularly the Monroe Doctrine.[45]

For Andrews, the league represented the embodiment of the international cooperation for which she had worked so long. She saw the covenant as "the only hope for an organized and peaceful world."[46] But she believed the draft could be improved. To that end she participated in two separate gatherings of nongovernmental observers in Paris. The first was the Conference of Delegates of Allied Societies for a League of Nations, a group hastily organized by LEP leaders in Paris to coordinate the work of like-minded associations in various countries. Representatives from France, Britain, Italy, and other nations as well as the United States met in Paris for a week at the end of January and again in London in March. Ultimately they called for greater authority for the General Assembly, relaxation of the provision for unanimity on the Executive Council, a stronger international court, and more specificity in the disarmament provisions.[47] Andrews also joined a group of women from the International Council of Women and the International Woman Suffrage Association that called themselves by the rather cumbersome name International Council of Women and Conference of Women Suffragists of the Allied Countries and of the United States. This group, according to Andrews, regarded the League of Nations "as the great hope of the world" and fully supported it. They felt it their duty, therefore, to respond to Wilson's "historic appeal to public opinion" to weigh in on the covenant. The group of women channeled their demands into five resolutions and presented them to Wilson and the League Commission on April 10, on behalf of the more than twenty million women around the world represented by the ICW.[48]

First, they asked for the league to be more representative. Given that it was "demanded by the masses of the people" that in order to be effective it had to be democratic and representative and that "half the people of the world are women," the group declared that "women should be equally eligible with men" to serve on the governing bodies and the permanent commissions. Second, they wanted specific provisions to curb prostitution and human trafficking. Third, given that the commission members purported to recognize "the right of peoples to a free self-determination" and that the league could not be fully representative as long as women lacked a political voice, they demanded that the covenant call for women's suffrage throughout the world. Fourth—this was where Andrews's influence was most evident—they called for the covenant to contain a provision for an international bureau of education. Finally, they requested a comparable international bureau of hygiene.[49]

These were demands of world citizenship. These women were asserting their right to help shape the League of Nations, and they demanded recognition of that citizenship in two forms: representation in the league bodies and an official call for equal suffrage around the world. In other words, they wanted not just to participate in the new international organization. They also wanted to ensure that it more accurately reflected and could more fully respond to the interests of women.

Andrews was generally pleased with the results of their efforts when the final draft of the covenant was presented on April 28. Article 7 explicitly stated that "all positions under or in connection with the League, including the Secretariat, shall be open equally to men and women," while Article 23 provided for the suppression of trafficking in women and children.[50] The covenant made no mention of suffrage, but Andrews reported that "the peace treaty gives full recognition [of that demand] in that it provides that in all the plebiscites to be taken under the League of Nations, women shall be consulted equally with the men as to the fate of their country." Nor did the covenant provide for a bureau of education, but she noted that members of the League Commission had expressed support for one. Based on this precedent of having their petitions heard, Andrews believed, women could look forward to continue playing important roles in the league once the treaty was ratified. U.S. women could join with others around the world to make the league "a living instrument for the betterment of the human race." Quoting Ishbel Aberdeen, president of the ICW, Andrews declared, "This is an opportunity for women to show the value of their new citizenship."[51]

Members of WILPF also made demands as world citizens, though they had a very different reaction to the covenant. Convening in Zurich in May 1919, WILPF strongly condemned the provisions of the Versailles Treaty. It benefited the "conquerors" at the expense of the defeated nations, demanded unfair standards for German disarmament, and condemned millions of people to "poverty, disease and despair, which must result in the spread of hatred and anarchy within each nation."[52] On the League of Nations itself, members were divided. One camp, headed by Mead, supported the league, arguing that despite its shortcomings—to Mead's mind, particularly its weaknesses on universal disarmament—it still represented the world's best hope for permanent peace. Another camp, led by socialist Ethel Snowden of Britain, believed the covenant beyond redemption, and urged the conference to condemn the league as "simply a League of Conquerors against the conquered."[53]

In the end, the Zurich delegates compromised. They applauded the league but argued that as written, the covenant "in many respects does not accord with the fourteen points laid down as the basis for present negotiations, contains certain provisions that will stultify its growth, and omits others, which are essential to world peace." Among the principles WILPF wanted the league to embody were open membership to any nation that wished to join, disarmament on equal terms for all member states, and "adherence to the principle of self-determination in territorial adjustments and matters of nationality." They also wanted to add specific terms to the covenant, including democratic elections of executives, protection of the civil and political rights of minorities, a requirement that "all backward races under the tutelage of more advanced nations should be put under the guardianship of the League," and the establishment of universal suffrage and full gender equality. Finally, while the delegates applauded the covenant for providing for women's participation in the league, they wanted more. WILPF demanded not only a statement of equality but explicit recognition of women's "service to the world not only as wage earners but as mothers and homemakers." In addition to suffrage they called for equal protection under the law, equal access to education and professional training, and equal pay.[54]

Despite having been a founding member of the Woman's Peace Party, Andrews was "not in sympathy with the meeting" in Zurich, as she told a friend. Given her strong, if qualified, support for the league, she was shocked by such an adverse reaction. She saw WILPF's critiques as nothing less than a condemnation of the entire covenant. "To my mind," she wrote her friend, "people who are standing against this instrument are deliberately obstructing the realization of the only plan proposed to save the world from anarchy and desolation."[55]

But the U.S. women in Zurich were not the only ones who believed the covenant was fundamentally unjust. Florence Guertin Tuttle, a writer and reformer from Brooklyn who would later go on to head the Woman's Pro-League Council, also called attention to the lack of equal representation for women. The covenant ignored the "first fundamental of democracy," she claimed, which was that "all the people shall be directly represented. No man, no group of men, can truly represent the manifold aspirations of women. Surely we have progressed beyond the argumentative platitudes of vicarious representation."[56] Lola Maverick Lloyd, a wealthy reformer from Chicago, pointed out the lack of not just women's voices but also the voices of the world's people in general. She called for more democratic control over the league through the direct election of national representatives. "Choosing our own agents, that's democracy," she wrote. "But the people's will is remote indeed from the proposed Supreme Council of the League of Nations."[57] Jessie Wallace Hughan, a socialist and radical pacifist who went on to found the War Resisters' League in 1923, particularly criticized the mandate system, which was the quasicolonial relationship set up after the war between European countries and territories in Africa and the Middle East. Hughan pointed out that there was no mention in the covenant of "curbing the sway of the imperial nations" or providing for "the self-determination of subject states."[58]

Despite their varying levels of support for the league as it existed and the differences in their criticisms, these women shared some fundamental concerns. They wanted the league to serve the people of the world, and they sought to ensure—through sufficient representation, direct elections, and equal suffrage—that the voices of those people would be heard in Geneva. It is important to note that these were not the typical critiques levied by male internationalists in the United States, who were more likely to be concerned with the lack of a clear system of international law. But while Wilson and other world leaders in Paris may have paid lip service to the idea that the league was "for the people" of the world, most of its mechanisms were, as Lloyd pointed out, "remote indeed" from ordinary citizens. These women remained undeterred, however; all three continued throughout the 1920s to try to influence the direction of the league.

Andrews likely would have agreed with Tuttle's critique, though it is doubtful she would have endorsed either Lloyd's or Hughan's. Andrews was an elitist, wary of too much democracy. She strongly supported the mandate system as proposed in the covenant; when she heard Wilson read that part of the draft in February 1919, she believed "every person in that vast hall in the French Foreign Office felt that a new plan for the treatment of the backward peoples of the world was really coming to pass." Despite not holding any of the official league mandates, Andrews believed the United States had a vital role to play in those parts of the world, particularly the Middle East. She cited the growth of American colleges in the region, noting that promoted "moral and intellectual betterment" in addition to "harmony and friendly cooperation among the different races." The United States' only interest in the region, Andrews asserted, was "the welfare of the inhabitants of the country. There is no oil question here."[59] This statement was either wishful thinking or naïveté, given that all of the world's major powers, including the United States, had a significant stake in the fate of the oilfields on the Arabian peninsula.[60] Andrews persisted, though, in proclaiming the United States' benevolent disinterest, urging her government to send a representative to sit with the league Executive Council during its discussions of the mandates.

But Andrews need not have worried about too much democracy within the league. The great powers had little interest in making it truly representative. The league's framers—Wilson not least—cared very little about the ordinary people of the world except in the abstract. The best evidence for that is the empty promise of "self-determination." While that phrase enjoyed global popular appeal in 1919, its applications were always intended to be limited.[61] Unfortunately for Andrews, members of WILPF, and others, those limits extended to women. Their demands for equal representation and participation, including their calls for suffrage, signified the same desire for self-determination as demands for national independence, but they would suffer the same fate.[62] Andrews's and other women's calls for equal world citizenship went largely unheeded in 1919, but they would continue to shape women's involvement with the league and their international organizing over the next two decades.

Like many American internationalists, Andrews knew the fight for the league in the United States would be hard, but throughout much of 1919 she remained confident the U.S. Senate would eventually ratify the treaty. Both the future peace of the world and popular will seemed to her to demand it. Despite her own political affiliation, Andrews supported Wilson and the league with unceasing devotion. Throughout the summer of 1919 she published several pieces refuting Republican criticisms of the covenant. The provisions for unanimity, the clear protection of the Monroe Doctrine, and the guarantee against interfering in national disputes should secure Republicans' support, she argued. "The treaty should be accepted as it is," she concluded. "The Covenant of the League of Nations marks an historic pledge of mutual confidence and proclaims a resolve to achieve peace for the world. The Preamble is a magna charta of freedom and equality. It should be committed to memory and should sink into the hearts of all of us."[63] Andrews was prepared to defend Wilson to such an extent that when the international president of the CODP published an article on "Wilson's failure" at Versailles, she promptly resigned from the organization to which she had dedicated herself for four years.[64] Despite her best efforts, however, the U.S. Senate rejected the treaty in March 1920.

The failure of the United States to join the League of Nations ended Andrews's commitment to world organization. Her vision of internationalism was predicated on U.S. leadership; her country could not lead the league if it was not even a member. She likewise lost enthusiasm for the American School Peace League after the war. After so firm a rejection of the international system, the league's arguments for world citizenship education no longer resonated. Its demise may also have been due in part to the first Red Scare, which reached its height in the United States in 1919. That year Andrews changed the name of her organization to the American School Citizenship League, noting that "the word 'peace' is inappropriate, I think, at the present time."[65] Andrews kept up a few of the group's activities, particularly its popular essay contest for high school and normal school students, until the late 1920s, but by 1930 the organization existed only on paper. Andrews herself embarked on another career; she earned a doctorate in international relations from Harvard University in 1923 and went on to study the League of Nations mandate system in the Middle East. This work allowed her to understand methods for, as she put it, "the betterment of backward peoples."[66] Even as Andrews's work for world organization diminished, her faith in the civilizational hierarchy persisted.

Andrews and her contemporaries saw their citizenship—soon to be recognized by the ratification of the Nineteenth Amendment, which gave white women the right to vote—as having an important international dimension. During the war, they felt themselves obligated to look toward the postwar peace. Once it came, their responsibility was to help maintain it and also to urge their country to help. But in addition, they expected recognition of their status as world citizens. Their demands for suffrage, for equal representation in the League of Nations, for full participation in its administration—all signaled that women were prepared to work with men to govern the global body politic. Whether the United States joined the league or not, internationalist women would continue to fulfill those obligations.

CHAPTER 3

Florence Guertin Tuttle Advocates
for the League of Nations

For Fannie Fern Andrews, the failure of the United States to ratify the Versailles Treaty in March 1920 signaled the end of her work for world organization. For other women, that was just the beginning. Many internationalists believed there was still hope that the United States could be persuaded to join the League of Nations, perhaps with reservations like the ones proposed by Henry Cabot Lodge in 1919. But whether the United States signed on or not, they saw the league as crucial to the maintenance of peace in the 1920s. A growing number of these internationalists were women. Inspired by the formation of the Woman's Peace Party during the war and reinvigorated by both the founding of the Women's International League for Peace and Freedom in 1919 and the ratification of the Nineteenth Amendment, women peace activists across the country mobilized in support of various causes, including not only the League of Nations but also international disarmament and "outlawry"—the campaign to make war illegal and punishable by international law. Florence Guertin Tuttle, who had served as a member of the New York branch of the WPP and spoke and wrote in 1919 about the links between women's suffrage and the peace process, enthusiastically joined these efforts to ensure that a disaster like World War I could never occur again. "Surely it is not an accident," she argued, "that the widespread enfranchisement of women and the hour of civilization's greatest peril coincide."[1]

For Tuttle, world citizenship for women meant bringing their maternal instincts to bear on the creation of a world federation, the germ of which she saw in the League of Nations. As mothers, she believed, women had a natural reverence for life and an instinct to protect it. The war had made them citizens of the world as well as of the United States, and as such they had a responsibility to further the development of humankind by supporting the league and encouraging the United States to join. The League of Nations was not Tuttle's ideal international organization; she wanted greater political and economic cooperation among nations as well as a world legislature and a system to enforce its laws. But it was a start, and it was the best one on offer at the time. And without U.S. membership, she warned, it would likely fail. Like Andrews, Tuttle urged her government to accept its responsibility as the leader of the new world order.

She established the Woman's Pro-League Council in 1921 to fulfill that mission. The council never achieved a large membership or reached a wide audience, but through the organization Tuttle was able to articulate her arguments for the league and encourage other women's organizations to keep U.S. membership on their agendas. Many groups, such as WILPF and the League of Women Voters, voiced support for the League of Nations, but for them it was one among many concerns. For Tuttle, however, there was no higher priority than U.S. involvement in the incipient world government. By the middle of the 1920s, she understood she was fighting a losing battle. But as Tuttle and other women internationalists turned their attention later in the decade to other peace causes, including disarmament and outlawry, it was clear how much the rhetoric of world citizenship had permeated their thinking.

The "Psychic" Side of Feminism

Tuttle was of the same race and generation as Mead and Andrews, but in many ways her origins and circumstances were distinct from theirs. She was born in 1869 to a privileged family in Brooklyn, New York. Her father, Pierre, was a French Canadian immigrant who became a successful merchant. Her mother, Lucy Henry, was the daughter of a prominent Virginia family and a descendant of Patrick Henry. The Guertins were well-connected in Brooklyn society. Florence attended the private Nassau Institute until her father encountered financial difficulties; she went to a local public school for a year before being invited back to the Nassau Institute tuition-free. She did not attend college, but like Mead she was an avid reader. In her early twenties she tried to become a professional writer, inspired both by her own passions and a desire to help her family financially. She published a few poems and short stories, but her literary ambitions remained largely unfulfilled. In April 1897 she married Frank Day Tuttle, a wealthy coal merchant, and the two settled in Brooklyn Heights. They

Figure 4. Florence Guertin Tuttle with her husband, Frank, in Palm Beach, Florida, c. 1909. Photo courtesy of the Sophia Smith Collection, Smith College.

had two sons, Frank Day Tuttle Jr., known as Day, born in 1902, and Winnslow Guertin Tuttle, known as Guertin, born in 1904. Florence and Frank were married very happily until the latter's death from pneumonia in 1926.[2]

As a mother, unlike either Mead or Andrews, Tuttle dedicated a considerable portion of her time and energy to the care and education of her children, especially while they were young, and the experience of motherhood profoundly shaped her worldview. The Tuttles could have afforded full-time child care, but Florence chose to supervise her sons' education herself, keeping them out of school until Day was twelve and Guertin was ten. "For me this work was the highest privilege of creation," she later remembered. But she acknowledged that it was not easy, and she lamented her lack of time and energy for her own creative pursuits, especially her writing: "I could not energize as wife, mother, daughter, food specialist, social secretary, director of the commissariat and department of repairs, and bring any but a gasping effort to creative work." Whenever she had a moment alone, she recalled, her mind was "too tired to function." Tuttle's pent-up creative energy burst forth once her sons went to school in 1914, however. "The rare privilege," she recalled, "that I had enjoyed of living closely to my little ones' mental development had given me an authoritative knowledge that I felt other mothers should share."[3] Her first book soon followed.

In *The Awakening of Woman: Suggestions from the Psychic Side of Feminism*, Tuttle presented her particular brand of feminism as a blend of maternalism and eugenics. "Psychic" did not connote anything paranormal; for her the "true meaning of feminism" was "mental and spiritual advancement." Freed by technological innovations from the toil and drudgery of bygone years, with minds awakened by new access to higher education, women now sought personal and social fulfillment. Society's support of their development was crucial not just for women themselves but also because they were the mothers of the race. The aim of feminism, therefore, was the evolution of women and, through them, their children. "The barque of womanhood," Tuttle wrote, "bearing the sacred freight of the children of the future, is turned in the same general direction of creative evolution as that of man. Together they sail on the same seas, moving toward the same goal—the port of a spiritually perfected race."[4]

Tuttle embraced eugenic philosophies, although she interpreted them to fit her understanding of feminism. She read the work of Herbert Spencer and Francis Galton, the Social Darwinists who applied Darwin's theory of natural selection to human societies. They argued for promoting reproduction among the "better" races so that they would more easily prevail over others in the struggle for existence. "I embraced these volumes like a sponge," Tuttle remembered. "Sometimes I became almost mentally inebriated."[5] Her enthusiasm, however, did not lead her to adopt all of Spencer's and Galton's arguments. Unlike many male eugenicists in the United States who decried declining birth rates among white women as "race suicide" and chastised white women to reproduce, Tuttle saw lower birth rates as evidence of "race sanity." For Tuttle the issue was quality, not quantity. In smaller families, parents could pay more attention to each child's education and moral development. Eugenics, in her interpretation, taught both women and men the importance of mothers' education and mental development. By fostering a sense of "race responsibility," eugenics offered a cure not only for overburdened motherhood but also for sexual depravity, the moral double standard, and absent fatherhood. "The spiritual ideal of the Woman's Movement," she wrote, by which she meant a more fulfilling motherhood as well as the general improvement of society, "cannot be embodied without a wider diffusion and comprehension of the science of eugenics."[6]

Tuttle's "Darwinian feminism" enjoyed a small but devoted following in the early twentieth century. While Darwin himself largely adhered to prevailing late nineteenth-century assumptions about women's intellectual inferiority, these women took their cue from a modified version of his theories that emerged in the United States. Unlike "social Darwinists," who used Spencer's take on Darwin to uphold racial and class hierarchies, "reform Darwinists" saw themselves as more progressive. They sought to help society evolve through such measures as worker's rights and women's rights. This approach appealed to Darwinian feminists frustrated with social and cultural traditions that devalued women's reproductive labor. They believed science, as they understood it, offered a more persuasive platform than morality or religion to argue for social reform. These feminists' ideology, like that of most white women at the time, was grounded in assumptions of white supremacy, but their arguments were more subtle than those of mainstream eugenicists, such as Madison Grant and John R. Commons.[7]

Tuttle was also influenced directly by some of the most prominent Darwinian feminists of the time. As president of the Avitas Club, a Brooklyn women's organization, she met Charlotte Perkins Gilman, whose views on the necessity of social support for motherhood Tuttle admired. Much like Tuttle, Gilman embraced eugenics not in the sense of "the ruthless slaughter of the unfit" but in the positive sense of improving the race through "the power and the glory of civilized motherhood." Raised by a single mother, Gilman argued in 1898 that women's economic dependence on men was detrimental to both sexes and that greater self-sufficiency for women, especially through participation in the workforce, would lead to better homes, better families, and a better society.[8] Tuttle never promoted women's economic independence to the extent that Gilman did, but she shared Gilman's views on the importance of motherhood and on the cost to society when mothers were exhausted and undervalued.

The centrality of motherhood was also driven home to Tuttle through her work with Margaret Sanger, whom she called a "noble woman but greatly misunderstood." This association occurred sometime before 1914, though its exact nature is not clear from Tuttle's autobiography. Sanger's work for birth control, Tuttle argued, stemmed from a belief that "over-population was one of the causes of war" and that the "unfit" who were "pouring out of the slums" were a tax on society.[9] Sanger was never an enthusiastic eugenicist, nor was she ever embraced by movement leaders in the United States, largely because they found birth control immoral and had little concern for women's autonomy.[10] Her central argument in *Woman and the New Race*, published in 1920, was that women should be able to control their own reproductive lives. She advocated for a lower birth rate in order to ensure better education and intellectual development and to reduce the number of women and children living in poverty. Tuttle particularly admired Sanger's belief in the transformative power of a free motherhood, allowed to work in its own way and in its own time. Free mothers, Sanger argued, could "save the precious metals of racial culture, fused into an amalgam of physical perfection, mental strength and spiritual progress. Such an American race, containing the best of all racial elements, could give to the world a vision and a leadership beyond our present imagination."[11] It is easy to imagine Fannie Fern Andrews agreeing with this sentiment; Tuttle likewise made the connection between eugenics and world politics.

These ideas were by no means marginal. They emerged among some of the leading women's rights advocates of the era. Carrie Chapman Catt, for instance, echoed many of Tuttle's sentiments about maternalism and race preservation. Arguments that women's suffrage would be defeated because of a natural division between the sexes had been proved false by the outbreak of war, Catt claimed in 1915. She pointed to the war as "a case where men's business of war and women's business of conserving the race have clashed, and women are helpless to defend their own." In such circumstances, Catt argued, "it becomes the terrible business of the mothers of the race to secure the right of a political protest in every nation." Not just in war, but in social causes throughout society, women had special domains to protect and reform, hence their "ceaseless and noisy agitation" for suffrage.[12]

Like Catt and millions of other Americans, Tuttle was shocked by the violence of World War I. She quickly channeled her energy into the peace movement, where her maternalist philosophies informed her perspectives on the need for suffrage as well as for a world federation to ensure lasting peace. She joined the Woman's Peace Party in late 1914, soon after its founding, and served as the vice chair of the New York City branch. It is possible that she met either Mead or Andrews, or both, through the WPP, though there is no record of any acquaintance. After the United States joined the war, Tuttle sided with Catt and others who felt a responsibility to support the U.S. war effort. While volunteering in a canteen at Camp Upton, an embarkation camp in Suffolk County on Long Island, Tuttle experienced an internationalist revelation. "The walls of my patriotism crumbled to include the peoples of the world," she later recalled. "I knew I could never again write of anything, work for anything, speak for anything but practical organization for permanent world peace."[13]

For the next few years, Tuttle devoted much of her energy to the cause of an international postwar organization. Her primary goal was to educate women, not only her colleagues in the peace movement but others as well, on the need for a world federation. In May 1917, as guest editor of the WPP's newsletter, *Four Lights*, Tuttle published a poem she called "A Call to Arms." She called on "humane," "inspired," "reverent" women to rise up and speak out against the "mad blood-letting of nations." She wanted "Patriot Women . . . / Women whose voices rise as National barriers crumble" to help shape "a new World State whose boundaries know no horizon."[14] As she urged women to support the cause, she also appealed to Woodrow Wilson to let them help. The fate of the world lay in his hands, she told him, but he did not need to bear the burden alone—the women of America stood at the ready. "We ask not only for peace, Mr. President," Tuttle wrote, "but also for a place at that peace table where America is to be authoritative. . . . We therefore ask you earnestly to strike off their political fetters that they may be able to aid in this great work of World restoration."[15] On behalf of the WPP, Tuttle asked Wilson for women's suffrage in order that she and her colleagues might help more concretely in the task of postwar reconstruction.

For Tuttle, maternalism, suffrage, and world organization were the integral components of women's world citizenship. As the war drew to a close, she made an explicit connection between America's emerging role as a global power and women's political power as emerging voters:

> Enfranchisement, at a normal period, would but have conferred
> a more direct responsibility toward the city, the state, the nation.
> Enfranchisement at this critical period of our national life, when
> America, urged by the world stress, has abandoned her policy of
> "splendid isolation" and joined forces with the battling nations of
> Europe, places a wider obligation upon the voting American woman.
> She is not merely the citizen of a country. She has become a citizen
> of the world. Her responsibilities are not merely local. They encircle
> the horizon itself. For wherever America now goes, the American
> woman must follow, and whatever moral covenants her country
> assumes, must be weighed, assumed or rejected by the voting Ameri-
> can woman as well.[16]

Women now had both an opportunity and a responsibility to rebuild the world, Tuttle believed. In the post–World War I context, voting was not purely a domestic political issue. As citizens of not just the United States but of the world, women were obligated to pay attention to global issues and to consider seriously how they wanted to support them—or not—through their votes. The end of the war thrust into their hands "the obligation to build the framework of a new world." Tuttle was not the only suffragist who felt this way; the League of Women Voters, successor to the National American Woman Suffrage Association, adopted international cooperation as one of its earliest objectives.[17]

In order to help American women weigh the "moral covenants" at stake in the peace treaty, Tuttle published *Women and World Federation* in 1919. Her goal was to educate women about the underlying principles of world federation so that they could more judiciously support the creation of the League of Nations and consider ways in which it might be strengthened and improved. Like Mead and WILPF, Tuttle advocated for a genuine world federation, not just a loose confederation of states like the league. In her book she reiterated earlier demands similar to Mead's for a world parliament with the power to make international law and in which representation would be "on the most democratic basis possible." She also called for "some sort of proportional representation" to protect national minorities, although she said nothing about representation for colonial populations or about the League of Nations mandates. Citing the extensive secret treaties among the great powers before 1914 that had dragged most of the world into the war, she echoed earlier calls for the democratic control of foreign policy. The people of those nations, she believed, would not have supported the agreements if they had known about them. To the argument that "the people" were not educated enough to understand those affairs, Tuttle responded, "It is doubtful whether ignorance could do any worse for us than the intrigues of carefully instructed diplomats have done." Finally, Tuttle echoed Mead's calls for disarmament and an end to compulsory military training. She supported the reduction of armaments through mutual agreements among nations, but she also wanted an end to private ownership of munitions plants. Those resources should be nationalized, she argued, so that investors could no longer profit from warmongering.[18]

Tuttle also echoed aspects of Andrews's perspective. She believed any world federation should be modeled on the United States and that the League of Nations would fail without strong American leadership. The problem facing the world was very similar to that faced by the American colonists, she contended. The question was how to unite diverse nations, get them to cooperate and defend each other, and structure their relations in a democratic way. The nations of the world had to follow the lead of the original American colonists, who had "dared to think of themselves not as subjects, but as citizens, dared to dream new ideals of the national federation that is a forerunner of that world federation which must ultimately be." The purpose of the world government, according to Tuttle, would be to regulate relations among nations without interfering in their internal affairs, just as the U.S. government did for the states. The world looked to the United States, she maintained, "to be the creator and guarantor of the new world's freedom."[19]

The League of Nations was not everything Tuttle had hoped it would be, but she saw in it the world's best hope for a true federation. She referred to the covenant as the "first framework of a federated world," likening it to the first steam engine on display in a museum, a far cry from mammoth machines of the present. Despite its shortcomings, however, the league had to be made to work, because no alternative plan existed to "check imperialistic ambitions" or forestall another world war. And she laid the responsibility for its improvement as much on women as on men. If the league was not "a human instrument for safe-guarding life" in its present form, then "women must help amend it as the Constitution of the United States has been amended, until it becomes a human instrument for guarding life."[20]

Where Tuttle differed most from Mead and Andrews was in her maternalist arguments, informed by her eugenic ideology, for women's participation in the world polity. Eugenics, she wrote, proved that there was a scientific basis for claiming women had a higher regard for life than men, because "a woman's body is the aqueduct of life to every mortal." Women's instinct to protect life would lead them to support the league, and that support would in turn help the "new world state" abandon the "ancient process of massacre." "Women," Tuttle maintained, "through maternity, have a genuine *race consciousness* that enables them to rise to a real race call." In other words, women's maternal instincts and strength—the same qualities that Tuttle had argued in 1915 were leading them to become better mothers and stronger feminists—would also compel women to support the new world organization in the interest of preserving and furthering the race.[21]

The maternalist and eugenicist emphases in Tuttle's worldview were not the only things that set her apart from many of her contemporaries. She was also influenced by Fabian socialism; she placed heavy emphasis on the "labor problem" and the need for "industrial democracy." For her, such a democracy meant an end to the exploitation of workers, more industrial cooperation, and wider and more equitable distribution of profits. Any woman interested in peace had an obligation to consider the labor problem, Tuttle warned, and to realize that "industrial peace is a fundamental of any genuine world peace." She saw the labor unrest around the world in 1919 as a clamor for justice and an opportunity to establish the new world order on an equitable basis. "The people are on the march," she wrote, "and though the march may be directed it may not with impunity be halted. The goal is industrial democracy. . . . To federate upon anything less is to invite and to perpetuate social chaos."[22]

Tuttle's combination of eugenics and a call for industrial democracy were common among the Fabians. Developed in Britain in the late nineteenth century and popularized in the early twentieth by George Bernard Shaw and Beatrice and Sidney Webb, Fabianism echoed Karl Marx's vision of a cooperative and equitable socioeconomic order but rejected his method of proletarian revolution in favor of gradual change through existing democratic channels. Fabians believed meaningful social change, especially the alleviation of ills caused by industrialization, could be wrought through the state, with economic and social policies designed to curb big business, protect workers, and create a more equal distribution of power. The height of their political influence in Britain came in 1918, when the new British Labor Party adopted the Webbs' *Labour and the New Social Policy* as its post–World War I platform.[23] Tuttle equated the Webbs' manifesto in importance to Wilson's Fourteen Points. Following its lead, she advocated for a national minimum wage; national ownership and control of transportation, communication, utilities, and other industries; a higher income tax; and the dedication of any profit surplus to the "common good"—to education, the arts, and so forth.[24]

She integrated these principles into her vision of a world federation. She wanted the parliament to be able to "equalize commercial opportunities" so that the waterways of the world would be open freely to everyone. She argued for removing barriers to access of raw materials so that no one country should be allowed access under special conditions nor prohibited by special limitations. And she called for the "open door" in all colonial territories rather than preferential trade for the "mother country."[25] Like Andrews's Minimum Program, Tuttle's plan for world federation thus focused more on ending mercantilism and economic competition among commercial powers rather than on any genuine concern for colonized people and their sovereignty.

Despite her focus on economic and industrial issues, Tuttle did not participate in or evince any knowledge of women's international labor activism in 1919. Neither in *Women and World Federation* nor in any of her subsequent writings and speeches did she mention the International Labor Organization (ILO), founded in 1919, or the International Congress of Working Women, which took place in Washington, D.C., in September of that year. Led by members of the National Women's Trade Union League, more than two hundred women from over a dozen countries attended the congress, whose purpose was to influence the international labor guidelines being formulated by the ILO. Both through that meeting as well as through direct participation in the various branches of the ILO, female labor advocates helped shape worldwide labor standards not just for women but for all workers.[26] The best explanation for Tuttle's apparent lack of interest may be simply that she, like Andrews, was an elitist, more involved with women and men of her own upper-middle class than with working women and more comfortable among armchair intellectuals than grassroots activists.

In the final chapter of her book, Tuttle reiterated her arguments that the League of Nations would fail without women's support and conversely that women's best hope for lasting peace to protect the lives of their children lay with the league. While both men and women had a responsibility to promote the league, women had more at stake in its success. Their biological imperative to preserve life endowed them with a greater drive than men to aid in the formation of an international organization to end war. "I have tried to show," she concluded, that "a world league, since it aims to safeguard

life, means more to women than to men, since women through motherhood stand more closely related to the humanities, being under compulsion
not only to create life but to preserve it." Without women's presence, Tuttle
feared the male diplomats of the world would simply fall back into their
great power patterns. Women were members of their national and international communities as well as their local and familial ones, she reminded her
countrywomen, and those memberships were not mutually exclusive: "Citizens are to be national and yet international, as a woman may be a devoted
wife and still be a good mother."[27]

Tuttle's vision of a world federation was thus even more vague than Mead's
or Andrews's. Tuttle had a tendency to confuse terms like *league*, *federation*,
world state, and *world government*, and she often used those terms inter-
changeably. She knew the League of Nations was not really a world federation,
but she offered no definite plan for how it might become one. In keeping with
her writerly ambitions, *Women and World Federation* was more of a literary
promotion of world citizenship and world government than a social scientific one. But the key for her was that women needed to support the league.
Just as women were becoming national citizens through enfranchisement,
the League of Nations presented an opportunity for them to become world
citizens. As such, it was their duty to convince Americans that it was time for
the United States to take its place in the world community.

Unfortunately for Tuttle, the U.S. Senate remained unpersuaded. But her
faith in the progress of humankind toward peace through a world federation was strong enough to carry her through the next few years of continued
advocacy for U.S. membership in the league. Like Andrews, Tuttle believed
world government was the natural result of gradual human development.
What Andrews called civilization, Tuttle called race progress, but they meant
the same thing. They both saw war as a marker of human degradation; truly
civilized, progressive people recognized its futility and barbaric nature. As
long as women could be convinced of their responsibility to aid human progress by supporting the league, Tuttle believed, its long-term success was still
assured.

The Woman's Pro-League Council

Despite the Senate's failure to ratify the Versailles Treaty in the spring of 1920,
many Americans' hopes remained high that the United States would not

only engage in international cooperation but eventually join the League of Nations. The defeat of the treaty spoke not to the United States' desire for isolation from world affairs but to its desire to engage in those affairs on its own terms.[28] Throughout the early 1920s, Tuttle focused her energy on that goal, even if joining meant doing so with reservations. "To say that America will have nothing to do with League of Nations," she argued, "is like Jupiter saying that it will have nothing to do with the solar system, or the heart telling the adjacent organs that it will not be part of the human organism. We *are* in the great world system of nations whether we acknowledge it or not."[29]

To persuade others of that fact, Tuttle founded the Woman's Pro-League Council (WPLC) in March 1921. Its stated aim was to promote international peace, and it favored the league as the best means of maintaining that peace and "terminating the insufferable burden of great military and naval establishments." Council members, according to their founding platform, would work by any means available toward U.S. entry into the league, recognizing that modifications to the covenant might be necessary to achieve that.[30] Tuttle recruited several prominent women to serve on an advisory committee, including Catt, Gilman, suffragist and WILPF president Anna Garlin Spencer, wealthy social reformer Florence Jaffray Harriman, and a young Eleanor Roosevelt, whose husband addressed the council members at a dinner in New York just after the WPLC's founding. But the bulk of the council's work was carried on by Tuttle and her close friend, suffragist and social reformer Harriet Burton Laidlaw. Within two months they had close to fifty local members and had established additional branches in Iowa and Colorado.[31]

What made Tuttle's council distinct from other internationalist women's organizations of the day was its exclusive focus on U.S. membership in the League of Nations. Other peace groups included general support for the league on their platforms, but they tended to concentrate on more specific campaigns to foster peace, such as disarmament. WILPF, which became a powerful force after 1924 under the leadership of executive secretary Dorothy Detzer, threw its energy not just into peace work but voting rights, antilynching campaigns, and the elimination of child labor. This broader agenda made it more effective than a group like the WPLC, but it did not advance Tuttle's cause of world federation.[32] Members of Tuttle's council also differed in their approach to international work from the handful of U.S. women in Geneva who worked at or closely with the league in its early years, as well as from groups like the National Woman's Party, which lobbied the league as part of its campaigns for equal rights.[33]

Tuttle and her colleagues had reason to be optimistic about their cause in the early 1920s. Opinion surveys in the spring of 1920 suggested that a majority of Americans still favored U.S. membership in the league in some form. Even the Republican Party, whose members had led the charge against the treaty, included in its platform in the summer of 1920 a call for "agreement among the nations to preserve the peace of the world." Though he was not prepared to reconsider U.S. membership in the league, the new president, Warren Harding, responded to popular pressure for disarmament by convening the Washington Naval Conference in 1921. Representatives from the United States, Britain, France, Japan, China, and four other European nations convened for three months in Washington, D.C., to negotiate the reduction of naval armaments among the world's powers. Many observers hoped it would be the first step toward a new association of nations.[34]

The WPLC's first order of business was to stimulate interest in the conference and to urge Harding to appoint a woman member to the U.S. delegation. They circulated leaflets, arranged town hall meetings to educate the public on the aims of the conference, and cooperated with the National Council for the Limitation of Armaments, a clearinghouse of national peace organizations established in the fall of 1921. They also wrote to Harding and Secretary of State Charles Evans Hughes to voice their concerns about the United States' disregard for parallel disarmament efforts at the League of Nations. They knew that the League Committee on Armaments had tried to communicate with the State Department about the need for global arms reduction. But U.S. officials refused to recognize any formal communications from the league. Without that input, the women felt their government was ill-prepared to carry out its duty at the conference. The remedy, they suggested, was to appoint a woman delegate. "As long as our Government is satisfied to appear before the World in international swaddling clothes," they admonished Harding, "at least one of our sex should be named as a delegate that we may help in the fashioning of a fuller and more becoming garment."[35] Their main concern, though, was that efforts at disarmament would only work within an organized world. "It seems to be the mission of the WPLC," Laidlaw wrote to members in October 1921, "to emphasize the emptiness of mere disarmament talk, without dwelling upon the self-evident fact that we can get nowhere in the solution of this or any other international problem unless we have international organization."[36] Members of the council celebrated the outcome of the conference—an agreement among the United States, Britain, Japan, France, and Italy to reduce their naval armaments—but lamented its lack of connection with the league. The moral of the Washington Naval Conference, argued Tuttle, was that "all international roads today lead to Geneva, where the first Parliament of the World is functioning to the satisfaction of fifty-one states—all the world except the recalcitrant nations—Germany, Russia, and the United States."[37]

Throughout its first year, the council focused on keeping the league in the forefront of Americans' minds. The council raised money, organized dinners to publicize disarmament, printed and distributed more leaflets, and sponsored a lecture series at the Women's University Club in New York on the League of Nations. It pressured political candidates to declare their support for U.S. entry into the league. And it continued to emphasize women's obligation as citizens to work for U.S. membership. "Before every other cause," wrote Tuttle to council members in June 1922, "this cause—the cause of world security—takes precedence. It is fundamental. It is more than a movement. It is a crusade. Upon every woman, for the sake of the children of the future, it lays a solemn obligation to do her share." In November 1922, the council responded to President Harding's Armistice Day address, in which he reminded the American people of their international responsibility to participate in the "wider concerns which involve the welfare of all mankind," by urging him to support U.S. membership in the league. They pledged their support for him in this effort, offering "to strengthen your hand by offering you every cooperation which citizenship commands in the fulfillment of your great task."[38]

Tuttle was well aware that while the majority of national women's organizations supported the cause of peace in general, few of them were as devoted to the cause of world government as the WPLC. At least six, she noted with pleasure, had by 1922 passed resolutions in favor of outlawing war; those groups, including the League of Women Voters, the Young Women's Christian Association, the National Women's Trade Union League, and WILPF, collectively represented more than six million women. But few of them had offered ideas on the international mechanisms to accomplish it or on what should follow. "No plan of world organization to effect these ends and maintain world peace is suggested" in their agendas, Tuttle noted. Other women's groups, by contrast, were still "provincial" in their outlook. As an example she cited the National Woman's Party, which, according to Tuttle's correspondence with president Alice Paul's secretary, did not "take a stand in international matters," though it took "a profound interest in all that concerns women." Tuttle interpreted this as a belief that "international politics do not concern women."

Within the National Woman's Party, she lamented, a "Feministic program" for equal rights had taken over to the exclusion of all other causes.[39]

While the WPLC fully supported outlawry and disarmament, they felt each was only "one plank in the world program." A stronger league was still required, with regular conferences, the power to make international law, and an executive machinery for enforcing that law. Throughout the early 1920s, Tuttle hoped the WPLC could evolve into a broad coalition of women's organizations working for peace and international cooperation. She believed the impulses that motivated other groups to pursue disarmament and outlawry could be mobilized in support of world government. All women internationalists demonstrated "an awakened world conscience," she maintained, and had "the same goal at heart—the safeguarding of posterity." And all were driven by the same sense of obligation. If the future of the league depended on "'a universal consciousness of duty' . . . then the League of Nations may rest in the hands of women, since duty is woman's long suit."[40]

To convince her internationalist compatriots to prioritize the league, Tuttle drew on her beliefs about maternalism and eugenics. The time had come, she told readers of the *Woman Citizen*, the premier women's rights publication, when every woman had to decide "whether she prefers the policy of isolation or cooperation with the rest of the world." For Tuttle the choice was obvious. World cooperation was a "woman's job," one to which they were particularly suited and in which they had a particular stake. "Let us not forget the object of the League of Nations," she wrote. "Behind every other purpose, in reality, it is a great organ for human conservation. It aims to underwrite the security of the children of the future. Race conservation always has been and always will be woman's chief charge."[41] While she generally tempered her eugenicist rhetoric in her WPLC work, her belief that women were the natural protectors of life and the conservers of the race still informed her arguments.

It is difficult to gauge the impact of Tuttle's arguments. The council never did collaborate closely with other women's organizations, and by the mid-1920s enthusiasm for the league cause had waned among many women internationalists. Tuttle and other members of the council gradually became involved in a new venture, the League of Nations Non-Partisan Association (LNNPA), which emerged in 1923 in an effort to encourage U.S. membership "under whatever terms seemed wise." Led by prominent internationalists, including journalist Hamilton Holt and retired Supreme Court justice John Clarke, the association quickly secured hundreds of members and tens of thousands of dollars in donations.[42] The WPLC initially decided to remain separate rather than join forces with the new group, but Tuttle agreed to chair the Greater New York Branch of the association, established in January 1924. Several other council members also accepted governance positions within the new group, with the result that its leadership was almost evenly split between men and women. Given that, it was perhaps inevitable that the Woman's Pro-League Council began to feel redundant. Tuttle resigned as chair of the executive committee in May 1925 in order to focus on her work for the LNNPA. The council disbanded soon after.[43]

Tuttle did not record her reaction to the council's demise, or if she did, it has not survived. It is likely she was disappointed, of course, not only that the United States had not yet joined the League of Nations but also that other U.S. women's organizations had not taken up the cause to the extent she hoped. But she was also glad to have a new organization, with more members and more money—and more men—join in the effort. She told Charles Bauer, a Democratic congressman and one of the organizers of the LNNPA, that she was happy to know the standard of U.S. membership in the league was "to be borne by stronger hands." "We believe," she wrote him, "that this is the greatest of causes for women—the protection of the children of the future. We believe also that it is the greatest of causes for men—to organize and stabilize the world."[44] Women and men each had their own purview in the cause of world organization, this statement implied, and while both were necessary to the cause, they would remain distinct. Tuttle did her part to make her gendered contribution as a woman; she chaired the New York branch of the association off and on through the early 1930s. Her attention, however, was soon diverted toward disarmament efforts at the League of Nations.

Alternatives to War

During the latter half of the 1920s and the early 1930s, there was little focused thinking about world government among internationalist U.S. women, but their work for other peace causes was still infused with world citizenship rhetoric. Among the major campaigns that absorbed their time and energy were those for disarmament, outlawry, and U.S. membership in the World Court. In the wake of the Washington Naval Conference, the great powers of the world continued to negotiate reductions in naval armaments, though their agreements remained difficult to enforce. The outlawry movement, meanwhile, coalesced around the Kellogg-Briand Pact, signed in 1928 by the United States, Germany, Britain, France, the Soviet Union, and almost fifty other nations. The signatories renounced war as "an instrument of national policy in their relations with one another" and pledged to settle "all disputes or conflicts of whatever nature or of whatever origin" through "pacific means."[45] The pact lacked any enforcement measures, but peace activists around the world saw it as a crucial achievement in the campaign to end war. The World Court finally had been established through the League of Nations in 1920, but membership was not tied to the league. To some in the U.S. government, joining the World Court meant relinquishing less sovereignty than joining the league because they could ensure its limited jurisdiction. World Court membership thus remained a viable internationalist cause in the United States for much longer than league membership.[46]

Women's peace organizations succeeded in mobilizing millions of Americans in support of these causes. In 1925 WILPF and other women's peace groups were joined on the national stage by the National Committee on the Cause and Cure of War. Carrie Chapman Catt organized the committee as a clearinghouse for the international relations activities of eleven national women's organizations, including the League of Women Voters, the General Federation of Women's Clubs, the Young Women's Christian Association, and the National Women's Trade Union League. Altogether the committee represented the interests of more than six million women. Between 1925 and 1930, two of the committee's main agenda items were building support for the Kellogg-Briand Pact and pushing the United States to join the World Court. The combined force of Catt's committee, WILPF, and other mixed-sex organizations, such as the National Council for the Prevention of War, produced the largest peace movement in U.S. history to that point.

Through these campaigns, U.S. women articulated their world citizenship by demanding to participate in shaping the world polity. Members of the Women's Peace Union, for example, testified before Congress in 1927 on the need to outlaw war, arguing that since suffrage had put women on the hook for future wars, they should be able to help prevent it. "Since we are now enfranchised," union president Elinor Byrns reminded the Senate, "we must share with the men citizens of the United States the responsibility for the next war, unless we do everything in our power to prevent that war."[47] The following year, more than 14,000 meetings of organized women across the country adopted resolutions in support of the Kellogg-Briand Pact. Observers at the time credited women's mobilization for the Senate's ratification of the pact.[48] In 1931 the International Council of Women circulated a "Polyglot Petition for Disarmament," which called for a gradual reduction of arms leading to the full implementation of the pact. Thousands of U.S. women, representing several different organizations, participated in the effort to gather signatures. U.S. women eventually collected more than half a million signatures out of more than nine million gathered worldwide.[49]

Women also asserted their obligation as citizens to work for these peace measures and encouraged other women to embrace that responsibility. "It is now the duty, therefore, of every patriotic American citizen to think for peace and work for peace, and to shun everything that leads toward war," argued Virginia Gildersleeve, dean of Barnard College, in an address on disarmament in 1929. "Women today are citizens, equally with men, and of course they share this duty with men. . . . Women now face a great responsibility and a great opportunity for playing a part in the cause of world peace."[50] Florence Allen, the first woman to serve on a state supreme court, told the First Conference on the Cause and Cure of War in 1925 that "the women of the world who believe that this evil can and must be abolished have to go out to change the conviction of men's minds, that war is legal and sanctioned and necessary, and that is primarily a task for women."[51] Mary Woolley, president of Mount Holyoke College, reassured one audience in 1932 that while disarmament might seem like a complex topic, through study and discussion it was possible "for the layman to become an intelligent world-citizen." Intelligent public opinion, in turn, could be mobilized and used to influence future efforts. The disarmament campaign represented a great opportunity, Woolley told her listeners. "I depend upon the women of America to realize the opportunity and shoulder the responsibility."[52]

Tuttle shared all these views. She devoted the bulk of her time in the late 1920s and early 1930s to the cause of disarmament. She wrote and spoke on the topic often, and in 1931 she published her final book, *Alternatives to War*, which emphasized disarmament as one of the most promising paths toward a "constructive peace." She still believed the United States should join both the League of Nations and the World Court and lamented the fact that it had not, but she took heart from the United States' willingness to sign the Kellogg-Briand Pact and to continue participating in disarmament negotiations. But more public education was still necessary to get the country to play its part as a world citizen and assume responsibility for world cooperation. Ordinary men and women likewise needed to adjust their mindsets: "Our understanding of changing events today depends on whether we think locally or universally. If you think locally, you may be a good citizen, but you will not be a world citizen, as is today demanded of you. To make any contribution to your age you must think of matters beyond your country's horizon."[53]

As she had in 1919, Tuttle still believed women had a particular role to play in this process, though she had softened her maternalist rhetoric. In an echo of Lucia Ames Mead, she aimed her book at women "not because the author cherishes illusions of feminine super-idealism, but because in the United States, at least, women have more leisure than men and are giving greater response to new ideas." The vote had empowered women, she argued, but along with that power came responsibility "not only to the home but to the nation and to that world which has become our larger home."[54] Twelve years after the Paris Peace Conference, Tuttle was still hoping to rally U.S. women to embrace their obligations as world citizens.

Along with thousands of other internationalists in the United States, Tuttle looked toward the World Disarmament Conference, scheduled to convene in Geneva in 1932, as the last hope for meaningful disarmament. The world situation was precarious. Japan had invaded Manchuria in 1931 as part of its mission to expand its power in East Asia. Tensions between France and Germany remained high. Authoritarian governments were consolidating power in Italy and the Soviet Union. And the onset of the Great Depression affected nearly every part of the planet, making armaments even more of a financial burden for many countries and limiting U.S. overseas investments that had provided a measure of stability in the 1920s. The ambitious goal of the conference was to hammer out details for the limitation of arms budgets and production. Prominent peace groups pressured President Herbert Hoover to appoint a woman delegate to the conference; he agreed to send Mary Woolley. Tuttle also attended as part of a special delegation from the League of Women Voters.

Tuttle was thrilled by much of what she saw in Geneva but ultimately, like many, disappointed. In a radio address broadcast in the United States just after the opening, she reported her delight at seeing "a sight altogether unprecedented—an American delegation sitting with the family of nations." To her the sight captured the United States' acknowledgment of its responsibilities to international peace. "There is no greater delusion today than the illusion of isolation," she reminded her listeners. "Let us [work] . . . for a new world order founded upon international law and justice. There is no other alternative. It is world organization or further world disinte-gration."[55] The delegates, to Tuttle's dismay, chose the latter. The conference was a major disappointment to internationalist U.S. women and to peace advocates around the world. The negotiations became bogged down almost immediately over a range of national security concerns from the French and demands for military parity from the Germans. Discussions were sus-pended numerous times, and in the end the conference dragged on for almost two years before ending without an agreement. The growing tides of fascism and militarism in Europe and Asia were simply too strong, and there was too much money to be made from the production of munitions and war materials for the powerful nations of the world to do more than pay lip service to disarmament.[56]

Like Lucia Ames Mead and Fannie Fern Andrews, Florence Guertin Tuttle saw world federation as the only hope for a peaceful future. The key to end-ing war lay in greater political integration. And, as world citizens, women had a particular obligation to further that task. Unlike Mead and Andrews, however, Tuttle brought a maternalist perspective to bear on her arguments for women's world citizenship. Informed by her reading in eugenics, Tuttle's views on what women could contribute to the world polity grew from her conviction that as mothers, women were more attuned to the preservation of life than men. Women should work for world federation, Tuttle argued, because it was the only logical way to ensure the preservation of human life. In 1919, Tuttle had cause for optimism; the new League of Nations seemed to her the germ of a genuine world federation, and she believed the United States could be convinced to participate in it. By 1932, however, her optimism proved unfounded. The United States never joined the league or the World Court, and both were proving increasingly ineffectual. Disarmament talks collapsed, and the Kellogg-Briand Pact rang hollow in the face of resurgent militarism around the world.

But Tuttle did not feel her work had been in vain. In a preface to an unpublished memoir of her time in Geneva, written in the early 1940s, she predicted that the United States would yet assume its world responsibility: "When World War II is won, world federation is to come up again, with the United States as one of its active leaders." When that time came, her experi-ences with the Woman's Pro-League Council and her books on world federa-tion and disarmament could prove useful. "If these feminine, social chapters," she wrote, "will interest women in a new world federation ... it will prove that every little bit helped." She then reiterated one last time the need for women to assume their global obligations. "Women as well as men will be responsible for the kind of world we build," she concluded. "So here's to the women of the world to realize their responsibility and to say God help us all to cooperate and succeed."[57] Whether or not other internationalist women read those words, they took up her charge in 1945.

CHAPTER 4

Rosika Schwimmer, Lola Maverick Lloyd, and a World Government of the People

While Florence Guertin Tuttle lamented the failures of the 1932 Disarmament Conference, other women castigated even such limited measures as too little, too late. "Chaos all over the world has reached a climax," wrote Rosika Schwimmer in the early 1930s, "which does not permit further waste of time with puny attempts to drench one fire while flames, ashes and lava are bursting from myriad other holes." As they were for many women of her generation, the memories of World War I were still fresh in Schwimmer's mind, though for her, as a Hungarian Jew rendered stateless in the war's aftermath, they were more personal than for some of her colleagues. "The human family is going insane," she warned. "It is in a frenzy of self-destruction." Citing Japanese atrocities in Manchuria, she declared, "International law is dead, dead as the sanctity of treaties. . . . Treaties, covenants are scraps of paper, and not honorable guarantees for peace."[1] What Schwimmer and her colleague Lola Maverick Lloyd wanted was to see ordinary women and men band together into a new kind of world organization, one that would do away with the hollow shell of the League of Nations and put an end to the escalating violence. While many of her contemporaries dismissed her hyperbolic rhetoric, Schwimmer's language conveyed the depth of her concern and the passion with which she dedicated herself to the cause of world government.

For both Schwimmer and Lloyd, being active world citizens meant forcing a radical restructuring of the political world order to make it absolutely pacifist and more responsive to ordinary people. Unlike Mead, Andrews, and Tuttle, they had little faith in national governments to further world integration. By the late 1930s, after working for over twenty years for various peace efforts, Schwimmer and Lloyd were convinced that the only way to end war permanently was to establish a populist world government. Their practice of world citizenship, therefore, was not so much a demand to participate in shaping the *existing* global polity; it was a call to form an entirely new one. They rejected the status quo of intergovernmental cooperation, especially as represented by the League of Nations, and proposed instead a new kind of global federation that was truly of the people.

Their 1937 pamphlet *Chaos, War, or a New World Order?* laid the ground-work for this "all-inclusive, non-military, democratic Federation of Nations." Schwimmer and Lloyd envisioned a federal system, governed by a world con-stitution, in which nations would retain sovereignty over their domestic affairs but would cede authority over international matters to the world government. It would be all-inclusive, with every nation in the world immediately invited to join and provisions made for the fair representation of colonized peoples. It would be nonmilitary; the central body would abolish all standing armies, end all weapons manufacturing, and outlaw state-sanctioned violence. All disputes among nations would be settled by the world government through negotiation and arbitration. And it would be democratic, based on an equita-ble system of voting and direct representation.[2]

Schwimmer and Lloyd's plan echoed earlier schemes, such as Mead's and Tuttle's, especially in that it was premised on active citizenship. But it also represented a significant departure from the liberal internationalist founda-tions of the League of Nations. Schwimmer and Lloyd believed in govern-ment, international law, and self-determination, but they had little patience with what they saw as the capitalist, imperialist underpinnings of Wilsoni-anism. And while women such as Mead proposed building blocks toward an eventual world federation, Schwimmer and Lloyd skipped the preliminary steps and sketched out the actual world government they wanted. Unsurpris-ingly, they found little support for their plan in the late 1930s and early 1940s, but the ideas they proposed would resurface after World War II and help shape the postwar world government movement.

Feminists for Peace

By 1937 both Schwimmer and Lloyd had long experience with peace activ-ism. They first met in November 1914, when Schwimmer was traveling through Chicago on a lecture tour. Born in 1877 into a distinguished Hun-garian Jewish family, Schwimmer became an activist at an early age and gained considerable fame in Europe as a feminist and pacifist. She traveled to the United States after the war broke out to try to convince Woodrow Wilson to mediate an immediate peace. She wanted him to form a committee of representatives from neutral nations to study the conflict and formulate peace proposals. After Wilson balked, Schwimmer pressed on, working for the next two years to promote neutral mediation. When Lloyd heard Schwimmer speak in Chicago, she was immediately drawn to her ideas. Born in 1875, Lloyd was literally a "maverick"; she was the granddaughter of the wealthy Texas landowner whose name became synonymous with all things independent and unorthodox. She married the son of Progressive journalist Henry Demarest Lloyd and eagerly absorbed her in-laws' political radicalism. By 1914 she was a wealthy, soon-to-be-divorced mother of four and eager for new outlets for her activism.[3]

Schwimmer and Lloyd became fast friends and worked together often over the next four years. Like Mead, Andrews, and Tuttle, they were both founding members of the Woman's Peace Party. They likely knew Mead and certainly knew Andrews, given that both Schwimmer and Lloyd attended the International Congress of Women at The Hague in the spring of 1915. Whether they knew Tuttle is less clear, and no record exists of any sustained relationship among the five women. After the Hague congress, it was Schwimmer's idea to send representatives as envoys to all the European heads of state to pressure them into negotiating for or mediating a peaceful settlement of the war.[4] Her efforts to promote neutral mediation ended rather ignominiously, but Schwimmer's dedication to "citizen diplomacy" illustrated her belief that it was not only possible but necessary for ordinary people to play a role in ending the war and shaping the peace.[5] From Schwimmer and Lloyd's perspective, strategies like outlawry and disarmament were a waste of time because they targeted the symptoms of the disease rather than the underlying illness. Disarmed fascists would still be fascists, repressing the will of their people in whatever ways they could.

In the wake of World War I, both women were critical of the Versailles Treaty and the League of Nations Covenant. While the league reflected in part the wishes of ordinary people, including peace advocates who had been envisioning a concert of nations since the late nineteenth century, the plan for its operation was in no way democratic. Toward the end of the war, while Schwimmer returned to Hungary to participate in postwar rebuilding, Lloyd devoted time to studying and critiquing emerging plans for the league. In all long-term peace efforts, she argued, "the people want control." She urged peace activists to organize themselves in order to exert influence over the peace process, to "be ready to guide into democratic channels all the deliberations of that deeply significant peace commission which can and will alter forever our whole international situation."[6]

Lloyd also argued that the league should be based on a system of direct representation. She demanded that citizens—women as well as men—be allowed to vote for the peace commissioners who would represent the United States. Knowing this was a long shot, she rallied her compatriots. "Is it historically probable," she asked, "that diplomats will extend for us the powers of the plain citizens of the world? The plain citizens had better bestir themselves!"[7] Her fears were confirmed as she read about plans for the league, to which delegates would be appointed rather than elected: "Choosing our own agents, that's democracy. But the people's will is remote indeed from the proposed Supreme Council of the League of Nations."[8] Unlike other world government theorists, who criticized the league for its lack of enforcement power, or peace activists, who criticized its reliance on collective security or the exclusion of Germany, Lloyd criticized its lack of representation. She demanded more democratic control of foreign policy, not just by having member nations represented fairly within the league but by allowing the people of the world more of a voice in who represented them.[9]

Schwimmer and Lloyd channeled their frustration with the league into the first draft of a plan for world government, which they hashed out in 1924. It included many of the elements they later developed more fully, including universal membership, democratic processes, and popular representation. To promote their plan, they formed the Union of World Patriots, later reincarnated as the Campaign for World Government. The constitution of the new organization opened with a statement that would guide Schwimmer and Lloyd's quest for the next twenty years: "We believe in the unity of the human family. We believe that the world must be organized into a safe home for all humanity. We believe that physical violence is always wrong in principle and disastrous in practice, and we believe that all conflicts of human society, whether between individuals, classes, races, or nations, can be solved by reason."[10] Their program encompassed world organization, physical as well as moral disarmament, and the establishment of social justice. Membership in their union would be open to all who accepted these principles. They were very clear that it was to be an organization of both women and men and that they would start small, gathering together interested individuals to exchange information and ideas.[11]

But the greatest influence on Schwimmer and Lloyd's thinking about world government in the 1920s was Schwimmer's battle for U.S. citizenship. She had fled Hungary in early 1920 under threat of persecution for having refused to serve in the Communist government of Béla Kun. Because of her friendship with Lloyd, she settled in Chicago, where she applied for citizenship in 1926. One of the questions on the naturalization petition asked, "If necessary, are you willing to take up arms in defense of this country?" The lifelong pacifist answered no. Her answer led to an official interview with the district director of naturalization. In the course of that interview, she proclaimed,

> I believe that national governments will continue on an individual basis, as the States have, that form the North American Union. I believe the national governments will increasingly organize for peaceful cooperation, as the 13 States have developed into a Union of 48 States. *I believe that future generations will arrive at something like the United States of the World.* Such an organization, to my mind, will permit every State to develop on its national lines, keep its own language and individual type of culture. Within all this variety, however, I believe the elements of common interest to all mankind will be ultimately organized so that all human differences can be solved without resort to war.[12]

Schwimmer's statement shows how her emerging thinking about world government informed her own struggle for access to U.S. citizenship. That thinking would later shape Schwimmer and Lloyd's articulation of world citizenship as a legal status within their global government.

What ultimately doomed Schwimmer's quest for U.S. citizenship was not her belief in world government, however, but her refusal to swear she would bear arms if asked to do so (an unlikely scenario, given that she was over fifty and women could not serve in the U.S. military in the 1920s). In response to an accusation that she had been a German spy during World War I, Schwimmer asserted that she would never have engaged in the conflict on either side as any kind of combatant. "I am an uncompromising pacifist," she wrote. "I have no sense of nationalism, only a cosmic consciousness of belonging to the human family."[13] For Schwimmer, that consciousness, that sense of connection to the "human family" that she and Lloyd had first articulated in 1924, was part of her mindset as a citizen of the world. For U.S. immigration officials, it was evidence that she was not sufficiently loyal to the United States.

After a lengthy legal battle, the U.S. Supreme Court denied her citizenship petition in 1929. Schwimmer had not adequately pledged allegiance to the United States, the court argued, citing specifically her "cosmic consciousness." According to the court, "Whatever tends to lessen the willingness of citizens to discharge their duty to bear arms in the country's defense detracts from the strength and safety of the government."[14] From the court's perspective, within the cultural context of the hyperpatriotic, anti-immigrant 1920s, the security of the nation far outweighed the imagined promise of Schwimmer's world federation. Schwimmer remained stateless until her death in 1948, largely unable to work and frustrated by her lack of civil and political status in the United States.[15]

Schwimmer's loss sharpened both her and Lloyd's sense of the need for world citizenship not just as a mindset and a practice but as a legal status. In the fall of 1934, as Hitler consolidated power in Germany and began persecuting Jews and other German citizens, Schwimmer argued "the establishment of world citizenship and world passports is a fundamental necessity, and the key to physical safety. This is essential not for Germans only, but for all others who are without a country, without rights anywhere, without that minimum of safety which is the birthright of the most miserable citizen in any civilized country." Prominent Germans were assured of asylum abroad, she argued, but what about the thousands of men and women who had no resources and nowhere to go? They might attain physical safety by leaving Germany, but they would not find security if they were left to the mercy of other countries' willingness to welcome them. Schwimmer pointed directly to the "Nansen Passport"—established by the League of Nations commissioner for refugees, Fridtjof Nansen, in the 1920s to serve as identity papers and allow refugees to travel more easily—as a precedent for her world passport. She was aware of its limits; at that time it was available only to Russians and Armenians. But for her it was "the embryo which should be developed into the most urgently needed world citizenship passport."[16]

Lloyd, for her part, had supported Schwimmer throughout her citizenship battle, both emotionally and financially. She channeled her frustration after 1929 into an effort to secure congressional legislation making it illegal to deny U.S. citizenship to pacifists. She formed the Griffin-O'Day Bill Committee, named for Anthony Griffin and Caroline O'Day, the two members of the House of Representatives who introduced the bill in every congressional session throughout the 1930s. At its height the committee boasted over five thousand members, including Jane Addams, John Dewey, and Felix Frankfurter.

Lloyd served as national chair and Schwimmer's protégée Edith Wynner as national secretary. The bill never advanced far in Congress, but it kept the issue of statelessness at the forefront of Schwimmer and Lloyd's agenda.[17]

Schwimmer and Lloyd's early formulations of a world government were thus informed both by their critiques of the League of Nations and by Schwimmer's battle for citizenship. They shared many of Tuttle's critiques of the league, such as its lack of real authority, but unlike her, they were not willing to wait for the possibility that the league might evolve into a more genuine world government. The peace of the world demanded action. As world citizens, Schwimmer and Lloyd felt they had not only the right but the responsibility to instigate that action on behalf of the world's people. As the 1930s passed and the world situation grew more precarious, both women felt an urgent need to refine and publicize their plan.

Chaos, War, or a New World Order?

By the early 1930s the weaknesses of the League of Nations were becoming daily more apparent. The failure of the disarmament conference at Geneva underscored that reality. Schwimmer and Lloyd were not the only ones who noticed; several world government theorists began in these years to propose alternatives to the league. Advocates of a true world federation (as opposed to a loose *con*federation such as the league) argued the only way to eradicate war was to bind the nations of the world more firmly together. Salvador de Madariaga, Spain's ambassador to the United States and a League of Nations delegate, argued in 1930 for an organization similar to the league but with universal membership and a greater relinquishment of national sovereignty. Nicholas Murray Butler, president of Columbia University and of the Carnegie Endowment for International Peace, wanted to federate the world into a "society of citizen-nations," modeled on Switzerland and the United States. Oscar Newfang, secretary of the World Unity Foundation, envisioned a similar federation but went even further than Butler in outlining its proposed legislative, executive, and judicial powers. And in 1939, U.S. journalist Clarence Streit, in his best-selling *Union Now: A Proposal for the Federal Union of the Democracies of the North Atlantic*, laid out a plan for a regional federation of nations that would eventually grow into a world union.[18]

Though they differed in detail, all of these plans began with governments and their representatives. They called for official delegates to come together to work out the structure and operation of the new system. Once the machinery was in place, the various legislative, executive, judicial, and other bodies would be staffed by national representatives appointed by their governments. In form they were thus similar to the league, although each author envisioned much greater authority for his organization than the league had ever had.

Schwimmer and Lloyd's vision for world government, on the other hand, centered ordinary people. The plan they laid out in their 1937 pamphlet *Chaos, War, or a New World Order?* differed not only from Mead's or Andrews's but also from contemporaneous ideas like Madariaga's or Streit's in almost every fundamental way. Where other plans stemmed from cooperation among government officials, Schwimmer and Lloyd's was built on the work of nonstate actors. Other plans, following the model of the League of Nations, relied on indirect representation; Schwimmer and Lloyd proposed a formula for the direct election of representatives to their world body. Finally, while other plans replicated existing global hierarchies based on race, gender, and other structural inequalities, Schwimmer and Lloyd did their best to ensure not only the equal participation of all women and men around the world but equal protection and security for all within the world system.

By far the most radical feature of Schwimmer and Lloyd's plan was that they envisioned a *democratic* world government based on the demands of the world's people. That was why their plan began with popular action, with steps that ordinary people could take to begin the world federation. If any governments or heads of state were willing to lead the way, Schwimmer and Lloyd invited them to do so, but they assumed none would. In that case, "organizations or individuals shall raise the necessary funds and invite a small group of experts . . . to [arrange] a World Constitutional Convention." The delegates to this convention would draw up a plan for the federation and present it to the governments of the world for adoption. If after one year none had accepted it, then "unofficial steps must be taken by the people to inaugurate the all-inclusive, non-military, democratic Federation of Nations."[19] The plan was short, and it glossed over a few key details—how all of this would work in practice, how funds would be raised, how they would secure support for their plan from diverse populations around the world. But the key was that this was not to be simply another effort at intergovernmental cooperation. These women believed it was time for a different approach.

Once the new federation had been inaugurated, a system of direct representation would ensure popular control. To achieve this, each nation would elect ten representatives, based on a voting system recommended by the committee of experts. Delegates would serve for a period of ten years and would be subject to recall during that time. Most important, from Schwimmer and Lloyd's perspective, the delegates would not be required to vote as a bloc. They expected internal divisions among national representatives and welcomed them, along with opportunities for cooperation across national borders. Schwimmer and Lloyd argued that "every important group in a nation can be represented among its ten delegates, and will find like-minded groups from other nations in the World Parliament, where divisions will consequently occur along lines of opinion, not lines of geography."[20] As opposed to the league, then, in which representatives were appointed by governments, Schwimmer and Lloyd envisioned a true world parliament, where delegates were directly elected and governments had no say in who would represent their nation.

Making their world government people-centric rather than state-centric also meant it would be nonmilitary, because reducing the role of the state, the two women argued, would eliminate the "war system." No military person would be allowed to participate in the world constitutional convention. Indeed, there would be no military anywhere; no national force would be necessary in a system where the world government adjudicated all disputes among nations. National armies and navies would be dismantled, both figuratively and literally. Men and women previously employed by the military, as well as those unemployed, would be available to work in new industries, while the raw materials and massive budgets previously devoted to militarism could be rededicated: "The abolition of armies, navies, air fleets, armaments and munition factories in all the states of the world will release for this vast reemployment scheme the scrapped war material and enormous sums heretofore provided in open and concealed war budgets."[21] Schwimmer and Lloyd had no patience with gradual plans for disarmament, like those that circulated in the 1920s and early 1930s. They demanded an immediate end to all forms of state-sponsored violence.

In order for Schwimmer and Lloyd's world government to be truly democratic, it had to be based on a fair and equitable system of representation. Their key adjective was "all-inclusive." First, all countries of the world were to be admitted immediately and on an equal basis. When Schwimmer and Lloyd talked about a world government, they meant a *world* government. In contrast to other plans that provided for a union of military allies—like the League of Nations, which initially excluded Russia and Germany—or for a union of existing nation-states—also like the league, which left out colonized populations—theirs included from the beginning every nation and every person. Schwimmer and Lloyd therefore included Germany, Japan, and the Soviet Union right from the start. "Why take it for granted," Lloyd argued in January 1940 to William Allan Neilson, chairman of the Commission to Study the Organization of Peace, "that Germany, etc.—the chosen enemy nations—will not welcome a practical and just line-up? None has ever been offered. An honest offer of cooperation without implied or open insult will reach the ears and hearts of Germans, Russians, Japanese."[22] Schwimmer and Lloyd proposed to isolate violent individuals like Hitler and Mussolini by distancing them from their own populations. They simply could not believe that ordinary men and women would not jump at the chance to forestall war by cooperating in such a "practical" effort.

Second, Schwimmer and Lloyd's system of popular voting and direct representation was designed to ensure not only democratic control of international relations but also that "every important group" would be adequately represented in the world body. Whether or not that was possible in practice, it shows they were cognizant of the need to extend political rights to women, racial and ethnic minorities, religious minorities, and other underrepresented or disenfranchised groups. They assumed a system of equal suffrage. As a member of the Women's Consultative Committee of the League of Nations, which was working in the summer of 1937 to amend the league's covenant to secure equal suffrage and other rights around the world, Lloyd argued, "Equality of suffrage within a nation is not entirely a domestic question, but has its international bearing. The governments of countries where women vote do in a certain sense represent women, and the delegates [to the League] chosen by such governments for the Council and the Assembly, even though they may all be men, are more truly representative than delegates from countries where women have no vote at all. And action in the League is affected by this fact."[23] In order for the world government to reflect the will of the people, all people had to have input on its actions.

By contrast, other world government theorists, even those frustrated with the League of Nations, saw little reason to change the basic system of representation under which the league operated in order to represent the diversity of the world's people. Madariaga argued in the 1930s that there was nothing wrong with the "machinery" of the League of Nations. He attributed the failures of the league not to its structure but to "an insufficient loyalty to its principles on the part of some major state."[24] American philosopher John Herman Randall devoted little attention to the mechanisms of a world government, but he emphasized the fundamental oneness of humankind. "The human mind is one, the whole world round," he argued. "Its activities everywhere conform to the same laws of mind; its power, given the same opportunities and an equal time for development, are practically the same for all men."[25] With such an assumption of global homogeneity, there was no need in these men's minds for equal suffrage or representation.

Schwimmer and Lloyd's inclusive intensions extended to colonized territories. They elaborated on this two years after the first appearance of *Chaos*. Not only did people living under colonial rule have a right to participate in a world government, they argued, but colonization was one of the chief causes of war that had to be removed. "Hungry" imperialist nations regularly attempted to steal the colonies of other nations because they knew that home populations in Europe would not care. Their world government would solve these problems by administering colonial territories itself rather than leaving them under the control of one nation. Leaders would ensure "adequate representation for native peoples" and establish concrete procedures for achieving statehood. Money that would have gone to military defense would be diverted into development, irrigation, sanitation, tax relief, and other initiatives. An economic commission would regulate the production and distribution of raw materials. Moreover, "certain constitutional guarantees could be given all native peoples," Schwimmer and Lloyd proposed, though they did not elaborate on what those might be. In the end, then, the great powers "would have nothing to fight over in the colonial field" since all territories would have protections "equal to any nation that was a member of the world federation."[26] In Schwimmer and Lloyd's minds, this approach rectified the shortcomings of the League of Nations mandate system by keeping colonial administration within the world government itself rather than divvying up territories among European nations.[27]

In some respects, this attitude toward colonies was an improvement from that of earlier women's. Mead and Andrews agreed with Schwimmer and Lloyd that imperialism was a chief cause of militarism, but, using their Progressive-era civilizationist rhetoric, they likely would have argued that colonial populations needed much more supervision and tutelage. Andrews in particular was a proponent of the League of Nations mandate system. Tuttle hardly mentioned colonies at all, aside from noting, in a comment on Article 22 of the covenant, that it was "possible that mandatary [*sic*] forms of government may lend themselves to exploitation. If so, it is another leak in the dyke for women to watch."[28] But all three shared the attitude that people in the Middle East, South Asia, Southeast Asia, Africa, and other regions needed guidance from more civilized nations before they were ready to participate in the world community.

Schwimmer and Lloyd, it is important to note, did not disagree. Their plan incorporated what was essentially a restructured mandate system in which the supervision of colonies was the responsibility of the world government rather than individual nations. They left vague what the administration of those territories would look like, how "adequate representation" would be measured, and what the procedures for achieving statehood might be. Schwimmer and Lloyd were by far the most radical of these five women, but as with many other white feminists and pacifists of their time, justice for people of color was not an integral component of their worldview. Jessie Wallace Hughan of the War Resisters' League, for example, worried about the voting power of nonwhite people in an international federation. Her solution was for the world parliament to recognize "only fully enfranchised citizens." African Americans and other disenfranchised people around the world would simply not be represented at all. Such attitudes were not unusual in the interwar period, even among radical pacifists.[29]

Mead, Andrews, Schwimmer, and Lloyd did, however, critique the imperialist system as it existed, which is more than can be said for other world government theorists of the day. Most did not address explicitly the question of how colonized populations and territories would be incorporated into a world federation. They took it for granted that the federation would consist only of previously existing nation-states. British economist J. A. Hobson, writing during World War I, proposed that internationalists looking to form a global political order should first seek to "obtain the adhesion to their main proposals of as many as possible among the eight Great Powers, and the minor European States, leaving open the question of the immediate or the later accession of the other States." Historian Arnold Toynbee envisioned a world union growing from a nucleus of original members into "a federal state embracing all the already democratic states in Western Europe and overseas." Under this model, nonsovereign areas and peoples would come into the union under the umbrella of whatever imperialist nation controlled them. India, for example, would be represented in the federation only through Britain, which meant that the interests of India's people would be voiced only to whatever degree Britain thought it necessary to do so. Clarence Streit was one of the few who did address the "colonial question"; his plan was quite similar to Schwimmer and Lloyd's. Article II of his draft constitution, "The People of the Union," stipulated that "the non-self-governing territory of these states and of all states admitted later to the Union is transferred to the Union to govern while preparing it for self-government and admission to the Union."[30] But Streit was an exception. While most authors critiqued myriad aspects of the League of Nations, the mandate system was not one of them.

The "all-inclusive" nature of Schwimmer and Lloyd's government extended finally to stateless people around the world. They envisioned not just moral or spiritual but *legal* world citizenship. Their plan provided for a commission on world citizenship "to regulate the rights and duties of citizens of the Federation of Nations." They further recommended that "in addition to equal world citizenship," every person should "automatically have the rights and duties of a citizen of the state where he resides." They envisioned a "world passport," based loosely on the Nansen passport of the 1930s but much more extensive. Passports would be available to everyone rather than only to certain nationalities, and they would provide not just freedom of travel but the right to resettle. Such countries as Britain and the United States would not be able to deny entry to world citizens based on their religion or nation of origin. Their goal was to offer some form of protection for refugees, exiles, and others who found themselves either stripped of citizenship at home or forced to travel abroad to ensure their safety.[31]

Statelessness was an increasingly dire international issue in the late 1930s as well as a very personal issue for Schwimmer. Her denial of citizenship by the Supreme Court in 1929 affected her for the rest of her life. By the time *Chaos* was issued in the fall of 1937, hundreds of thousands of Europeans had left or had been forced to leave their homes to seek safety in other countries, just as Schwimmer did in 1920, and those numbers only increased with the outbreak of war. They were vulnerable not only to persecution from fascists and Nazis but also to the economic hardships of the Depression and the reluctance of many Western European countries to absorb them.[32] Both Schwimmer and Lloyd were also familiar with another aspect of statelessness, one to which women were particularly vulnerable in the 1930s. By the early twentieth century, in many countries around the world women lost their citizenship when they married noncitizen men. Depending on the laws of their husband's country, some women gained citizenship status in his country automatically upon marriage, but many did not. At the 1930 League of Nations–sponsored Conference on the Codification of International Law, representatives from around the world debated several issues, including universal terms of nationality. But the terms they agreed on were deeply gendered;

women who married foreigners could still be stripped of their national citizenship. Despite vigorous lobbying by several international women's organizations, the conference delegates refused to budge. Although formal passage of an international Nationality Treaty was delayed by the United States (not because the United States supported women's equality but because it was reluctant to join any international agreement), it was eventually adopted in 1937. Thus the year Schwimmer and Lloyd first distributed their plan for world government was also the same year that women were formally denied equal nationality around the world.[33]

Statelessness was not a concern for most world government theorists, who focused on relations among governments and gave little thought to the role or status of individuals within the world system. For Madariaga and his colleagues, world citizenship was a mindset rather than a legal status.[34] Besides Schwimmer and Lloyd, the only other theorist whose plan for world government made explicit mention of world citizenship was Streit. In a riff on the Fourteenth Amendment to the U.S. Constitution, Streit wrote, "All persons born or naturalized in the self-governing states of the Union are citizens of the Union and of the state wherein they reside."[35] Streit thus wanted to extend birthright world citizenship to all individuals born within member nations—but that included only the United States, Britain, and other "Atlantic" states that joined the union. It did not include Germany, Eastern Europe, or the rest of the world.

In its protections against statelessness as much as in its promises of popular control and equal representation, Schwimmer and Lloyd's plan was far more radical than any other before World War II. Like Mead, Andrews, and Tuttle, the two women began with a liberal internationalist faith in democracy and global cooperation, but from there their plan took a harder left turn. Their vision was not only populist and egalitarian; it was anti-imperialist, socialist, and absolutely pacifist. Schwimmer and Lloyd believed the United States could serve as a model for the new world federation, but unlike Andrews and Tuttle, they did not see their plan as a method of advancing the status of the United States or making it a world leader among nations. Their goal was not U.S. supremacy. Their aim was to promote justice and end war permanently.

Immediate reactions to the plan, from friends and colleagues to whom the two women sent it, ranged from skepticism to outright dismissal. Carrie Chapman Catt found it naive and redundant; there was "nothing practical, new, or appealing in it," she wrote Lloyd. She wondered what they proposed to do about the League of Nations, which she believed was "not much unlike" their world government. And she thought the idea of a new constitution preposterous: "No American . . . would dream of a World Constitution and the very mention of such a proposal would cause a National smile!"[36] By contrast, Elinor Byrns and Alice Thacher Post, both longtime pacifists, approved the idea in theory but doubted its feasibility. Byrns questioned the plan's ability to balance the authority of the world government with the autonomy of member states, while Post wondered how the "present isolationist temper of the American people" could be overcome. Post also pointed out that given the spread of fascism in Europe, "to hold up the prize of a super-state which could dominate the world, would seem to invite universal *Untergang* [downfall]."[37]

In general, Schwimmer and Lloyd responded to critiques like these by doubling down on the idea that once the people of the world understood what was being proposed, they would welcome it. Schwimmer in particular was often carried away by her own zealotry for world government, even to the point of alienating colleagues and supporters. She never seemed to understand why the concept of world government was not as obvious a solution to everyone else as it was to her. It fell to Lloyd to try to keep her in check. "Our proposition takes a bold and reckless mind," she reminded her friend. "Don't let's 'kid' ourselves. It's not popular. . . . It will save time and friction if we keep on the realistic plane—just between ourselves, I mean. I get depressed when dear friends expect of me the impossible."[38] Lloyd's comment is revealing. It suggests she knew that while she and Schwimmer were right that the people of the world were tired of war and worried about another potential conflagration on the scale of the Great War, both the virulent nationalism around the world and the commitment to neutrality within the United States were too strong to be overcome in the late 1930s. Nonetheless, they set out to plant the seed of world government in people's minds.

The Campaign for World Government

Schwimmer and Lloyd officially launched the Campaign for World Government (CWG) in September 1937. It was not a membership organization; the two women wanted to keep the group small and agile. To assist them they hired Edith Wynner, a young woman who had been working for several years as Schwimmer's private secretary, and Caroline Lexow Babcock, whose experience in the peace movement included stints with WILPF and the War Resisters' League. Within a year they brought on board Lloyd's son, William Lloyd

Figure 5. Rosika
Schwimmer, left, and
Lola Maverick Lloyd,
1937. Photo courtesy
of AP/Wide World.

Jr.; her daughters Jessie, Mary, and Georgia also volunteered their time at
various points. Schwimmer and Lloyd distributed copies of *Chaos* to friends,
colleagues, organizations, potential supporters—anyone they thought might
take an interest. They corresponded with people across the country who had
read the plan and wanted to know more. But the two main projects on which
the campaign focused its efforts in the late 1930s were lobbying members of
Congress to introduce legislation that would set the wheels of their plan in
motion through governmental channels and reaching out to other peace and
internationalist organizations to convince them to integrate the Schwimmer-
Lloyd plan into their platforms. Lloyd Jr. took the helm on the first project,
with help from Babcock; Lloyd and Wynner steered the second. Lloyd bank-
rolled most of the work, while Schwimmer frequently weighed in on policy
and strategy.

The campaign began lobbying public officials to endorse its plan, at both
the state and national levels. Throughout the 1938 midterm elections, Babcock sent dozens of letters to various state chairs of platform committees for
both parties, urging the adoption of a resolution to urge President Franklin

Roosevelt to call a world constitutional convention. "The world is looking to you, the party which freed the slaves," she wrote to the platform committee chair of the Republican convention in New York, "to free mankind from the greatest slavery of all, the tyranny of war."[39] Babcock and Lloyd Jr. even wrote directly to Roosevelt. "The world needs a new deal too," they argued. Roosevelt had it in his power to solve the present crisis if he would only call a convention, which could "apply our own tested principles of federal organization to [the] establishment of a world federation, giving the peoples continuous and direct contact through [a] world legislature instead of through antiquated diplomacy." World organization, they told him, "is [the] next logical step in human progress."[40] These efforts met with very little response.

Lloyd Jr. spearheaded most of the campaign's work on Capitol Hill in the hope that congressional support would signal the legitimacy of Schwimmer and Lloyd's idea. He spent considerable time in Washington in 1938 and 1939 trying to gauge the interest of various members of Congress who he thought might be willing to introduce legislation urging Roosevelt to issue a call for a world constitutional convention. But it was an uphill battle against a Congress that, while divided among noninterventionists and those who wanted more decisive action against fascism and Nazism, would never have supported a multilateral initiative on the scale of Schwimmer and Lloyd's world government.[41] He finally achieved a small measure of success in June 1939, when Democratic congressman Jerry Voorhis of California introduced House Concurrent Resolution 27: "Resolved . . . that the President of the United States hereby be memorialized to take without delay the necessary steps to prepare a plan for the calling of a world convention which shall draw up a constitution for an all-inclusive, democratic, nonmilitary federation of nations."[42] The campaign immediately swung into action to try to drum up support for the Voorhis resolution. They put out an emergency edition of their newsletter to announce the measure and encourage people to flood their representatives with messages in favor of it. They reached out to other peace groups to try to gain endorsements. They knew the resolution was a long shot, but they hoped at least that it would win a hearing within the House Committee on Foreign Relations. On August 31, Lloyd Jr. urged Voorhis to bring the matter of a world convention to Roosevelt, "now that the European tension has eased a little bit."[43] The next day, Germany invaded Poland and World War II began. Despite continued lobbying from Lloyd Jr. and other members of the campaign, the Voorhis resolution was never debated in Congress. Lloyd Jr. tried in vain to interest other members of Congress until he was drafted in 1943.

He registered as a conscientious objector and spent the rest of the war in a Civilian Public Service camp in California.

The second prong of the CWG's strategy was to build networks with other organizations and then persuade them to advocate for Schwimmer and Lloyd's plan. These included women's peace groups, such as WILPF; mixed-sex groups, such as the United Pacifist Committee; and other world government organizations, such as Clarence Streit's Federal Union. The peace movement as a whole, however, had suffered during the 1930s. The economic crisis had greatly diminished the amount of time and money that supporters were able to donate to the cause, and the growing threats in Europe and Asia made some doubtful of a cause that felt like acquiescing to militarist regimes. Peace advocates were increasingly divided between those who remained staunch pacifists and wanted the United States to maintain strict neutrality and those who believed the United States had to work with the League of Nations and allied forces in order to halt the aggression and violence. The latter, led by internationalists including William Allen White, James Shotwell, and Clark Eichelberger, reorganized themselves into prointerventionist groups like the Committee to Defend America by Aiding the Allies.[44] Schwimmer and Lloyd wanted nothing to do with such men; their adherence to pacifism steered them more toward the strict neutralists.

Lloyd's long-standing ties to WILPF, as well as that organization's stated commitment to neutrality, made it an obvious place to start. She was still an active member of the Chicago branch and joined the national executive board sometime in the early 1930s. Given her long tenure and her status as a founding member, she was widely respected, but she was not universally liked. Unlike many other members, Lloyd was a self-described militant feminist who was active in the National Woman's Party and campaigned for the Equal Rights Amendment. Dorothy Detzer, who had served as the executive secretary of the U.S. section since 1924, referred to her as a part of a small minority of "absolutists" and "inflexible humorless zealots."[45] Given Detzer's power within the organization, Lloyd faced an uphill battle when she introduced the Schwimmer-Lloyd plan in early 1938. She reminded her colleagues that WILPF had critiqued the League of Nations Covenant in 1919 and argued they now had a chance to help shape a new world organization.[46] WILPF briefly took up the cause; the national board passed a handful of resolutions calling on the Roosevelt administration to convene a world constitutional convention and encouraging members to study and publicize various plans for world government.[47] But it was never the priority Lloyd wanted it to be.

Detzer made it clear to Lloyd that she personally was not committed to the cause, and she had extensive power to set the organization's agenda. She often left world government causes, such as support for the Voorhis resolution, off of her regular circulars to members, despite frequent protests from Lloyd.[48] While Detzer agreed that the United States should play an active role in working toward an organized world, she referred to world government as "an issue which did not have immediate relation to the present political realities in the world." Lloyd resigned permanently from WILPF in the spring of 1942.[49]

Schwimmer and Wynner, meanwhile, looked to the United Pacifist Committee (UPC). Labor activist and Christian pacifist A. J. Muste had formed the UPC in 1938 as a clearinghouse for absolute pacifist organizations in the New York area. Wynner and Babcock met with Muste in early October of that year; both reported back to Schwimmer that Muste was supportive of the campaign's plan. He agreed to bring the idea before the committee and told Wynner and Babcock that he believed he could organize a delegation to President Roosevelt to ask him to call "the right kind of world conference." Schwimmer subsequently wrote to Lloyd that "that fine A. J. Muste ... is entirely for our plan." Her hopes were soon dashed, however, by the final version of the UPC's resolution, which demanded a "World Conference to work out solutions for the basic economic difficulties in connection with access to raw materials, currency and tariff policies, etc., the tragic problems of refugees, and other pressing economic and social issues." There was no call in the resolution for any kind of world government. Discouraged, Wynner reported to Schwimmer that the committee did not really believe in the cause, but she conceded that the resolution "begins to circulate certain essential conditions of a future conference."[50]

Finally, given the popularity of Streit's *Union Now*, it made sense to Schwimmer and Lloyd to see if they might cooperate with him. When Schwimmer first read the book, she was enthusiastic. "For one who has spent a life-time propagating World Government and is just about despairing of its realization," she wrote to Streit in March 1939, "your book and your lectures are more than a tonic. I can't tell you how happy I am to know that you are as determined as the few of us are to get World Government *now*." She regarded the differences between their plans as slight. Where Streit's plan was limited to the fifteen democracies, the Schwimmer-Lloyd plan called for *inviting* all nations of the world to join immediately, but Schwimmer recognized that not all would do so. To her the all-inclusive invitation was a significant gesture to the people of every nation, regardless of the attitude of their government toward the world body. Schwimmer requested a meeting with Streit to "straighten out the seeming differences in our plans." Streit agreed that the two plans had enough in common that they should all be able to cooperate.[51]

Schwimmer's optimism about Streit did not last. She found him a poor public speaker, uninterested in entertaining criticism or engaging in debate. This impression was reinforced during a private meeting between the two in March 1939. Streit wanted only to convince her that his plan promised immediate success. He had no patience, Schwimmer reported, for her concerns. More significantly, to her mind, the two disagreed on the role of European colonies in the new world government. Schwimmer characterized Streit as "rigidly pro-British Commonwealth" and told Lloyd Jr. that he "nearly ferociously refused" to consider including India in his federal union. "He has no conception," she argued, "of the human psychology involved in telling the people of all the nations and also of colonies and dependencies that we consider them our equals, of whom some may need assistance while growing into self-governing nationhood." Schwimmer presented another aspect of this critique in her published refutation of Streit. Limiting the federal union to only fifteen countries would be disastrous, she argued: "He does not seem to realize that to start with a *power group of nations*, labelled Union of Democracies, would provoke a Union of the rest of the world in hostile opposition."[52] Any potential for cooperation between Schwimmer and Streit foundered on the latter's rejection of "all-inclusiveness."

In their efforts to collaborate with WILPF, the UPC, and Streit, as well as other groups including the National Woman's Party, the War Resisters' League, and the National Council for the Prevention of War, the Campaign for World Government refused to compromise. Not only the idea of world government in general but also their plan in particular had to be accepted absolutely. This rigid stance emanated from Schwimmer. She had been uncompromising since the days of her interactions with Woodrow Wilson, and the intervening years had only crystallized her faith in her own convictions. Despite the best efforts of Lloyd and her children to temper Schwimmer's fervor, she continued to be as bold and demanding as ever.

Over time, debates over whether and to what extent the CWG should compromise its stance in order to build coalitions strained existing tensions between Schwimmer and the Lloyds. Throughout the late 1930s and early 1940s, Schwimmer repeatedly tried to distance herself from the daily work of the campaign, declaring she was wholly absorbed with finishing her autobiography. But her frequent correspondence with Lloyd and Lloyd Jr., often on a daily basis, revealed her inability to cede even a modicum of control over the campaign's mission and strategy. Lloyd Jr. especially found her frustrating. His impulse was to be cautious and cooperative; Schwimmer's was to be combative. In February 1940, for example, Lloyd Jr. discovered that Schwimmer and Wynner had been sending out postcards to their acquaintances in New York, urging them to fight against Streit's Federal Union plan. Lloyd Jr. argued they should not dissuade people from *any* world government plan until the general idea had caught on. Schwimmer's response was typically melodramatic. She wrote to Lloyd, "I will not question him, but I must know whether we are giving up and are lining up the campaign with those organizations which believe that anything but direct action can save the world. Please let me know clearly and definitively where we stand, because then I shall fold up and declare myself dead from the point of view of efforts for world peace."[53] Lloyd, who often found herself in the middle of these struggles between her old friend and her son, did her best to appease both, but the disagreements over emphasis and strategy continued to the point that the campaign was virtually paralyzed by 1942.

The outbreak of war tested people's commitments to world government. On September 4, 1939, Schwimmer wrote to Albert Einstein, asking for a meeting to confer with him on "world peace action." Einstein had become increasingly outspoken on the need for an international body to regulate armaments. But in response, he admonished Schwimmer to "rejoice that the English and the French have at last plucked up the courage. I, at least, acknowledge this thankfully and it is my intention to keep my mouth shut. I advise you to do likewise."[54] Schwimmer, of course, would do no such thing. Where the war made some question their commitments to the machinery of peace, she doubled down on world government. "There is only one peace aim," she told Lloyd, "and that is to make war impossible in the whole world through the creation of such a world organization which makes war unnecessary, even from the militarist point of view."[55]

If the outbreak of war had made the CWG's work more difficult, U.S. entry into the fray in 1941 made it virtually impossible. "The Japanese attack of Sunday will be good immunity against all sectors of the peace movement in this country for at least fifty years," Lloyd Jr. presaged on December 10.[56] For Schwimmer, Pearl Harbor signaled the time to abandon any hope of working with governments and turn exclusively to the people of the world. As during

World War I, she called for an immediate cessation of hostilities as "the one gesture which would ensure the attention of all the peoples in the world."[57] Even in early 1942, she was still convinced that if offered what she saw as a real opportunity to end the fighting, the people of the world would jump on board. Schwimmer never seemed to grasp the extent to which Americans—to say nothing of the rest of the world—saw World War II as a just, necessary war. Over the next few years, the campaign existed only on paper and perhaps in Schwimmer's mind.

Even taking into account Schwimmer's intransigence, their plan's vagueness, and the campaign's lack of direction and resources, Schwimmer and Lloyd embodied all three facets of world citizenship as defined in this book. They called for the formation of a new kind of global polity and began shaping it in the pages of *Chaos*. As absolute pacifists, they were determined to abolish the use of force within the new federation. And while their plan for colonial territories came with civilizationist undertones, their commitment to an "all-inclusive" world community went far beyond what either their predecessors or their contemporaries envisioned. Their federation of nations did not garner much support in the late 1930s. But as World War II progressed, more and more people became interested in planning for the peace, and women and men across the United States and around the world formulated their own ideas on what that peace should look like. Schwimmer and Lloyd's vision of a populist, egalitarian democracy found a new audience among postwar world federationists and critics of the newly created United Nations. Although the full radical potential of Schwimmer and Lloyd's plan was never realized, their beliefs helped shape future debates over world organization.

CHAPTER 5

Esther Caukin Brunauer and Collective Security for the World Community

On Friday, February 24, 1933—less than a month after Adolf Hitler was sworn in as chancellor of Germany—thirty-two-year-old Esther Caukin Brunauer arrived in Berlin to begin a year's residence as a research fellow of the Oberlaender Trust of the Carl Schurz Foundation. Brunauer had a PhD in European history from Stanford University and extensive experience with European politics through her work for the American Association of University Women (AAUW), and she planned to conduct research at the Reichstag Library on "Women in the Civic Life of Germany" and "German Political Parties and the Foreign Policy of the Reich." The Reichstag fire on February 27, which Hitler claimed was set by Communists and used to consolidate his political control, changed her plans. Instead, given the changing situation in Germany, she decided to focus her efforts on gathering material on the Nazis' rise to power. To that end, she spent hundreds of hours reading back issues of German magazines and newspapers. She traveled around the country, attending meetings and events and interviewing local and national public officials. She spoke with university women, not just in Germany but also in Poland, Austria, and Hungary, to gain a sense of the struggles they were facing. And she interviewed as many Nazi Party leaders as she could, including the chancellor himself. Unfortunately she left little record of the meeting. "The interview with Hitler," she later reported, "just a couple of days before Christmas, was an interesting experience and valuable in helping me to understand the psychology of the man."[1]

Brunauer's experiences in Germany affected her deeply. "Even though the transition from the republic to the national socialist state was not marked by the usual outward accompaniments of a revolution, it was no less profound and no less soul-shaking," she told her AAUW colleagues. She was disturbed by the implications of the German revolution for other Western countries, including the United States. "If it could be done in Germany," she believed, "it could be done in any other country." Both as a historian and as a human being, she saw this as a grave development for humanity: "This mass movement simply sets aside as of no value many aspects of modern culture which seem to us of greatest importance, and in that sense it may mark a turning-point as vital as was the renaissance of five or six hundred years ago—but in the other direction."[2]

Brunauer was a prominent member of a cohort of politically active women in the 1930s who argued that the rise of Nazism and fascism in Europe and Asia demanded active resistance. At a time when the vast majority of Americans believed U.S. intervention in World War I had been a mistake and that the country should take all measures to keep out of any conflicts brewing in Europe or Asia, Brunauer spoke for a small but concerned minority.[3] For them, neutrality represented an abandonment of the world community. Instead they promoted collective security, a phrase that became widely used in that decade to signify the need for an international organization of nation-states pledged to aid each other in the event of an attack. What Brunauer and her colleagues wanted was a world system based on mutual defense—and the full participation of the United States in it. They believed both they as individuals and the United States as a country had a responsibility to the rest of the world. Active citizenship in that world required challenging Nazism and fascism. Throughout the 1930s and the early years of the war, women like Brunauer and such organizations as the AAUW, the Young Women's Christian Association (YWCA), and the National Committee on the Cause and Cure of War (NCCCW) worked tirelessly to sway public opinion in their favor.

Like Andrews, Tuttle, and other women who had campaigned for U.S. membership in the League of Nations, Brunauer and her contemporaries believed women had a particular responsibility as world citizens to work for peace. Before 1939, fulfilling that obligation meant opposing neutrality; after 1939, it meant collaborating on plans for a postwar international organization that would rectify the shortcomings of the league. Even before the United States entered the war, women began strategizing on how to participate in shaping the postwar polity. Brunauer did not provide details on how she thought that polity should be organized, but she echoed two principles from other women world citizens. Like Schwimmer and Lloyd, she argued that any postwar body had to be all-inclusive and democratic in structure, and like Andrews, she thought its creation had to be led by the United States. Brunauer was convinced the United States had to play a more active role in the world—a military role, if necessary—to ensure peace. Unlike Mead, who was staunchly antimilitarist, and very much unlike Schwimmer and Lloyd, who were absolute pacifists, Brunauer expressed few qualms about the use of force when necessary. To her mind, the violence and chaos of the 1930s demanded full engagement on the part of the United States, not just in the war but in rebuilding the world community after it.

Opposing Neutrality

Brunauer's opposition to neutrality stemmed not only from her time in Germany but also from her family and her education. She was born near Jackson, California, in July 1901—making her a generation younger than all the women profiled in this book except Edith Wynner. Her father's work as an electrician kept the family from settling anywhere permanently; Brunauer and her younger sister moved frequently and often stayed with friends and relatives. The extent to which her parents' political beliefs influenced her as a child is unclear, but her father was a "strong liberal whose beliefs verged on socialism," and her mother was a dedicated suffragist who later worked for the United States Land Office—one of the earliest women appointed to a federal position. Brunauer graduated from Girls' High School in San Francisco in 1920 and enrolled at Mills College. While there, she enjoyed a close relationship with Mills president Aurelia Reinhardt. Reinhardt served as president of the AAUW from 1923 to 1927; it was likely she who connected Brunauer with the association, which later financed her graduate study. Brunauer received her BA in 1924 and completed a PhD in modern European history and international politics at Stanford in 1927. After graduating, Brunauer took a position in Washington, D.C., as a research associate with the AAUW, serving as the director of their international education program and also as secretary of their International Relations Committee until she left the association in 1944. In 1931 she married Stephen Brunauer, a chemist who had immigrated from Hungary ten years earlier. The couple's first child, their son, Lewis, was born in 1934 but died at the age of three following an acute infection. They later had two more children: Kathryn, born in 1938, and Elizabeth, born in 1942.[4]

Upon their return from Germany in early 1934, Esther and Stephen Brunauer settled in Washington, D.C., and Brunauer went back to work full

Figure 6. Esther Caukin Brunauer. Photo courtesy of the American Association of University Women.

time for the AAUW. The association had been established in 1921, formed from the combination of the Association of Collegiate Alumnae and a handful of smaller groups dedicated to promoting women's education and fostering community among women college students and alumnae. Throughout the 1920s, the association expanded its mission to include professional training for and promotion of women as civic leaders and social reformers. Members also took an interest in global affairs; the International Relations Committee, chaired by Mary Woolley but directed largely by Brunauer, focused on educating Americans about U.S. foreign policy and U.S. relations with the rest of the world. The committee circulated study materials for local associations and campaigned for women's representation on international bodies. Herbert Hoover's appointment of Woolley to the U.S. delegation to the 1932 Disarmament Conference in Geneva was one of their major successes. Members of the committee, including Woolley and Brunauer, also represented the AAUW within the International Federation of University Women and the NCCCW. Brunauer's work with the former increasingly involved maintaining contacts with women threatened by violence in Europe, while her work for the latter included sponsoring study groups on international questions and sending representatives to its annual conferences.

Though most did not call themselves feminists in the 1930s, AAUW members believed wholeheartedly in gender equality. As the organization representing the most highly educated women in the country, the association advocated for every woman to have a full opportunity to exercise her intellectual capabilities. To that end they promoted women's education—Brunauer's time in Germany was sponsored by an AAUW fellowship—and professional advancement, especially in public service. While some individual members supported the National Woman's Party and the Equal Rights Amendment (ERA), many did not, and the association did not take an official stand on the ERA until the 1960s. For Brunauer, it was a question of priorities. She did not oppose the amendment on principle, but she felt that working for it cost time and energy that could be better spent elsewhere.[5]

As it did for many activist white women in this period, the AAUW's belief in equality had racialized limits. Like other organizations, the association passively rather than actively discouraged the membership of non-white women. Black women, for instance, were eligible to join if they were college students or graduates. But they rarely opted to become active in their local chapters because AAUW leadership allowed local chapters to follow the social patterns of their communities—which could mean discrimination and segregation, even within chapter meetings. Black women thus often became members at the national level, which made it difficult to find any real sense of fellowship within the organization. Opposition to Nazism before and during the war, in addition to cooperation with women of color in postwar planning efforts during the early 1940s, gradually led the AAUW to take a stronger stance on racial equality after 1945. Though there is no record of it, it is possible that Brunauer's research on Germany in the 1930s and her ongoing crusades against Nazism aided that process.[6]

Her position with the AAUW afforded Brunauer an excellent vantage point from which to observe political developments in Washington, across the United States, and in Europe and East Asia. Public sentiment against any kind of foreign intervention was high in the mid-1930s, even in the face of increasing Italian, Japanese, and German aggression. The United States officially established its neutrality policy in 1935 and renewed it in 1936 and 1937. The first Neutrality Act imposed a general embargo on trading arms and war materiel with any nations in a state of war. Additional acts in the following years added a prohibition on loans to belligerent nations and a "cash-and-carry" policy meant to avoid the complications of transporting goods on neutral ships: in other words, warring nations could purchase munitions from the United States provided they paid in full and moved them themselves.[7] Franklin Roosevelt, for his part, pushed for amendments that would impose an arms embargo only on aggressor nations, but Congress was determined to maintain strict neutrality. These measures were widely popular, especially in the wake of the Nye Committee investigations, which stoked beliefs that weapons manufacturers had steered the country into World War I for the sake of their own profits.

Throughout the 1930s Brunauer was frustrated with what she saw as the entrenched refusal of the American public to engage meaningfully with the world. "Why is it," she asked, "that in spite of all the work that has been done these past sixteen years, we are still so far from having developed in the American citizen the international consciousness needed to make the United States function effectively and intelligently in the society of nations?" Citing the enormous amount of research that had been done on global topics and institutions, she wondered if internationalists had been "a little naïve in believing that all we had to do was to say, 'Here are the facts,' and that the public would thereupon revise its preconceived notions and throw away its prejudices." She called on her colleagues to put more effort and money into "interpreting the results of the research work in terms of the experience of the ordinary person" and reshaping "those elements of opinion that rest upon emotion and not upon fact."[8] Greater education about international affairs, she believed, could help ordinary citizens not only understand the stakes involved in opposing Nazism and fascism but also recognize their ability to influence government policy.[9]

While Brunauer's main focus in her role with the AAUW was to educate members on the neutrality issue in a way that would allow them to come to their own conclusions, it is clear from many of her writings in the 1930s that she not only opposed neutrality but also favored a system of collective security. The term is often associated with U.S. debates over joining the League of Nations but was not widely used until the 1930s, when Japanese and German expansion gave the phrase particular resonance. People rarely defined the term, but it generally represented the notion of an international organization of states characterized by the collective pledge of members to defend each other against attack. A world government premised on collective security thus differed greatly from the nonmilitary one envisioned by Schwimmer and Lloyd. In the event of an armed attack on any member nation, other states in the union would respond not just with condemnation or economic sanctions but with force.

Brunauer was clear, however, that not all applications of force would be acceptable. It was particularly important for her to make this plain in the context of the late 1930s, when totalitarian regimes used force indiscriminately. The United States, she told the delegates to the Fourteenth Conference on the Cause and Cure of War in January 1939, should rethink the relationship between diplomacy and the use of force. Recent years had shown that dialogue and persuasion alone were ineffective against nations such as Germany. The only option for anyone who wanted to see lasting peace in the world, Brunauer argued, was to "find some combination of *force with reason* that will eventually accomplish the two objectives most essential to the preservation of peace based on law: A way of restraining the independent use of force to achieve national aims, and a means of assuring a measure of justice to those nations which feel that they labor under serious handicaps."[10] Nations, in other words, should not be allowed to use force unilaterally; only in situations where it was necessary to ensure justice would there be a collective use of force. Nonetheless, this support for the use of force at all distinguished her approach from earlier arguments like Mead's, which called only for a very limited international police force, and from contemporaneous plans for world organization like Schwimmer and Lloyd's, which was adamantly nonmilitary. For Brunauer, in the context of the 1930s and the advance of fascism and Nazism, prohibiting the use of force entirely was not an option.

Brunauer's argument for "force with reason" was a clear endorsement of collective security, including the use of sanctions. Its application, through a coordinated international effort, would over time reduce the need for the use of force by individual nations in their own defense. "A successful collective policy," she suggested, "would involve not only willingness to use economic sanctions and even military force in some contingencies, but also the development of a sense of responsibility and a certain sophistication in regard to international policies that is now lacking in our national psychology."[11] The only hope for ending war around the world, she told an audience in 1938, "lies in the direction of collective responsibility for peace, as a substitute for national defense."[12] In other words, all women and men would have to exercise greater world citizenship and accept the attendant obligation to work for peace.

Brunauer's belief in that collective responsibility, not just on the part of the United States but of U.S. women in particular, was heavily influenced by Mary Woolley. After attending the Disarmament Conference in 1932, Woolley continued to serve as president of Mount Holyoke College until her retirement in 1937. She was one of Brunauer's closest colleagues at the AAUW, and the two worked together on the International Relations Committee throughout the second half of the 1930s. Woolley emphasized that U.S. women, as citizens of the world, had specific obligations to the world community. "Every normal woman," she argued in 1935, "whatever her vocation . . . has a community responsibility inherent in the fact that she is a citizen. Today that community responsibility has widened, widened to a world community."[13] In order to meet that obligation, according to Woolley, women needed to educate themselves about world affairs and then make their voices heard—by participating in political discussions, by contacting their representatives, and by influencing others wherever possible. But she had an even more specific goal in mind: a world system based on collective security. "The principle for which liberal, far-sighted, world-minded citizens of Great Britain, in fact, of Europe, are struggling, is the principle of *collective security*, the only security in a world that has become a neighborhood. And we, here in the United States of America, have a chance to 'aid and abet'—or to undercut—that effort for the security of the future." In the long term, Woolley hoped that chance would lead to the development of a stronger international government, but in the short term she advocated measures such as the enforcement of the Kellogg-Briand Pact.[14]

Together Woolley and Brunauer steered the AAUW toward collective security. In May 1938, the International Relations Committee recommended that the association withdraw from the National Council on the Prevention of War on the grounds that the council had "adopted an increasingly isolationist attitude toward foreign affairs" and its campaigns had "become increasingly hysterical and emotional." The AAUW, they noted, "had been feeling more strongly than ever the need of working for closer collaboration by the United States with other nations in measures to prevent and suppress war." The association's executive committee accepted the committee's recommendation and withdrew from the council.[15] These moves were not without opposition; one member wrote Brunauer an angry letter urging the "younger women" of the committee to study the 1915 Hague Congress and to promote neutral mediation. But the majority of the AAUW membership supported Brunauer's stance.[16]

This rejection of isolationism and strict neutrality in favor of more active internationalism was increasingly common among many of the most prominent national women's organizations in the late 1930s. Two illustrative examples are the League of Women Voters (LWV) and the YWCA. At its national board of directors meeting in November 1935, the LWV rejected isolation and decided not to support the Neutrality Act. The national body followed suit at its 1936 convention.[17] National president Marguerite Wells was a strong proponent of collective security, but she recognized that the majority of the LWV's membership was concerned primarily with keeping the United States out of war. In October 1938 she wrote to Louise Leonard Wright, chair of the International Relations Committee, that "all nations, including our own, must arm in the emergency of threats from fascist countries." She encouraged Wright to focus the committee's work on educating LWV members on the possible necessity of armed intervention.[18] Wright, for her part, agreed with Brunauer and Woolley that the United States had a responsibility to work for peace, even if that meant going to war to ensure it. In its support for Kellogg-Briand, its leadership of disarmament efforts, and its support for the International Labor Organization, Wright argued, the United States had already taken significant steps toward the position of "world leadership" it now had to embrace wholeheartedly.[19]

The YWCA, meanwhile, had been actively interested in U.S. foreign relations since its inception in the 1860s. Throughout the 1920s and 1930s it had maintained ties with the League of Nations Association and campaigned actively for U.S. membership in both the league and the World Court. The U.S. National Board's international program in the 1930s was directed largely by Emily Hickman. Hickman was born in Buffalo, New York, in 1880 and graduated from Cornell University in 1901. After earning her PhD in history from Cornell in 1911, she taught for sixteen years at Wells College in Aurora, New York, before being appointed professor of history at the New Jersey College for Women in New Brunswick. She taught there full time throughout World War II.[20] Like Brunauer, she was also active in the NCCCW and many other organizations through this period, but her organizational home was the YWCA.

Hickman and the International Relations Committee of the YWCA shifted toward collective security more gradually than did Marguerite Wells and Louise Wright. They supported Roosevelt's neutrality legislation and urged local associations to pressure the administration to enforce it.[21] Hickman's own views began to change during a tour of the country from January to June of 1938. She met with members of thirty local YWCAs, scattered across the country, from Nashville, New Orleans, and Los Angeles to Seattle, Minneapolis, and Providence. She also met with other local groups, spoke at high schools, gave radio addresses, and wrote for local newspapers. Those travels convinced her that while the desire to eliminate war was widespread, most YWCA members had little knowledge about the actual methods needed to do it. Members were open to various programs for peace, she noted, but they often could not distinguish among different proposals. As an example, she cited simultaneous interest in the programs of the isolationist Keep America Out of War Committee *and* the internationalist League of Nations Association.[22]

As a result of her trip, Hickman began to formulate a new approach to international relations, one that would in turn influence the direction of the YWCA. In several speeches and reports regarding her trip, she argued the most pressing task facing humanity was the "establishment of a world community." By this, Hickman meant not only a shift in cultural attitudes away from "complete independent sovereignty" and the right of nations to "enforce their individual will wherever they choose to do so." She had in mind a much more concrete community, one characterized by such political institutions as the League of Nations and the World Court, such economic programs as international currency regulation and the reciprocal lowering of trade barriers, and a legal system of disarmament and sanctions to forestall future wars.[23] Her journey across the United States had convinced her that more and more Americans supported the idea of international cooperation, at least in the abstract, although her perspective was likely skewed by the fact that most of her interactions were with members of the YWCA—an organization that had had an internationalist orientation since before World War I.

Brunauer, Wells, Hickman, and many of their colleagues brought their concerns into the NCCCW. In the mid-1930s its daily work was directed by Josephine Schain, a suffragist and social worker who had held prominent positions in several national women's organizations, and a small group of leaders that included Brunauer. The theme of women citizens' responsibility for peace permeated the committee's discourse throughout these years. "With us, as citizens," Schain told members in 1937, "rests the responsibility to see that the policies of our government do not run counter to the efforts being made to establish a world order on a peace basis."[24] Eleanor Roosevelt struck a similar note two years later when she addressed delegates to the Fourteenth Conference on the Cause and Cure of War on the obligation of all citizens to educate themselves about the world situation and to stand against the use of force to settle disputes. "We, here in this country," she told the attendees, "know that democracy is based on individual responsibility. I have an idea that we are not quite as well aware of the fact that peace is based on recognition of individual responsibility, nor are we aware of the fact that each and every one of us must put ourselves into a frame of mind where we can bring to bear the force of our belief that we must settle questions at home and abroad by methods of reason and not by force."[25] Hickman endorsed Roosevelt's arguments at the same conference: "To carry out our program, each member of this group must accept the kind of individual responsibility about which Mrs. Roosevelt talked. . . . Each one of us must take the leadership for intelligent and aggressive action in our community."[26]

The NCCCW did not endorse collective security until after the war began in 1939, but it did oppose strict neutrality. In January 1937 the group resolved to support revision of the neutrality policy in order to allow the president to limit the arms embargo to aggressor nations.[27] Brunauer later referred to this as the moment when the entire organization's ethos shifted. The 1937 conference marked for her the moment when "we moved from a study of causes of war *in general* and cures of war *in general* to a recognition that the war that was then in the making was due to one decisive cause, and that by that time there was only one cure for it."[28] From that point on, the committee worked to support the Allies. The following year, Hickman summarized the mood of the conference by noting the pervasive belief among delegates that "war anywhere is the concern of all" and that for the United States "to do nothing," by maintaining strict neutrality, "would be futile and wicked."[29]

By early 1939 the mood of the country was beginning to change. A poll taken in February found that nearly two-thirds of Americans believed that if war broke out in Europe, the United States should do anything it could, short of entering, to aid Britain and France.[30] Spurred by Japanese expansion in China in 1937 and the German occupation of Austria in 1938, internationalists formed several new organizations to pressure Congress and the Roosevelt administration to revise U.S. neutrality policy and take a stronger stance against the advance of fascism. The popular campaign for neutrality revision was led by the American Union for Concerted Peace Efforts, which emerged in March 1939 from several strands of other organizations. The Senate remained dead set against the idea, but the House Committee on Foreign Affairs conducted hearings throughout April 1939. Brunauer, who served on the union's executive committee, and several of her colleagues testified during the proceedings.

Brunauer spoke in favor of limiting the embargo to aggressor nations. Such a change, she argued, would "establish a principle of nonmilitary action

to restrain aggression, and thereby make a tremendously important contribution to the prevention of international war right now and to the establishment
of a permanent peace for the ages." Drawing on her own experiences in and
knowledge of Germany, she argued that the strict neutrality policy actually
aided Hitler because it made the United States seem indifferent. In contrast,
"benevolent neutrality"—by which she meant a firm statement that the United
States would throw its "moral support" and "gigantic economic support"
behind the victims of aggression—might be just the "balancing force" needed
to avoid war. That possibility obligated the United States to act. Brunauer
took advantage of the opportunity to drive home her point about the United
States' responsibility to the world community. The United States had always
been entangled in European affairs, she argued. There was no choice but to
accept it. Whether hard-line neutrality supporters liked it or not, "the United
States plays a role in international affairs by its mere existence. . . . Because
the United States is a disinterested nation it can make its power count on
the side of peace and justice." The United States had a responsibility not just
to people living in the world in 1939, Brunauer asserted, but to future generations to take up its proper role on the world stage and support the Allies
against Germany and Japan.[31]

Despite Brunauer's testimony, however, and considerable pressure both
from internationalist organizations and President Roosevelt, Congress rebuffed
all efforts at neutrality revision before September 1939. From Brunauer's perspective, members of Congress had abrogated their obligation to the world
community to oppose Nazism and fascism. As she followed the news of the
German invasion of Poland and the onset of war, Brunauer must have felt as
though all her efforts on behalf of collective security had been for naught. She,
Woolley, Hickman, and other women had been beating the drum of *responsibility* for years, trying to persuade people that the United States had to oppose
aggression in Europe and Asia. It would take two more years and a direct attack
on their own soil to convince most Americans of that fact.

Women's Plans for World Organization

Once the war began, internationalist organizations like Americans United
focused on convincing Congress to repeal the Neutrality Acts altogether—
which they finally did in late September—and fully support the Allies. Leading this charge were prominent, well-connected men who enjoyed close

access to Roosevelt and Congress and the considerable resources of foundations such as the Carnegie Endowment for International Peace. But most of them were focused on the short-term objective of Allied support; they gave little regard to the long-term role of the United States in the world or to the possibility of establishing a new world organization after the war. The events of the late 1930s, and particularly Hitler's stunning seizure of France in June 1940, seemed to confirm the futility of an intergovernmental organization designed to maintain peace.[32]

There were exceptions. The most widely known was Clarence Streit, whose *Union Now* was a best seller in 1939. The most coordinated effort was launched late that same year by James Shotwell, Clark Eichelberger, and others as the Commission to Study the Organization of Peace (CSOP). The commission gathered dozens of scholars, journalists, former politicians, and others to "engage in a thorough and comprehensive study of all aspects of the problem of international peace, with special emphasis on plans for a future world organization to maintain peace and to promote the progress of mankind."[33] Women made up ten of the original seventy-four members of the commission; that number included Brunauer, Hickman—who was also the only woman on the eight-member executive committee—Virginia Gildersleeve, and Josephine Schain. However, while the commission published regular reports beginning in 1940, it kept its more concrete plans for world organization private until 1943.[34] Likewise private were early discussions at the State Department and the Council on Foreign Relations—discussions that would develop after 1942 into official postwar planning efforts.

Internationalist women, meanwhile, were thinking specifically and publicly about world organization as early as 1939. Even before the United States entered the war, Brunauer and many of her colleagues devoted their precious energy and scarce resources to planning for the postwar world—a world they were determined to help shape. Their two most notable efforts shared similar names and an affiliation with the NCCCW, although they overlapped very little. The first, the Commission on a Permanent World Society (CPWS), existed throughout most of 1939 and 1940. Its members dedicated themselves to studying existing models for world organization and determining the key features any postwar body should have. Those included, they decided, collective security, universal membership, democratic relations among nations, and economic justice. The second endeavor was more specific. Convened as part of the Woman's Centennial Congress in 1940, members of the Commission on World Peace Through World Organization designed an actual structure for a world government, and to the other commission's list of key features added greater curtailment of national sovereignty. Brunauer, although she did not participate extensively in either effort, published her own thoughts on world organization throughout this period and agreed with many of both commissions' conclusions.

The first notable effort was the emergence of the CPWS from the Fourteenth Conference on the Cause and Cure of War in January 1939. Its mandate was to study the best methods and processes for organizing the world. "Whatever the cause, whatever the proposed remedies," the conference delegates stated, "there will be no elimination of war itself as an instrument of national policy until all nations unite in a cooperative endeavor to set up permanent machinery whereby the common concerns of national states can be dealt with on an orderly basis of law and justice."[35] Chaired by Edith Ware, a longtime associate of Brunauer's at the AAUW, the commission included representatives from all member organizations of the NCCCW. Emily Hickman served as the commission's secretary throughout 1939, and Josephine Schain took an active role in its discussions.

After spending the summer of 1939 studying existing plans for world government—the list did not include Schwimmer and Lloyd's, for reasons that are unclear—as well as other plans for peace, such as Kellogg-Briand and various disarmament treaties of the 1920s and 1930s, members of the commission arrived at two conclusions. First, any world organization would falter without the active participation of the United States. Second, they therefore should focus their efforts on studying methods of world organization that seemed to offer the greatest likelihood of popular support in their own country. At Schain's recommendation, the commission based its first "unit of study" on inter-American cooperation, believing that the "better society of nations in the Western Hemisphere" could serve as a model for a global society.[36] Throughout the fall and winter of 1939–1940, the commission members spent considerable time compiling a detailed study outline of inter-American relations for discussion among NCCCW member organizations.

The commission published its conclusions in the summer of 1940, in which they called for "active peace" and the embrace of collective security. In contrast to a negative peace, characterized only by the absence of war, they called for constructive action, similar to that employed for national defense: "It seems clear that peace needs its planning board, no less than war, and that the building of peaceful relations must be a commitment no less than defense. . . . The achievement of peaceful relations between nations will be a by-product of constructive change for improvement of standards of living, coincidentally and mutually advantageous to all the parties touched by any adjustments proposed. The only peace that can be enduring will be a cooperative peace." Such a cooperative peace could not, however, be *imposed* on the nations of the world, nor could any one nation assume a position of dominance. Democratic relations among states would have to be ensured.[37]

The commission also stressed the need for recognition of global economic interdependence and a system of organization to ensure economic justice. Technological innovations, especially in transportation and communication, had drawn the world closer, CPWS members argued, and nations were now more interdependent than ever before. That state of affairs required concomitant political cooperation to ensure universally beneficial trade relations, support for proposals to improve economic conditions, and a commitment to raising the standard of living around the world. The collective security they envisioned was closely tied to economic stability: "Security cannot be found until every country is able to provide adequate opportunities for earning a livable living, and until each country can develop its economic resources through unfettered trade relations with other countries. Such economic prosperity for one nation will not mean security unless all countries enjoy similar opportunity."[38]

This suggests a sensitivity toward the potentially negative impact of sanctions, especially economic sanctions, as a method for enforcing collective security. Edith Ware, for example, noted in one discussion that she had strongly supported sanctions until they were proposed against Italy. She then saw that "if Greece and Rumania, for example, lived up to what was expected of them, if complete sanctions were applied, people in these countries would starve unless the United States and Britain, or other strong countries, carried their economy. The application of sanctions," she concluded, "involves much other cooperative action." An international system of collective security would only succeed, Ware argued, if the international economy were "planned to absorb inequalities, so that countries would not suffer under sanctions."[39] The CPWS thus advocated relinquishment not just of some degree of political sovereignty but of economic sovereignty as well. One of the things they found in their study of U.S.–Latin American relations was that developing countries needed outlets for their goods; the United States, they believed, had a responsibility to provide those outlets in the interest of hemispheric prosperity and stability.[40] They asserted over and over throughout 1940 that improvement in standards of living around the world was necessary in order to achieve lasting peace. Moreover, they argued repeatedly that the United States had a particular responsibility to ensure economic security and prosperity for all.

Brunauer attended a few early meetings of the CPWS but was never heavily involved in its discussions. Her own published writings from these years indicate, however, that she agreed with many of its key findings. She professed reluctance to propose her own blueprint for world organization, but her observations on the strengths and weaknesses of the existing international system were indicative. She praised the League of Nations, the Permanent Court of International Justice, the ILO, and the Pan American Union for fostering public discussion and encouraging cooperation. Their weaknesses, on the other hand, included "the requirement of unanimity on vital questions," their failure to make "much of a dent in the doctrine of national sovereignty," and the fact that "enforcement of their obligations on members is almost impossible." Brunauer did not devote as much time as the CPWS to the issue of sanctions and economic security, but she did argue that any world organization should promote the "twin ends" of peace and justice. The outstanding question, as she saw it, was "how can all nations be brought within the system and subjected to its influence?"[41]

Both Brunauer and the CPWS also argued that any postwar international organization had to be universal in membership, unlike the League of Nations. This was the key point on which they would have sided with Schwimmer and Lloyd against Streit, whose *Union Now* proposed a federation only of North Atlantic democracies. Members of the CPWS agreed that Streit's provisions for popular elections and enforcement mechanisms were points in his favor, but they were very concerned about the union's limited membership. Schain, for instance, argued that any nation willing to abide by international law should be eligible to join.[42] Brunauer, while she praised Streit for provoking discussion about the idea of world government, was not convinced his plan for a union of democracies was the right one. In particular she worried that the failure to admit all nations on equal terms would spell doom, as it had done for the League of Nations.[43] Both the CPWS and Brunauer advocated for a global organization, into which all nations would be invited as members, rather than regional blocs based on geography or type of government.

Above all, Brunauer wanted "democracy in world affairs." The particular form any international organization took was less important, she argued, than the character of that organization. She was wary of any system in which some member nations exercised disproportionate power over others. All nations in the world community had to have equal rights and responsibilities within it. Further, any postwar international system had to center on developing "appreciation of human beings as persons and . . . respect for standards of truth and justice," "loyalty to the free community," and "habits of democratic behavior" and on removing "the causes of greed and selfishness." As for the United States, finally, it now had an opportunity to exert its leadership for world democracy, to harness its new global power not for "self-gratification" but "to serve the cause of human freedom."[44] Brunauer's vision was vague on specifics but clear on principle. Any world organization set up after the war needed to differ from the League of Nations in two key respects: in an echo of Schwimmer and Lloyd, it had to be universal in organization, and it had to be democratic in structure. She did not want a body that simply replicated the old great power politics in a new form.

The second notable effort among women to promote world organization produced a more concrete plan. In November 1940, Carrie Chapman Catt convened the Woman's Centennial Congress in New York City. The purpose was twofold: first, to celebrate one hundred years of women's activism since Lucretia Mott and Elizabeth Cady Stanton had been denied entry to the World's Anti-Slavery Convention in 1840, and second, to issue a new "declaration of purpose," loosely modeled on the Declaration of Sentiments from the 1848 women's rights convention at Seneca Falls, that would outline goals for the next hundred years of women's activism. Five separate commissions carried out the work of preparing the declaration. Their topics included economic and social welfare, government and politics, and postwar peace. The last commission, known as the Commission on World Peace Through World Organization, was made up of thirteen women, including Catt and Schain, and chaired by Louise Laidlaw Backus. Backus was a prominent member of the League of Nations Association and the daughter of Harriet Burton Laidlaw, who had worked with Tuttle on the Woman's Pro-League Council. Like the other commission, this group met regularly throughout 1940 and prepared an extensive report, which was then submitted to the congress attendees for deliberation. "In this dark hour of history," they proclaimed, "it behooves every citizen of a free nation to consider most profoundly his relationship to his country and to the world." The women of the United States in particular needed to assume their "rightful responsibilities," and rise to their "full stature" in order to help meet the present crisis.[45]

The commission stressed the "necessity of world government" and articulated nine basic principles on which it should be based:

1. Universal membership and equality of status for all nations.
2. An international Bill of Rights guaranteeing certain basic freedoms to all people.
3. A solidarity and unity of purpose in solving problems common to all nations.
4. Respect for treaties and international law.
5. Renunciation of force as an instrument of national policy.
6. Collective responsibility for the maintenance of international order.
7. International justice through peaceful settlement of disputes.
8. International progress through peaceful change.
9. Curtailment of national sovereignty.[46]

This list had much in common with earlier ones. Phrases such as "respect for international law" and "peaceful settlement of disputes" had appeared in world organizations schemes since before World War I. Mead, Schwimmer, Lloyd, and others had long stressed the renunciation of force, albeit to varying degrees. And the curtailment of national sovereignty was implicit in all such plans—though again, to varying degrees. Other points evolved more out of the context of the 1930s. The sixth point, for instance, was a logical extrapolation of increasing calls for collective security, while the notion of universal membership became more popular after the confirmed failure of the League of Nations.

As with many of these principles, the commission's recommendations for the structure of the new world government also echoed earlier models, including the league. They envisioned some kind of executive branch, charged with carrying out "the will of the legislative body" and made up of international civil servants answerable only to the world government. That legislative body was key to their program; they suggested a bicameral legislature, with the lower house made up of representatives directly elected by the people and responsible to them. There is no evidence members of the commission read Schwimmer and Lloyd's plan, though they certainly reiterated its central premise that any world government had to represent the world's people. But whatever system prevailed, the commission maintained that it must "be universal and representative of all parts of the world on some basis of equality."[47] The legislature also had to have broader powers than the League of Nations Assembly and should not be "hampered" by the rule of unanimous consent. Finally, the commission recommended a judicial system to settle disputes and an international police force to maintain order.

The most intriguing of the nine points was a harbinger rather than an echo. The commission did not elaborate fully on what they meant by an "international bill of rights," but the notion that individuals should be protected in some measure from war and violence resided implicitly in the Hague Conventions of 1899 and 1907 as well as the League of Nations Covenant.[48] That notion evolved during discussions over the United Nations into a demand for what became the Universal Declaration of Human Rights. The commission's report in 1940 addressed the role of the individual in the world government, and in the process it hinted at what commission members meant when they talked about an international bill of rights. "All government should exist only insofar as it can serve the individual within its domain," the report emphasized. But individuals had obligations to that government in return: "As the world becomes increasingly interdependent, the individual must become increasingly aware of his dependence upon, and his responsibilities to, and his rights as a member of the world community. While remaining loyal to his town, state and nation, he must develop loyalty as a citizen to the world government." If she ever read that, Fannie Fern Andrews must have smiled. But this report went further than she had. In exchange for loyalty, the world citizen would be "guaranteed protection from international violence" and "left undisturbed in working out for himself and his country, the benefits of a higher standard of living."[49] Thus while individuals had to learn to see themselves not just as members of their town or their nation but of the world community, in turn they could expect security and relative autonomy.

Perhaps unsurprisingly, given this concern for human rights, the Commission on World Peace Through World Organization also promoted a liberal policy on decolonization. "National imperialism," the report declared, "must be superseded by a recognition of the principle of independence for all peoples." Commission members were not prepared to call for immediate independence, however. They recommended a new system of mandates as a "transitional step" and even suggested that some territories could be administered directly by the world organization.[50] This idea was very similar to Schwimmer and Lloyd's. And members of this commission, like Schwimmer and Lloyd, apparently had not sought or considered input on this policy from any colonized people or from any people of color within the United States.

Still, the commission's approach was more liberal than that of Mary Woolley or Brunauer, both of whom treated the issue of colonies as one that affected only the colonizers. Woolley believed the "question of colonies" should be "settled in accordance with principles laid down in the League of

Nations."[51] Presumably by this she meant the mandate system, to which colonies themselves had not agreed and which by 1939 had largely dissolved in chaos. Brunauer, for her part, declared that in a world system that guaranteed free trade and access to raw materials, colonies would become less important and less sought after. Gradually they would cease to be a source of conflict. She made no mention of potential independence for colonized people or the possibility that they might want to control their own natural resources.[52] Despite the fact that Brunauer recognized many fundamental shortcomings of the League of Nations, such as its lack of universal membership, when it came to colonies, both she and Woolley were operating within a mindset still very much shaped by the league's mandate system—a mindset centered on colonial powers and their needs rather than on colonized populations.

Members of both of these commissions, like Brunauer, envisioned a postwar world organization based on universal membership, democratic relations between nations, relinquishment of national sovereignty, and collective responsibility for peace. Most notably, unlike their male colleagues in Americans United and other organizations, they were thinking publicly about the ideal form of a world organization even before the United States entered the war. They wanted global, not regional, federations, and they wanted to ensure that the postwar world would not be dominated the great powers, as the League of Nations had been. Most of them likewise envisioned an end to colonial empires, though they were not clear on how that might come about. Above all, they believed they as individual citizens and the United States as a country had a responsibility as members of the world community to help ensure that any postwar organization would finally secure lasting peace. But for as much as she emphasized the need for women to take responsibility for building that new world order, Brunauer—like Mead, Andrews, Tuttle, Schwimmer, and Lloyd before her—did not consider ways in which *all* women might participate in that endeavor or the impact it could have on people of color around the world. It would fall to Black women over the next few years to bring those issues to the table.

While women internationalists were sketching ideas for a universal, cooperative world government, official postwar planners had something very different in mind. Early efforts, conducted largely in secret and led by the State Department and the Council on Foreign Relations, did not include anything resembling what became the United Nations. The men involved in those efforts envisioned not a global organization but a close relationship with Britain that would ensure Anglo-American global supremacy. It was only the weak reception of the Atlantic Charter in August 1941 that led U.S. planners to explore more "universal" options for a world organization. Even then, however, the United States made sure to structure the United Nations so that it would still be able to dominate international relations through the guise of an equitable body.[53]

As these official plans became public after 1942, the contrast between organized women's visions of equality and democracy and official planners' visions of U.S. dominance only grew more stark. But despite the fact that the latter was destined to win out, Brunauer and her colleagues, including Woolley and Hickman, continued to dedicate themselves to the postwar planning process. The work they did between 1935 and 1941—Brunauer's arguments for collective security and the work of the two commissions on world organization—laid the groundwork for women's increased demands to participate in shaping the global polity between 1942 and 1945. As world citizens, they had an obligation to make sure *this* attempt at world organization would endure. Their efforts, along with popular pressure from around the world, succeeded in making the United Nations more responsive to the needs of ordinary people than it might otherwise have been.

In July 1941 Brunauer published a short piece titled "Women on the Ramparts: What Total War Demands of the American Woman." For the past twenty years women's organizations had been educating their members on international cooperation and key foreign policy issues, she argued. Those efforts, according to Brunauer, had created the "climate of opinion" within which the Roosevelt administration was able to revise the neutrality policy, pass the Lend-Lease Act, and aid the Allied war effort against the Axis. Women had always lent their service to national war efforts, Brunauer pointed out, and they would continue to do so in the future. But their greater degree of education and awareness since World War I had led to the feeling among American women "that it is a privilege as well as a duty of their citizenship in the American democracy to help with the concrete, specific things that must be done to defend that democracy and also to take part in formulating the policies behind the defense effort."[54] As planning for the United Nations accelerated, women were determined to play their part.

CHAPTER 6

Mary McLeod Bethune's Plans
for a Just Postwar Peace

"My dear Mr. President," wrote Mary McLeod Bethune, president of the National Council of Negro Women (NCNW), to Franklin Roosevelt in June 1940, "at a time like this, when the basic principles of democracy are being challenged at home and abroad, when racial and religious hatreds are being engendered, it is vitally important that the Negro . . . express anew his faith in your leadership and his unswerving adherence to a program of national defense adequate to insure the perpetuation of the principles of democracy." To Roosevelt's program of national defense, Bethune pledged the support of herself and her organization, and urged the president to make use of the services of "qualified Negro women" in order to "assure the thirteen and a half million Negroes in America that they, too, have earned the right to be numbered among the active forces who are working towards the protection of our democratic stronghold."[1] Over the next five years, Bethune and members of the NCNW made good on that pledge, participating in information campaigns, local Civil Defense Councils, and war service organizations like the Women's Army for National Defense.[2]

For Esther Brunauer, active world citizenship in the late 1930s and early 1940s meant advocating for collective security in a postwar international organization. For Bethune, it meant that and more. Bethune's letter to Roosevelt proved not only that she was ready to defend democratic principles but also that she recognized the opportunity presented by the war for African Americans to advance their own arguments for citizenship. Over the next five years Bethune articulated her demands for national citizenship within an international context. As the war progressed, and especially as the postwar planning process ramped up, Bethune and other Black Americans merged their calls for racial justice at the national and international levels. They demanded an end to racism at home and abroad, white supremacy, and colonial domination. In other words, Bethune's arguments for world citizenship—her demands to participate in shaping a just and inclusive global polity—were heavily informed by the racism and discrimination she faced within the United States. Unlike several of the other women profiled in this book, Bethune's belief in equality was not abstract or theoretical. She demanded a full realization of citizenship's equalizing potential.

And she wanted to see it realized within the United Nations (UN). Bethune was among many U.S. women who took an active interest in postwar planning during this period. As plans for what became the UN took shape between 1942 and 1945, organized women paid close attention and sought to influence those plans as much as possible. They pressured the Roosevelt administration, met with Department of State representatives, and cooperated with other nongovernmental organizations to exercise that influence. Though their interests varied, they all believed women's participation was integral to ensure a just and lasting peace. That was true as well of Bethune and her colleagues in the NCNW, but they also believed such a peace demanded racial equality, not only for themselves but for women and men of color around the world. Through their wartime activities as well as their attendance at the UN Conference in 1945, Bethune and the women of the NCNW asserted their world citizenship.

Fighting for Full Citizenship

Bethune was almost exactly the same age as Schwimmer and Lloyd, but her background was very different. Mary Jane McLeod was born in Mayesville, South Carolina, in 1875, the fifteenth of seventeen children of two formerly enslaved people, Samuel McLeod and Patsy McIntosh. She attended a local mission school until she earned a scholarship to Scotia Seminary in North Carolina, where she graduated in 1894. Bethune taught for several years throughout the South, often moving with her husband, Albertus Bethune, whom she married in 1898. The couple had one child and separated in 1907. In 1904 she opened the Daytona Institute in Daytona Beach, Florida, a normal and industrial school for girls. The school, renamed Bethune-Cookman College in 1929 and still in existence today, became Bethune's lifelong project and her proudest legacy. "Very early in my life," she wrote, "I saw the vision of what our women might contribute to the growth and development of the

race—if they were given a certain type of intellectual training." She expected
her students to shoulder their share of responsibility for uplifting all African
Americans.[3]

While education was her first passion, Bethune also devoted considerable
time and energy to other causes, especially later in her life. She was involved
with the National Association of Colored Women from an early period,
eventually serving as president of the organization from 1924 to 1928. She
traveled throughout the country and internationally, promoting interracial
cooperation and encouraging Black women to join public service efforts. This
experience led to a series of federal appointments in the late 1920s and early
1930s that culminated in her membership in Roosevelt's "Black Cabinet" as
director of the Division of Negro Affairs of the National Youth Administration. Throughout her education and public service, Bethune gained a wealth
of experience with working with white people and building interracial alliances, skills that helped her cultivate white patronage and exploit white paternalism. She aspired to be a "bridge between worlds."[4] As such she was more
involved throughout her life in the mainstream civil rights movement than
leftist anticolonial and Pan-Africanist movements, though she was a member
of the Council of African Affairs. By the late 1930s she had become a "shrewd
politician and a power broker with few equals."[5]

Bethune founded the National Council of Negro Women in 1935 as an
umbrella group for Black women's organizations across the country. She
designed it as a political operation, focused not on nurturing Black womanhood but on lobbying on behalf of all African Americans on issues ranging
from full employment to desegregation to voting rights. One of the council's
first campaigns was for citizenship training for Black women, to teach them
that politics involved more than voting or running for office. It encompassed
everyday needs: "Politics means food at prices you can afford to pay; housing
at prices you can afford to rent or buy; adequate educational facilities and
equal educational opportunities for your children . . . and many other citizenship rights which should be enjoyed alike by all Americans."[6] Through the
council, Bethune encouraged Black women to see themselves as members of
a national body politic rather than just of their families or local communities,
with a responsibility to be an informed and active citizen of that body. For
her, building Black women's capacity for citizenship as well as community
and national leadership was the best path to effecting change.[7]

After 1939, in the context of World War II, it was not hard for Bethune to
expand that body politic to encompass the world. Her own internationalism

Figure 7. Mary McLeod Bethune. Photo courtesy of the Library of Congress, Prints and Photographs Division, Carl Van Vechten Collection (LC 12735 and 12736).

had been growing since the early 1920s. She was a member of the International Council of Women of the Darker Races, founded in 1922, which devised reading lists for Black women's clubs and participated in events like the 1927 Pan-African Congress in New York. That same year Bethune undertook an international goodwill tour as president of the National Association of Colored Women, traveling to nine European countries to gain firsthand knowledge of the "true conditions" of racial oppression abroad. She brought these experiences to bear on her leadership of the NCNW, establishing connections with women in Haiti and Liberia. And as she had promised Roosevelt, she spurred the council members to action in support of the war after U.S. entry in 1941.[8]

Like Brunauer and so many other women internationalists, members of the NCNW began looking to the postwar settlement process almost as soon as the war began. At a symposium on "The Political Scene of 1940," Addie W. Dickerson, NCNW member and president of the International Council of Women of the Darker Races, declared that "because the United States is the leading Neutral of the world its voice will be one of the most influential at the Council Table. Therefore the Negro women of America should so organize themselves that they can exert such influence on their respective parties that their collective voice will be heard in the postwar settlement."[9] Throughout the early years of the war, especially as the likelihood of U.S. involvement grew, the NCNW focused much of its energy on the contributions of Black women to national defense and the entrenched racism they faced while making those contributions.

The leadership of the NCNW worked hard to convince Americans of the threats posed by Hitler, just as Brunauer had done throughout the 1930s. But unlike most white women, Black women drew attention to the racialized nature of those threats. "Never has it been so clear that the Negro people are endangered by Hitlerism at home and abroad," declared Audley Moore, a Black Nationalist and member of Marcus Garvey's United Negro Improvement Association, in the fall of 1941. "To Negro Americans, Hitlerism means the lynch mob, the denial of jobs, and the right to vote and serve on juries. American Hitlerism means the whole systematic curtailment of their rights and liberties as guaranteed to them in the Fourteenth and Fifteenth amendments to the Constitution."[10] Where for Brunauer, Hitler represented a serious threat to peace, for Moore, Hitlerism was even more insidious because of its manifestations within the United States. Moore classed African Americans with Jews and others who faced discrimination and persecution within Hitler's worldview and explicitly tied their struggles for liberation and equality to the world's fight against the Nazis. Moore recognized herself as a world citizen in the sense that she understood what was at stake for African Americans. Combating Hitler abroad and fighting racism at home were two fronts of the same war.

Once the United States joined the war, Bethune emphasized Black women's responsibilities as citizens to support the war effort. "As a significant part of the womanhood of all America," Bethune wrote to council members in early 1942, "with characteristic fortitude and vision, we will shoulder our full share of responsibility."[11] At the group's annual conference that year, the committee on planning for the postwar peace echoed Bethune's call for every Black woman to participate in the civilian national defense programs but also reminded the council of the need to look ahead. In 1919 Black women had found themselves "largely through our own shortsightedness and lack of interest . . . without representation at the peace conferences where we could seek a part in the plans for peace." Determined not to repeat that experience, the commission pledged to "do all in our power to see to it that Negro men and women are integrated into all of the various organizations that are drawing up plans for a postwar society."[12]

Bethune articulated the particular world citizenship obligations of African American women in her annual report to the council in October 1943. The women of America and of the world had a crucial role to play not just in winning the war but in uniting all of humanity behind the forces of freedom. "The problems of oppressed women in far off Ethiopia," Bethune argued, "soon become the problems of the women in our own community. Their effects are inescapable. This world cannot remain half slave and half free." She urged all NCNW members to "assume our full responsibility in bringing about the unity, the security, and the freedom which the peoples of the world, who subscribe to the principles of democracy in action, are now seeking."[13] Like Brunauer and others, Bethune spoke of "responsibility" and "interdependence," both buzzwords of world citizenship. She believed that Black women had the same obligation as white women to help shape the global polity in order to ensure lasting peace. But her conception of world citizenship also took racism and oppression around the world into account. Liberation had to be part of the peace. While women like Andrews, Schwimmer, and Lloyd paid lip service to the need for a new system of mandates or colonial administration governed by an international body rather than individual nations, they did not go so far as to advocate for anticolonial nationalist movements. They would not have seen the same parallels between the oppression of Ethiopian women and the oppression of African American women that Bethune saw. Bethune's vision of world citizenship also represented her own commitment to interracial cooperation rather than separatism and Black Nationalism, which were powerful strains in the anticolonialist movement around the world both before and after World War II.[14]

Throughout 1942 and 1943, Bethune and the NCNW cooperated with several other women's organizations that were working on international and postwar planning issues. She drew attention to this work in her 1943 annual report, noting the council's ties to such groups as the Committee on Interracial Cooperation, formed after World War I to combat lynching and promote better race relations; the Joint Canadian-American Women's Committee on International Relations; and the United Council of Church Women. Bethune also highlighted the council's work with two key organizations with rather cumbersome names: the Women's Action Committee for Victory and Lasting Peace and the Committee on the Participation of Women in Postwar

Planning.[15] Both represented the efforts of broad coalitions of women—white as well as Black, mainstream liberals rather than radical pacifists—to influence the new era of international cooperation they all anticipated would follow the war and to ensure that women and their concerns would be central to the planning process.

They faced an uphill battle. Official postwar planning remained within the State Department, conducted behind closed doors. In early 1942, Undersecretary of State Sumner Welles established an "advisory committee on postwar foreign policy," made up of State Department officials and private citizens with expertise on diplomacy, many of whom had worked for the Council on Foreign Relations.[16] Initially, the only woman invited to participate was Anne O'Hare McCormick, a longtime columnist on foreign affairs for the *New York Times* and a staunch supporter of the Roosevelt administration. Other women did not begin to participate in State Department planning until 1944. A few nongovernmental efforts included women. Brunauer worked with the Commission to Study the Organization of Peace, though they did not begin to make their findings public until 1943. The best-known woman in foreign policy circles was Vera Micheles Dean, research director at the Foreign Policy Association. The association, though, focused less on devising its own plans and more on helping the U.S. government sell the United Nations. Dean, for her part, argued that the form of any postwar organization was less important than its ability to ensure collective security, integrate the world politically and economically, and safeguard the welfare of ordinary people.[17]

Many other groups took an interest in the idea of postwar planning, but they almost never made an effort to include women in the process or considered women's status as an issue. In 1942 the International Federation of Business and Professional Women conducted a survey of nongovernmental organizations' postwar planning activities. Almost as an aside, they asked whether "the various subjects are considered at any point from the so-called woman's point of view?"[18] Out of more than thirty responses, only four acknowledged the question, and only one person said his group had considered it. That one was Pierre Waelbroeck, chief of the Employment and Labour Conditions Section of the ILO, who reported that he believed "the position of all the women who have thus been absorbed into wartime employment will constitute one of the most urgent social problems in the period immediately after the war, and it will be the duty of this Office to devote very special attention to it."[19]

Both the Women's Action Committee for Victory and Lasting Peace and the Committee on the Participation of Women in Postwar Planning sought to remedy the lack of attention to women's issues. The former emerged from the ashes of the National Committee on the Cause and Cure of War, which dissolved in March 1943. Vira Boarman Whitehouse—a former suffragist, longtime women's rights activist, and one-time colleague of Rosika Schwimmer—assumed the chair; Brunauer accepted a position as vice chair. "The basic purpose of the Women's Action Committee," wrote Brunauer, "is to unite American women to work for full participation by the United States in international efforts to build a world of peace and justice under law."[20] The new committee's first action was to pass and send to Congress a strong statement in support of the Ball Resolution for a Global Assembly, proposed by Senator Joseph Ball of Minnesota: "We appeal to the U.S. Senate to endorse at once the basic principle that the United States accepts its full responsibility for participating with the United Nations and nations of like mind in a system of collective security. We believe this will hasten the winning of the war and build toward a lasting peace."[21] Over the next two years the committee focused its efforts on educating women about postwar planning and mobilizing them to pressure U.S. policy makers to make the United Nations a genuine instrument for international cooperation. Bethune was excited about the new committee and sent representatives to its meetings, and NCNW members contributed to its education and lobbying efforts whenever they could.

The second postwar planning effort took shape in October 1942 under the direction of Mary Woolley. She was less interested in devising plans for a postwar world organization than in securing "representation of the woman's point of view in shaping world policy after the war."[22] Convinced that "women had less interest in war, as a game, than men," she believed the most valuable contribution they could make to the postwar world was to exercise their influence wherever possible on all the committees and commissions already being organized. To that end, she convened a day-long meeting to discuss "women's opportunity to make full contributions to planning and establishment of world cooperation."[23] Thirty-two women, representing twenty-five different organizations, gathered at the YWCA headquarters in New York. Brunauer and Bethune were both invited, although neither was able to attend. Those present agreed with Woolley that their duties as citizens encompassed an obligation to participate in postwar planning in both formal policy-making and informal educational roles. To do that, they formed the Committee on Women's Participation in Postwar Planning under the leadership of Emily Hickman. The idea was that any time a formal planning initiative was announced, the committee would identify a woman or women who were experts in the relevant fields, and then mobilize all affiliated individuals and organizations to pressure the Roosevelt administration to appoint at least one woman as a U.S. delegate to the meeting or conference. For example, the committee's first successful effort was to get a woman appointed as a U.S. representative to the United Nations Conference on Relief and Rehabilitation.[24]

In addition to joining both of these new organizations, Bethune and the NCNW formed their own postwar planning committee. Theirs, however, focused not on a new international organization but on the domestic challenges the United States would face in the wake of the war. "It is particularly significant to citizens members [sic] of minority groups," wrote committee chair Inabel Burns Lindsay, "that they can speak frankly in urging greater recognition and opportunity to share the privileges of a complete democracy. To conserve whatever gains are made now, and to use these as a foundation for a just and prosperous peace, post war planning becomes of paramount importance."[25] Black women, Lindsay argued, had to assume their full responsibility to strengthen postwar American society. To that end, the committee followed closely the work of the National Resources Planning Board, which had already begun publishing proposals on public housing, health, education, transportation, and employment, and agreed to look for ways Black women could aid in those efforts.[26]

As Bethune did throughout the war, the NCNW committee framed its work in a global context. "We must now demonstrate to the world," wrote Lindsay, "and to America in particular that we are capable of, not only carrying our share of responsibility in the present need, but also of contributing to basic active democracy of the future."[27] NCNW members never lost sight of what was at stake in the war for Black women and all Black Americans. Even as they concentrated many of their efforts on their demands for full national citizenship, they kept that global context in mind. "We are engaged in a great struggle," the national committee declared in October 1943, "to perpetuate the principles of democracy on the face of the earth."[28]

Planning the Postwar World

In 1944 Bethune contributed a piece to *What the Negro Wants*, an anthology of essays by Black intellectuals edited by Howard University historian Rayford W. Logan. In the most important year of the postwar planning process, Bethune again demanded full citizenship for African Americans as part of the peace settlement. Citing violence and discrimination against Black soldiers, veterans, and workers, Bethune called on the federal government to protect civil rights, extend federal programs that provided social services, guarantee equal suffrage and equal employment, and promote interracial cooperation. In doing so she tied Black Americans' struggles to nationalist and anticolonial activism around the world: "Just as the Colonists at the Boston Tea Party wanted 'out' from under tyranny and oppression and taxation without representation, the Chinese want 'out,' the Indians want 'out,' and colored Americans want 'out.'" Her arguments echoed those of many Black activists during the war who tied their own struggles for racial equality to anti-imperialist movements around the world. But as the end of the war came in sight, Black women took heart from that sense of international solidarity. "We see now more than a glimmer of light on the horizon of a new hope," Bethune wrote. "We feel behind us the surge of all women of China and India and of Africa who see the same light and look to us to march with them."[29]

Bethune brought this demand for an equitable postwar peace to bear on her reactions to the emerging plans for what would become the United Nations. Over the course of 1942 and 1943, various committees and subcommittees within the U.S. State Department worked on draft after draft of a postwar international organization.[30] By the summer of 1943 an early version of what would become the UN Charter was in place, and Roosevelt spent much of the rest of the year persuading the British, the Soviets, and the Chinese to support it. By February 1944 they had all agreed in principle to a United Nations made up of a Security Council, a General Assembly, an executive Secretariat, a World Court, and various subagencies. After the liberation of France in June, the end of the war seemed finally to be close, and organizations across the United States—representing religious groups, lawyers, workers, educators, and others, as well as women—looked forward to the peace process with renewed enthusiasm.[31]

Like Bethune, many African Americans were prepared to support such an organization, but only if it included them in substantive ways and only if it brought an end to racial discrimination and colonial oppression around the world. In the summer of 1944, leading Black organizations issued a message to the Republican and Democratic national conventions on behalf of the "Negroes of America." "Victory," they declared, in an echo of Audley Moore, "must crush Hitlerism at home as well as abroad." In addition to the elimination of the poll tax, antilynching legislation, and desegregation of the military, they demanded a cooperative foreign policy that promoted economic as well as political security for all. This included putting an end to colonial exploitation everywhere, recognizing China as an equal world partner, and unequivocally opposing any form of imperialism "based upon 'white superiority'" or that gave "economic or political advantage to the 'white' nations at the expense of the two-thirds of the people of the earth who are brown, yellow, or black of skin." Finally, the message called on the United States to appoint Black delegates to the peace conference. Twenty-six organizations signed it, including the NCNW and the National Association for the Advancement of Colored People (NAACP).[32]

The NCNW also took an active role in the summer of 1944 in efforts to ensure that women would be appointed to the plethora of committees and commissions established to coordinate postwar planning. In June, Bethune attended a conference at the White House titled "How Women May Share in Postwar Policy-Making." Convened by members of the National Federation of Business and Professional Women and the AAUW and supported by Eleanor Roosevelt, the conference gathered over two hundred women, including Brunauer, New York lawyer Dorothy Kenyon, and Bethune, representing seventy-five organizations. "The tasks of war, of peace, of nation-planning must be shared by men and women alike," the attendees declared. "Women have been called upon to share the burdens of war, to stand side by side with men on the production line and to complement men in the fighting services. So women must share in the building of a postwar world fit for all citizens—men and women—to live and work in freely side by side."[33] After the conference a small committee led by Emily Hickman compiled a Roster of Qualified Women—a database of names that could be provided to any governmental or bureaucratic agency at a moment's notice. When it was finalized in January 1945 the roster had over 250 names. Bethune was among the very few women of color; it also included Brunauer and Kenyon.[34]

As official postwar planning proceeded among diplomats, women became more determined to participate. Between August 21 and October 4, representatives from the United States, Britain, and the Soviet Union met at Dumbarton Oaks, in Washington, D.C., to hash out a plan for the "general international organization" to which Roosevelt, Winston Churchill, and Joseph Stalin had committed themselves. Those present agreed to call the new organization the United Nations and to provide for the creation of a General Assembly, a Security Council, and an administrative Secretariat, as well as an International Court of Justice. They also agreed to establish an Economic and Social Council (ECOSOC) that would facilitate "solutions of

international economic, social, and other humanitarian problems" and promote "respect for human rights and fundamental freedoms."[35] They did not
agree, however, on several measures that would determine the extent of the
UN's authority and effectiveness, including, most importantly, the use of the
veto on the Security Council. They also came to no agreement on the status
or disposition of colonies and territorial possessions around the world, and,
contrary to the hopes of many observers, they made little mention of human
rights beyond the establishment of ECOSOC.[36]

Thousands of organized women, despite their anger at the fact that none
of the almost sixty diplomats and advisers who attended the conference was a
woman, joined the campaign to publicize and rally support for the Dumbarton Oaks proposals. They faced no great challenge, and when they were
released on October 7, the proposals met with general approval. Ninety percent of Americans favored joining some kind of international organization—a
notably higher percentage than in 1919. The League of Women Voters put out
a pamphlet to explain and promote the proposals. The General Federation of
Women's Clubs pledged the support of its 2.5 million members. The AAUW,
the YWCA, and the Women's Action Committee all joined the effort.[37]

Not all reactions were positive, however. Some women saw in the proposals little more than the replication of great power politics, in which the
powerful nations controlled the Security Council and granted little authority
to the General Assembly, ECOSOC, or the international court. Those on the
left were particularly frustrated. Jessie Wallace Hughan of the War Resisters'
League called the proposals "the frankest assertion of power-politics that has
appeared since the Quadruple Alliance of Metternich." WILPF protested the
lack of any mention of disarmament as well as the United States' plan to continue peacetime conscription. Edith Wynner, Rosika Schwimmer's protégée
and a stalwart member of the Campaign for World Government, lambasted
the proposals: "Dumbarton Oaks offers the form of international government
without the reality. Its Assembly cannot legislate, its Court is a shadow, and
its Council of great powers can act only against the weak. . . . It is limited to
enforcement of peace by means of war."[38]

The most prevalent critiques of the proposals centered on two concerns. First, they lacked any kind of international bill of rights, and second,
they lacked a concrete plan to transfer control of all colonies directly to the
United Nations. The NAACP and the NCNW were among those who levied
these critiques. W. E. B. Du Bois characterized the proposals as "intolerable,
dangerous," and irreconcilable "with any philosophy of democracy." In his

mind they said "to six hundred million human beings, if not to a majority of mankind, that the only way to human equality is through the philanthropy of masters."[39] Bethune and the NCNW issued a similar statement. "The Dumbarton Oaks proposals," the council pointed out, "do not give assurance to the non-white peoples, the dependent peoples, and the minority groups of the world that a new page of history affecting their welfare is about to be written." The council acknowledged that the proposals were a starting rather than an ending point, but they called on the authors to realize "that there is growing doubt and skepticism about their intentions in the minds of the hundreds of millions of non-white peoples who make up the preponderance of the world's population."[40]

The NCNW outlined three principles that it believed must be part of any postwar program for peace. They included a declaration of the equality of all races and nations, a liberalized system of colonial administration dedicated to self-government and independence, and strong leadership from the United States. While the NCNW foregrounded its concerns on behalf of all colonized and nonwhite people around the world, it also protested the absence of women at Dumbarton Oaks and supported Emily Hickman's ongoing efforts to get women appointed to future conferences. "The women of America have a formidable task before them," the NCNW acknowledged. "They must be a strategic and articulate segment of the citizenry and they cannot escape the responsibility for being competent citizens." But as Black women, council members also had a more specific task. In addition to acting as responsible citizens themselves, they had an obligation to reach out to and educate African Americans across the United States: "The members of the NCNW must reach every man and woman in their community and expose them to ideas that will eventually gain for them and their posterity the opportunity to become citizens of the world in every sense of the word."[41] In the same breath Bethune and the NCNW both made demands and acknowledged their responsibilities as world citizens. They called for the postwar global polity, in the form of the UN, to establish universal equality and end colonialism. At the same time, as both women and African Americans, they would continue their own active world citizenship and compel others to do the same.

Some of these critiques seemed to resonate at the State Department. On October 16, Bethune attended a meeting at which Secretary of State Edward Stettinius and other members of the U.S. delegation to Dumbarton Oaks listened to feedback on the proposals from representatives of over one hundred nongovernmental organizations. Stettinius emphasized that the proposals were "neither complete nor final" and welcomed input from citizens across the country. "Throughout this process," he told the attendees, "there is need for wide, intelligent and maturing consideration of the proposals on the part of the American people and of all other peace-loving peoples."[42] Stettinius, in other words, claimed the very opportunity internationalist women had been demanding—the opportunity to help shape the global polity. Bethune went back to her membership with that in mind. She implored local branches to ensure that consideration of the proposals "is a 'must' on your council program. . . . Today's decisions are creating tomorrow's world." She encouraged all members to form study groups in their communities to read and discuss the proposals to go door to door if necessary to spread the word about the United Nations and the need for action.[43] What Bethune did not say, however, was that Stettinius did not promise that women would be directly engaged in the official peace process, nor did he indicate that the revised proposals would include a greater degree of colonial sovereignty.

Unlike most organizations dominated by white women, the NCNW built their demands for equality explicitly into their conception of world citizenship. The two were inseparable; their demands to participate in shaping the world polity were inextricable from their demands for colonial liberation, economic freedom, and racial equality. Where other women advocates of international government in this period—even ones as radical as Schwimmer and Lloyd—went no further than some kind of system of trusteeship or supervision with eventual independence, Bethune and the NCNW made clear that gradual or partial measures would not suffice. Colonized populations had to be guaranteed not only independence but full equality within the world community, and all people of color everywhere had to be promised freedom from all forms of oppression.

The NCNW also went further than the NAACP, the Committee on African Affairs, or any other Black organization in pointing out that *women* had a particular role to play in the peace process.[44] "The postwar world also offers a challenge to women as a group," wrote Gertrude Martin, editor of the *Aframerican Woman's Journal* in March 1945. "Negro women, that twice oppressed minority, . . . have stepped into new roles of importance in the last few years, appraised their position and found many obstacles ahead." They still faced employment discrimination and segregation in the military, but they had contributed nonetheless. The end of the war presented yet another opportunity for women to shape the global polity and assume responsibility not only for peace but for justice.[45] More determined than ever, Bethune and members of the NCNW looked forward to the 1945 United Nations Conference in San Francisco as a chance to exercise that responsibility.

The United Nations Conference on International Organization

From April 25 to June 26, 1945, delegations from fifty countries met in San Francisco to draft the UN Charter. Those delegations were supplemented by hundreds of official advisers, consultants, and observers from around the world. The U.S. State Department was determined not to repeat what it saw as one of the mistakes of the Paris Peace Conference, when citizen organizations had been shut out of the proceedings and therefore could not help the government build a broad base of popular support for the League of Nations Covenant. Stettinius asked forty-two organizations, including the League of Women Voters, the Women's Action Committee, and the NAACP—but not the NCNW—to send two official consultants to San Francisco. Bethune was not among the leadership of any of the women's organizations invited, so none chose her to attend. But she was a vice president of the NAACP, which designated Walter White and W. E. B. Du Bois as its representatives. Bethune, frustrated that among the consultants there was no Black woman, contacted Eleanor Roosevelt, who in turn reached out to the State Department. Assistant Secretary of State Archibald MacLeish asked the NAACP whether they would appoint Bethune as one of their representatives, since the State Department was reluctant to add any other organizations to its list. The association agreed, and Bethune set out for California.[46]

For her, the conference represented the culmination of Black women's struggles during the war for greater involvement in shaping the postwar world and for the equality of their race within it. She wrote with optimism to her friends and NCNW members. The conference, she proclaimed, marked the dawn of a new era, in which the nations of the world would perfect the blueprint for global democracy. She was heartened by the presence of people of color and of women. The former, Bethune reported, agreed that the United States had a great deal of work to do to improve its treatment of African Americans before it could claim to contribute anything to a "world program of freedom and brotherhood." The latter, meanwhile, had inserted themselves at almost every level of the proceedings. Women served as delegates and consultants as well as stenographers and canteen workers. Their presence,

Bethune argued, signified their growing consciousness of themselves as "citizens of the world."[47]

Women's participation in San Francisco stood in marked contrast to their marginal presence at the Paris Peace Conference twenty-six years earlier. No woman served as a national delegate to that summit, and few went as official representatives in any capacity, as Andrews did. Those who traveled to Paris generally did so as members of nongovernmental organizations such as WILPF or as attendees of the concurrent Inter-Allied Women's Conference or Pan-African Congress. Mary Church Terrell, for instance, cofounder of the National Association of Colored Women and charter member of the NAACP, went to Europe as a member of the U.S. delegation to the WILPF meeting in Zurich, and afterward spent three weeks in Paris during the last weeks of the peace conference. Terrell did not support the League of Nations; as the brainchild of Woodrow Wilson, a racist Southerner from a segregationist party, she did not see how it could present opportunities for freedom or justice for people of color. By 1945, however, her perspective had changed. She believed the UN was different. She saw it, particularly the Commission on Human Rights, as a chance for Black women to bring the issue of racism in American society before the world. That was precisely what Bethune hoped to accomplish.[48]

But not everything had changed since 1919. The San Francisco Conference did present more and better opportunities for women's involvement. The sheer volume of their presence, as Bethune noted, was a demand to participate in shaping the global polity and evidence of the obligation they felt to work for peace. However, while the white U.S. women in attendance all professed a belief in equality, they did not understand it in the same ways. Some, for example, led by U.S. delegate Virginia Gildersleeve, argued women's equality was implicit in the language of the UN Charter and therefore women's rights did not merit any special mention. Others sided with several women from Latin America who demanded an explicit statement of equal rights. But few white U.S. women—and few women at the conference in general—incorporated demands for decolonization and racial justice into their vision of equality. As a Black woman, Bethune was one of the only U.S. Americans at the conference concerned with securing in the charter both racial and gender equality. Her conception of world citizenship demanded no less.

U.S. women's presence in San Francisco was due in no small part to the work of those who had attended the White House Conference and assembled the Roster of Qualified Women. In early January, Charl Williams, one of its creators, sent the roster to Roosevelt and the State Department. Acting Secretary of State Joseph Grew expressed his gratitude for the list, calling it a "valuable service" to the government.[49] In February the Roosevelt administration announced the members of its delegation to San Francisco. Among them was Gildersleeve, the lifelong educator and international activist who served as dean of Barnard College from 1911 to 1947. Williams was in Chicago when the news broke. She reported to Eleanor Roosevelt that the women she was with had cheered and that all of them attributed Gildersleeve's selection to the impact of the White House Conference. "All the women that I see and hear from," she reiterated a week later, "think that the White House Conference was directly responsible for the appointment of Dean Gildersleeve!"[50] Organized women seemed finally to have won a significant victory in their battle to help shape the postwar world.

The victory proved somewhat hollow. First, other members of the U.S. delegation saw Gildersleeve's as a token appointment; they discounted her contributions and assigned her to marginal committees.[51] Second, Gildersleeve had particularly gendered ideas about how women should contribute to international governance that did not represent the views of all U.S. women. She invoked, for instance, the ideal of republican motherhood as a motivation for women's contributions to peace. Noting the "immense influence" that mothers exercised over their children, she argued that in order to instill in them the "right attitude of mind," women must "know ourselves something about the world order, other nations, their problems, their needs, how our country can cooperate and how together we can implement the peace in a new world."[52] Within Gildersleeve's framework, women were republican mothers not just for the nation but for the world. Her imagery harkened back to the early years of the century, when Mead and Tuttle were invoking maternalist arguments for women's participation in international affairs. Gildersleeve's selection as a delegate also angered many feminists in the United States because she was an advocate of protective labor legislation and feared those laws would be eroded by pressing for equal rights in the charter. In other words, Gildersleeve and her allies wanted to shape the world polity, but they wanted to do it in their own gendered ways. Advocates for women's equal rights, frustrated by Gildersleeve's refusal to hear their concerns, turned to women at the conference from Brazil, the Dominican Republic, Australia, and other nations to collaborate on a plan to insert explicit provisions for women's rights into the charter. Although their efforts were blocked by the major powers—the United States not least—they did succeed in adding Article 8, which declared the UN "shall place no restrictions on the eligibility of men and women to participate in any capacity and under conditions of equality in the principal and subsidiary organs."[53] With that line, women won recognition of their right to participate in the UN, though not of their equal rights.

Bethune supported the efforts of the equal rights advocates, but she was no less concerned with racial equality and anticolonialism—causes to which most women representatives in San Francisco paid only lip service, if they mentioned them at all.[54] Both as president of the NCNW and a vice president of the NAACP, she had been involved in discussions leading up to San Francisco about what Black Americans wanted out of the conference and the charter. Articulated primarily by Du Bois, their demands centered on a strong international bill of rights that would hold the nations of the world accountable for "how they treat people." The NAACP also expressed its frustrations that the future of "750,000,000 persons of color living under colonial governments" had been ignored in the Dumbarton Oaks proposals and that the San Francisco delegates had no stated intention of discussing racial equality. They pointed out that the responses of Black Americans to the UN Charter would depend heavily on its provisions for colonial independence. White, Du Bois, and Bethune issued a statement to similar effect just before the conference, noting that "what happens to even the most exploited of these [colonial peoples] has direct bearing upon the future of Negroes in the United States."[55]

But once they arrived in San Francisco, it quickly became evident they would not get very far. White and Du Bois had a hard time rallying support for decolonization among other mainstream nongovernmental organizations and even other Black nations, including Haiti, Liberia, and Ethiopia. The major powers, meanwhile, paid only lip service to human rights and carefully avoided any mention of decolonization. The United States, for its part, was maneuvering to limit the influence of the Soviet Union in the new body. To do that it had to maintain the support of Britain and France—in part by promising not to give the UN too much authority over colonial issues. On top of that, Stettinius and other members of the U.S. delegation were fully aware that Southern Democrats dominated the Senate, and they would need to be placated in order to ratify the treaty. In the end, the UN Charter included the promise of "fundamental freedoms for all without distinction as to race, sex, language, or religion," and set up a trusteeship system for colonial territories but made no plans for enforcing the promise and no mention of which colonies would be part of the system and which would not.[56]

Sue Bailey Thurman, who attended the conference both as a member of the NCNW and as a correspondent for the *Aframerican Woman's Journal* and the *Chicago Defender*, captured the situation. There was a "great scene" being enacted in San Francisco, she reported; the curtain was rising on the new postwar world. But Thurman wished the play had been cast differently. She celebrated the presence of delegates from China, the Philippines, and Ethiopia, but she could not help but note the absence onstage of any representation from Indonesia, Burma, or the two hundred million "indigenous peoples of Africa," while Britons represented India and Afrikaner Jan Smuts represented South Africa, where Blacks outnumbered whites four to one. Smuts presented statements to the conference recognizing "fundamental human rights," which Thurman noted rang hollow when contrasted with his statements to a town hall meeting in New York in 1930, where he famously said that "next to the ass, the most patient of all animals is the Negro." "We see him go on stage here in San Francisco," Thurman lamented, "and wonder what ironic fate has done the casting in this drama."[57]

Marginalized by white women as an African American and by Black men as a woman, Bethune held her ground. Throughout the conference she remained cognizant of the fact that her status as a consultant was in "recognition of the colored women of America."[58] She refused to see the gains Black women had made during the war, especially in employment opportunities, taken away. "Negro women will not go back to the kitchen," she declared.[59] Sidelined by White and Du Bois, she instead nurtured connections with women like Eslanda Robeson, the unofficial representative of the Council on African Affairs, and Vijaya Lakshmi Pandit, an official delegate from India. She spoke to African American clubwomen at a large gathering in Oakland and gave several other speeches in the area. Overall, her experience at the conference radicalized both her own politics and those of the NCNW. It heightened her awareness of the global connections among African Americans' oppression in the United States and the struggle for freedom among people of color around the world.[60] In 1947, when the NCNW sought consultative status at ECOSOC, Bethune drew on those connections. "The darker women," she contended, "not only in the U.S., but all over the world have added handicaps which are not the concern of other women. Therefore, since our organization is the only one in the world of its kind and character, devoted not only to the study of the problems of women in general, but of the darker minorities, we feel we have a definite stake in and a definite contribution to make to the deliberations of the Social and Economic Council and its various organizations."[61] Bethune's world citizenship had expanded to encompass a demand to participate in shaping the polity not just as a representative of African American women but all Black women and women of color around the world.

Two gatherings held in the early summer of 1945 captured the differences between Bethune's reactions to the conference and those of many white U.S. women. On May 19 representatives from eighteen local and forty-two national women's organizations met in San Francisco at a United Women's Conference to discuss the topic "Women's Share in Implementing the Peace." They were joined by all eight official women delegates and several other prominent observers, including Ruth Bryan Rohde, the first U.S. woman ambassador and a former congresswoman, and Jan Masaryk, foreign affairs minister of Czechoslovakia.[62] Catharine Sibley, director of public service for the National Broadcasting Company, chaired the executive committee. "It occurs to me that there are two ideas whose time has come," she told the attendees. "One is that of international organization and, the second, that women shall play a real part in the governing of that world which this international organization is to set up."[63] The speeches that day centered on the contributions women could make to the new United Nations, especially through ECOSOC, which they saw as the most appropriate outlet for their concerns for women, children, and humanitarian causes. Most speakers made little mention of racial equality, either at home or abroad. Bethune did not attend, choosing instead to spend the day addressing African American groups in the Bay Area.[64]

A month later, representatives from thirty-four Black organizations gathered at the NCNW headquarters in New York to voice their frustration with the UN Conference and chart a path forward. Bethune chaired the proceedings. The conference's failure to deal seriously with questions of decolonization and human rights, she argued, proved the extent to which Black Americans were "still, to a large extent, a subject people—men and women with little more than colonial status in a democracy." But the global gathering in San Francisco had also shown that ordinary people were demanding their rights within the new postwar world community, one in which they would no longer acquiesce to white domination. "*World unity cannot become a reality as long as the old traditional order remains,*" Bethune proclaimed. The war had stirred a desire for freedom among men and women the world over, but in the United States, African Americans still faced entrenched discrimination and segregation in employment, in education, at the ballot box, and even within the military they had served so faithfully. If the United States and other nations wished to avoid another world conflict, they had to demonstrate "the stabilizing power of a far-sighted united leadership."[65]

The UN Conference thus meant different things to different women world citizens. For some white women it was a victory, a culmination of their wartime work to shape the global polity, symbolized by Gildersleeve's appointment and by women's participation throughout the two months. Many of them left California in high spirits, looking forward to cooperating with the UN in the months and years to come. Other white women were disappointed that the charter did not go far enough to secure women's equal rights. For Bethune, that disappointment was compounded by the utter failure of the San Francisco delegates to engage in any meaningful way the issues of decolonization and racial justice. She and the NCNW had worked tirelessly in the years leading up to the UN conference to shape a just and equitable world polity. Bethune's presence at the conference demonstrated the full scope of her world citizenship—her demand to participate in the formation of the UN, her sense of responsibility to work for peace and justice, and her belief that without a genuine commitment to equality on the part of world leaders, there would be no lasting peace. Despite the fact that her efforts largely failed, she took heart from the connections she forged in San Francisco and the sense of solidarity the conference gave her. For the remaining decade of her life, she channeled that sense into fighting for Black women's rights and recognition within national and international women's organizations as well as the UN.[66]

For all its weaknesses, both with regard to equal rights and as an international governing body, the United Nations was here to stay. Over the next few years some U.S. women made it the focal point of their work for world citizenship, using—and modifying—its structure and exploiting its global reach. For those women to whom the UN represented a genuine chance to participate in shaping the global polity, the late 1940s offered a new period of opportunity.

CHAPTER 7

Dorothy Kenyon and World Citizenship
Through the United Nations

In June 1949, Dorothy Kenyon, the United States' representative on the United Nations Commission on the Status of Women, gave the keynote address at the annual convention of the American Association of University Women. U.S. women had important responsibilities in the post–World War II era, she told her audience, and they could not allow geography to limit their vision. "Our frontier is now the world," Kenyon told the AAUW. "Not Latin-America, in respect to which we are becoming an increasingly good neighbor, nor Canada; not Europe of the Atlantic Pact; not even the sharp line of demarcation laid down by the Iron Curtain. . . . Nowhere, nowhere in the world can we draw any line." Citing a recent trip to Lebanon, she noted that even as advances in air travel were drawing the world closer together, "epidemics" such as "bad social conditions, low standards of living, illiteracy, poverty, [and] anti-democratic ideas" threatened international cooperation. Educated women, she argued, had a "special responsibility" to aid women in other parts of the world.[1]

And the United Nations was their best means of doing it. Women's duty was to lend a helping hand to regions where concern for human rights was lacking. "That hand," argued Kenyon, "can be extended by us through the United Nations, the tool created to handle our new world frontier, and which is in itself another new frontier for experimentation in world government."[2] U.S. women had an opportunity to fulfill their obligations as world citizens by helping all nations realize what Kenyon saw as the key promise of the UN Charter: "Fundamental freedoms for all, without distinction as to race, sex, language or religion."[3]

This chapter centers on Kenyon and others like her who saw in the United Nations their best hope for world government and their best platform for world citizenship. They shaped the global polity, worked for peace, and advocated for women's equality through the UN, especially its Commission on the Status of Women (CSW). Kenyon recognized the UN's weaknesses—she detested the veto power, and she knew very well that it had little real authority—but she still saw it as "the hope, and the only hope, of the world."[4] She and her contemporaries in mainstream women's organizations, such as the AAUW and the League of Women Voters, urged President Harry Truman to strengthen it as an instrument of world peace. And even as they worried about communist expansion in the late 1940s, they were concerned about U.S. policies that seemed to undermine the UN by further entrenching the adversarial positions of the United States and the Soviet Union.

Kenyon's emphasis on the responsibilities of citizenship in her speech to the AAUW was common among internationalist U.S. women in the post–World War II period, just as it had been before the war. In addition to helping the nation readjust after the war, many felt an obligation to uplift women around the world. To Kenyon, the CSW seemed the best vehicle for doing that. As her speech indicated though, her sense of obligation to other women tended to carry classist and racist undertones. In that regard, Kenyon's perspective harkened back to the civilizationist discourse of Mead, Andrews, and Tuttle, though Kenyon was more focused on advancing women's status than they had been. While this tendency was not uncommon among white women of her era, it was still problematic and limited the CSW's effectiveness. Despite Kenyon's and other women's determination to bolster the UN, however, the onset of the Cold War in the late 1940s hampered their efforts in more ways than one.

The United Nations and the "Special Interests of Women"

Kenyon was one of many women eager after World War II to assume the mantle of responsible world citizenship. Born in 1888 to a life of privilege, she grew up on the Upper West Side of Manhattan and spent summers at her family's home in Connecticut. She graduated from Horace Mann High School in New York in 1904 and from Smith College in 1908. She described herself as a "bookish little girl," but it was not until after college that she experienced what she would later characterize as an awakening to social injustice. She enrolled in New York University Law School, one of the few law schools in the country to admit women, and graduated in 1917. She practiced law throughout her

life, mostly in New York, and volunteered her services to organizations ranging from the League of Women Voters to the American Civil Liberties Union.
She also served on numerous public commissions in the city and was among
the first women to earn admittance to the New York bar in 1937. Unlike all
the women in this book except Edith Wynner, she never married; like Mead,
Andrews, Schwimmer, and Wynner, she had no children.[5]

"I'm interested in all kinds of people who are in one way or another dis-
advantaged," Kenyon told an interviewer near the end of her life.[6] That fact
explains much of her life's work, including for the UN. In both her paid and
unpaid work she dealt with issues ranging from public housing and minimum wage legislation to racial discrimination and legal aid for the poor. As
a member of a generation that associated "feminism" with the militant equal-
rights approach of the National Woman's Party, Kenyon did not identify as a
feminist, but she consistently fought for women's rights, including married
women's equal nationality, women's right to serve on juries, and equal educational and economic opportunities. At the same time, she was a staunch
opponent of the ERA until the early 1970s. She did not see these positions as
contradictory; rather she believed in fighting for women's rights on an issue-
by-issue basis rather than with a blanket ERA, the impact of which was difficult to predict. Throughout much of her life Kenyon also retained something
of her privileged class perspective on social reform, as the quote above illus-
trates, viewing herself as a benevolent benefactor helping the less fortunate.

During World War II, Kenyon argued that U.S. women like her also had an
obligation to participate in postwar planning not just because of their privileged
class position but because of their status as Americans. In a tone reminiscent
of Mead and Andrews, she cast her world citizenship—her demand to participate in shaping the global polity—as the logical extension of American excep-
tionalism and Manifest Destiny. "Ever since the earliest times the movements
of peoples have been westward . . . to the New World," she declared in 1942.
"Here we have made for ourselves a free land. The tradition of freedom is in
our blood. For we all came here in ships . . . mostly from Holland, England, Ire-
land and France, adventurous sea-faring people every one of us. And once here
we conquered the wilderness as adventurous hardy pioneering stock is bound
to do. . . . No wonder that democracy flourishes here and that our example
helps to inspire the rest of the war-torn world."[7] Beginning in the nineteenth
century with the acquisition of Alaska and Hawai'i and continuing through
the war against Spain in Cuba and the Philippines, the pursuit of the "open
door" in China, and U.S. entry into World War I, Kenyon traced the increasing

involvement of the United States with the rest of the world. The United States' neutral stance and refusal to join the League of Nations and the World Court was a disappointment, she admitted, but the tide had turned. Americans were now acknowledging that their "heritage of courage" came with an obligation to help in the Allied struggle. "Leadership has passed to us," she avowed. "In our hands lies the future. In the long pages of history our moment has come. We are now the people, this is now the country, of destiny. May we prove worthy of that destiny, may we stay humble in the face of that responsibility."[8]

Kenyon brought this conviction that the United States was destined to lead the new world order to her international work at the war's end, along with a significant degree of practical experience. She was one of the women who had pressured the League of Nations in the 1930s to take more seriously the problem of married women's nationality and women's rights more broadly. When the league finally established its Committee on the Status of Women in 1937, Kenyon was one of the seven people named to it and played a key role in the committee's initial efforts to study the legal status of women around the world. That study was cut short by the outbreak of World War II, but for Kenyon it was an important introduction to international work. She established her authority in the field of women's legal status as well as networks of colleagues and resources she would draw on again after 1945.[9]

At the end of the war, the chances seemed high that the United Nations would have the popular support it needed to effect change. Eighty-five percent of Americans polled in 1945 supported an organization that would "marshal the forces for understanding among the peoples of the world."[10] In a sign of how much things had changed since 1919, the U.S. Senate ratified the UN Charter on July 28, just over a month after it had been signed in San Francisco, by a vote of 89 to 2. The *New York Times* editorialized, "The vision of Wilson, the leadership of Roosevelt, and the steadfast faith of many of their countrymen that a day would come at last when the United States would be ready to assume the responsibilities that fall naturally to a great world Power, are honored in the Senate's vote."[11] Mainstream women's organizations, including the Women's Action Committee for Lasting Peace (the group shortened its name after "victory" was achieved), the League of Women Voters, the American Association of University Women, the National Council of Negro Women, and others, saw great promise in the UN and mobilized on its behalf. Proud of the work they had done in San Francisco, they turned their attention in the summer of 1945 to rallying support for the new body and figuring out how they could best contribute to it.

Figure 8. Dorothy Kenyon, right, with Eleanor Roosevelt next to a CARE package display, c. 1945. Photo courtesy of the Sophia Smith Collection, Smith College.

Many focused on work they felt particularly suited them as women. Some organizations were especially interested, for instance, in the work of the Economic and Social Council. Article 55 of the UN Charter stated that the UN "shall promote . . . . conditions of economic and social progress and development" and "solutions of international economic, social, health, and related problems" in order to create the "conditions of stability and well-being which are necessary for peaceful and friendly relations among nations."[12] One of the things that distinguished the UN from the League of Nations was the recognition of its founders that safeguarding human welfare was key to maintaining peace. The Economic and Social Council, the body created to fulfill the charge of Article 55, was designed to serve in part as a bridge between the short-term humanitarian relief efforts begun in 1943 by the UN Relief and Recovery Administration and the long-term development efforts of the World Bank, the World Health Organization, and other agencies.[13] Perhaps its most important work, at least in the eyes of many women activists in the United States, lay in overseeing the Commission on Human Rights, the group tasked with realizing the charter's promise of "fundamental freedoms for all."

In her public speeches following the San Francisco Conference, Virginia Gildersleeve did more than anyone to establish the theme of mainstream women's organizations' relationship to the UN throughout its first five years: responsible citizenship, both national and international, demanded women support the UN. "It is now the privilege and the obligation of all women," she told the General Federation of Women's Clubs (GFWC), "to play their part as responsible citizens in supporting and developing our new world organization."[14] And like many members of her audience, not least Florence Guertin Tuttle, Gildersleeve believed that sense of obligation arose from women's instinctual desire to preserve life. "Women have generally a stronger instinct for creating and preserving life and developing it," she argued in *Woman's Home Companion*. "So war, with its destruction of life, naturally seems even more terrible and more unreasonable to women than it does to men. They instinctively hate it."[15] That hatred, she argued, should steer them toward ECOSOC, which Gildersleeve saw as the best instrument for postwar humanitarian efforts. The council's work involved "an immense field of human welfare, of health and happiness, of the well-being of children, and of the family—subjects peculiarly the concern of women." She was thus certain that women would play integral roles in the economic and social work of the new UN.[16]

Kenyon did not echo Gildersleeve's gendered arguments to the same extent, but her work for the League's Committee on the Status of Women made her only too aware of the importance of getting women's status on the agenda of the new UN. With that in mind, she was eager to participate in the work of several organizations that coordinated their efforts in the fall of 1945 to strategize about how they could best ensure women's participation in the new body. On September 19, members of the AAUW, the GFWC, the

National Federation of Business and Professional Women (NFBPW), and the League of Women Voters convened a Conference on the United Nations and the Special Interests of Women. More than fifty prominent women attended the day-long session, including Esther Brunauer, Mary McLeod Bethune, and Kenyon.

The meeting had both an explicit and an implicit agenda. The explicit agenda, which is the focus here, was a discussion of how to use the UN to oversee and safeguard women's interests, based on the belief that "despite differences women spoke a universal language of human rights and fundamental freedoms."[17] The implicit agenda, which several other scholars have explored, was to figure out how to keep the National Woman's Party and other supporters of equal rights from dominating any committee on women's status set up by the United Nations. This battle between "equal rights feminists" and "social feminists" (sometimes referred to as the "Women's Bureau coalition" because so many adherents were connected to that office) stretched back to the 1920s and still exerted a disproportionate force on women's politics after World War II. The latter group, which included Kenyon and was responsible for the September 19 meeting, feared that an equal rights agenda would threaten protective labor laws that recognized women's status as wives and mothers. As a result, many of the "special interests of women" discussed at the conference were traditionally liberal, individual rights, such as suffrage, education, and equal pay. The attendees had no desire to see a blanket equal rights platform anywhere near the United Nations.[18]

The conference's explicit agenda, on the other hand, centered on strategies to get women involved in UN work. Brunauer, Bethune, and others who had attended the San Francisco Conference shared information on what they had accomplished there, especially the establishment of ECOSOC. Kenyon brought the attendees up to speed on the work of the League of Nations Committee on the Status of Women and urged them to call for a continuation of that committee's work as part of the new UN agenda. Several of the women present called attention to Emily Hickman and the wartime work of the Committee on the Participation of Women in Postwar Planning—newly renamed the Committee on Women in World Affairs—to ensure women's presence at important gatherings. The precedent Hickman's committee established, of compiling lists of qualified women and distributing them to government agencies, should be continued, they agreed. They also discussed various ways to cooperate with the International Labor Organization, the Food and Agriculture Organization, and the proposed educational and cultural organization (which would become the UN Educational, Scientific, and Cultural Organization, or UNESCO).[19]

Following the precedent set by the United Women's Conference in San Francisco four months earlier, there was no mention at the September gathering of racial injustice or the legal and political rights of women of color. It was left to Bethune to raise the issue; during a discussion of defining women's special interests, she called attention to "existing discriminations and abuses in the United States," such as the poll tax, "which must be cleared up if we are to be consistent."[20] Just as she had in San Francisco, Bethune readily connected struggles for racial justice at home and abroad. During Kenyon's report on the League of Nations committee, Bethune underlined on her copy the references to "special sections on Mohammedan and Hindu law" and to the inclusion of "the near East and Indo-China and . . . India." She wrote at the bottom, "We have a responsibility to the women of the world." She then added a word: "*all* the women of the world."[21] But Bethune's perspective had little influence on the conference. As in San Francisco, most white internationalist women were slow to see racial equality as part of their responsibilities as world citizens.

In the end, the attendees agreed on a series of proposals. First, they celebrated the provisions in the charter urging fundamental freedoms and ensuring women would not be restricted from participating in the UN, and they pressed for women's full inclusion in its work. Second, the conference called for "the prompt and effective recognition of women as equal citizens in every country of the world." They were careful to avoid the language of equal *rights*, calling instead for recognition as equal citizens, which, for them, limited the field of vision to women's legal, civil, and political status. Third, the attendees called not for a committee on the status of women but for the creation of a "consultative committee of experts to the Economic and Social Council" that would "concern itself with implementing the terms of the Charter with respect to women . . . and maintain relations helpful thereto in the countries of the world." This was an effort to thread the needle between ensuring that women's issues were heard at the UN but not calling for the establishment of a full commission. But they did encourage U.S. women's organizations to collaborate with international colleagues, and they called on the UN to sponsor a conference on the special interests of women in 1946.[22]

Just as others had done before and during World War II, these women came together to articulate their demand to participate in shaping the global polity. They supported the creation of the UN and were determined to be part of it. They expressed repeatedly their sense of responsibility as citizens, not only to safeguard the world against another war but also to advance women's status around the world. And, like Kenyon, they took women's civil and political equality as a given, even though—as other white women internationalists had done before them—they marginalized the problems of racism and used "Western" standards to measure that equality. In other words, they focused on such issues as suffrage, legal status, and equal employment rather than decolonization or human rights more broadly. But the dominant theme of the conference was the obligations of world citizenship. The attendees agreed with Kenyon that the time had come to act "as responsible adult citizens of the United States and of the world."[23]

Both at the conference and beyond it, much of this rhetoric about citizenship and its responsibilities was heavily gendered and relied on post–World War II tropes about domesticity. Echoing Progressive-era arguments for women's activism in the public sphere as a form of "municipal housekeeping," the Women's Action Committee in 1946 published an article titled "Global Housekeeping." In it they extended the domestic metaphor to the entire world, arguing that the work of ECOSOC to coordinate postwar relief and reconstruction was essential for long-term peace. While other aspects of the UN's agenda were being held up by political maneuvering, the council's work had to be allowed to continue, they argued. Its purview was "the kind of global housekeeping that must be carried out day by day, so that peace may be made possible within the family of nations."[24] It went without saying that those best suited to this daily work were the ones who had always done it within the family—women.

Kenyon also reiterated this theme. "Even those women whose interests center around the home find nowadays that the home is not just the four walls it used to be," she argued in April 1947. The home had expanded into the community and the community into the world. A good homemaker therefore had to concern herself not just with the needs of her family but of her neighbors and fellow human beings as well. "In other words," Kenyon argued, "a good mother must also be a good citizen."[25] Kenyon herself never married nor had children, but like many women of her generation she was well aware of the prevalence and power of traditional expectations about women's "sphere," and she drew on those expectations even as she argued for broadening that sphere.

Finally, after the United States bombed Hiroshima and Nagasaki in August 1945, women's rhetoric about responsible citizenship often included references to atomic weapons and the need to control them. Many women's organizations supported the Atomic Energy Act of 1946, which established the Atomic Energy Commission and put nuclear weapons under civilian rather than military control.[26] The Women's Action Committee reminded its members that the stakes involved in supporting the UN were even higher than those involved in supporting the League of Nations after World War I. "This time," they warned, "the responsibility rests squarely on our shoulders. Make no mistake, this is the last chance. If we fail now, the atomic bomb may destroy the whole world."[27]

Kenyon rarely mentioned the nuclear threat in her public speeches, but like everyone else at the time she would have been only too cognizant of it. The atomic bomb made world citizenship more necessary than it had ever been, and Kenyon as much as anyone felt the corresponding increase of responsibility to work for peace. For her, that meant working to bolster the United Nations. "We as women, as well as citizens," she told one audience, "have a special responsibility. . . . Let us see to it that that great potential force for good in the world, the United Nations, is strengthened and empowered to create for us a new world of international peace, security and freedom."[28]

The Commission on the Status of Women

Kenyon looked to the Commission on the Status of Women to discharge her obligation to support the UN and advance women's status. The commission had been formed in San Francisco over the objection of Gildersleeve and other U.S. women who argued that "women's issues" could be safeguarded by the Commission on Human Rights. Although they lost out to the persuasive arguments of Bertha Lutz and other Latin American delegates, Gildersleeve and her allies did succeed in keeping it a subcommission rather than an independent body within ECOSOC. After San Francisco, the Women's Bureau coalition—the same women who organized the September 19 conference—mobilized to try to keep equal rights feminists from dominating the commission.[29]

Kenyon's appointment to the CSW was a victory for the coalition, and the commission in its early years focused much more on issues near and dear to liberal feminists, such as suffrage, access to education, and equal pay, than it did to a blanket equal rights platform or to more radical issues like anticolonialism.[30] It enjoyed some notable successes. As the Commission on Human Rights was in the process of drafting what became the Universal Declaration on Human Rights, members of the CSW successfully lobbied to change the phrase "all *men* are created equal" to "all *human beings* are created equal." They also proposed several conventions that were eventually adopted by the General Assembly, including the 1951 Convention on Equal Remuneration for Men and Women for Work of Equal Value, the 1952 Convention on the Political Rights of Women, and the 1957 Convention of the Nationality of Married Women.[31] But the CSW—like the UN as a whole—had little power and few resources to enforce those conventions, and, as Kenyon often pointed out, it met for only two weeks once a year. Even under those constrained circumstances, however, Kenyon and her colleagues did help set the tone for the post–World War II world polity, making clear that women's status would at least be part of the conversation.

The work the commission accomplished in its early years was important, though circumscribed, and Kenyon did everything she could to publicize it in the United States. She hosted events, circulated literature, and corralled editors of women's magazines to publish features and interviews related to the CSW.[32] Her public speeches and remarks during her tenure as the U.S. representative make clear the extent to which she engaged in this work as a world citizen. She sought not only to improve women's status but also to use the CSW to make women's concerns an integral part of the UN. At the same time, her words illustrate her racialized and Westernized assumptions about what equality looked like and how to measure it. As a world citizen, Kenyon's dedication and sense of obligation were strong, but her belief in equality was not absolute.

The core task of the CSW, Kenyon repeatedly argued, was fulfilling the charter's promise of "fundamental freedoms for all." To that end, she and the other commissioners decided to concentrate their energy on women's political rights, especially suffrage. They believed, as Kenyon argued, that "the key to human rights for women is the vote. With the vote woman has the power to open for herself all the other doors to freedom." Given that only 60 percent of UN member nations allowed women to vote in 1945, the emphasis on women's suffrage was significant. This work led to the 1952 Convention on the Political Rights of Women, which declared women should be equally eligible with men to vote and run for office.[33]

Kenyon's public remarks also made clear the sense of responsibility she felt to women around the world, which she tried to instill in as many U.S. women as possible. If the principle task of the CSW was the fulfillment of the promise of fundamental freedoms, then U.S. women had a stronger obligation than others to further that task. In this she echoed her arguments during World War II that American women had to lead the way in the postwar world. "We of the United States must see that task through," she argued. "As members of the greatest and most powerful country on earth, we Americans, and particularly we American women, have a special responsibility to see it through. If we fail I am almost prepared to say the United Nations fails."[34] In other words, the entire fate of the UN and world peace rested on the shoulders of U.S. women.

But there is another aspect of Kenyon's perspective that is important to consider, and in her public speeches it often went hand in hand with her concern for advancing women's status and her sense of global responsibility. In 1948 she addressed a group of graduating college seniors:

> Here in this country the battle for women's freedom is practically
> won. Most of us think now in terms, not of our rights, but of our
> responsibilities (which is the way it should be) and the thought of
> battling for women's rights may seem to you somehow outdated and
> a little unreal. . . . But that isn't true of all parts of the world. Even
> now there are areas of the world where women live a kind of slave
> life our great, great grandmothers never dreamt of, where they don't
> vote, aren't considered to rate even an elementary education, are
> economically in bondage to their husbands or families and some-
> times in physical bondage as well. It is hard for us to realize what
> the veil and purdah mean in [terms] of the subjection of women. So
> there is still work to be done, human beings still to be freed, if we
> are to release the potentialities of people everywhere and to per-
> mit everyone to walk in dignity and freedom. That is the job of my
> Commission.[35]

With these remarks, Kenyon tapped into a long history in the United States of white women's perception that they needed to "liberate" other women around the world. While her belief that veiling and purdah were equivalent to slavery was common among white women of her time, it showed their unwillingness to hear the arguments of women from Egypt, India, and other regions who had long sought to educate white women about the complex social, cultural, and religious contexts of women's lives outside the West.[36] It is also worth noting that Kenyon, an expert on women's legal and political status, likely knew she was overstating her case that U.S. women's freedom was "practically won," but this was a commencement address, and she was trying to rally her listeners to public service, even going so far as to draw on the rhetoric of responsible citizenship prevalent in the post–World War II period.

Another useful way to analyze Kenyon's remarks is in the context of the CSW's focus on suffrage in its early years. Using suffrage as a barometer for women's equality meant measuring all non-U.S. societies by a narrow standard, one generated in the United States and Western Europe. It was not that women in other parts of the world did not care about suffrage, but for them it was not an isolated priority. Women outside the United States tended to have much broader conceptions of equality that included national liberation, social and economic development, and higher standards of living in addition to civil and political rights.[37] They also recognized that in undemocratic political systems, suffrage would do women little good. Kenyon and the other women on the CSW who concentrated on the vote were working to expand women's world citizenship as they understood it but not in ways that would have resonated with a large portion of the world's women.

This was illustrated clearly at the Third Session of the CSW, which took place in Beirut in the spring of 1949. Though there was no Lebanese representative on the commission, the Women's Committee of Lebanon took advantage of the publicity generated by the gathering to petition both the commission and the Lebanese government for greater women's rights. What they wanted in particular from the commission was an expanded *definition* of women's rights. Lebanese women urged Kenyon and the others to broaden their conception of rights and recognize that many women, such as themselves, saw the family, not individuals, as the foundation of society. They urged the commission to abandon the dichotomy of "East" and "West" and advocate for all women in ways that would help them rebuild their families and communities after World War II.[38]

Kenyon absorbed this request but only to a limited extent. Shortly after arriving home, Kenyon wrote to Ibtihaj Qaddura, president of the Women's Committee of Lebanon, to thank her for her hospitality during the commission's time in Beirut. Kenyon appreciated that Qaddura and her colleagues had brought their concerns to the commission's attention. "We learned much about your problems," she wrote, "and the special difficulties that women face there. Women face difficulties everywhere but they take different forms and have to be handled differently."[39] This polite but vague acknowledgment of the Lebanese women's petition also appeared in a speech Kenyon gave several times after the conference and eventually published in the *Women Lawyers Journal*. Despite the petition, the title of the article was "Beirut: East and

Figure 9. Dorothy Kenyon, center, with members of the UN Commission on the Status of Women, Beirut, 1949. Photo courtesy of the Sophia Smith Collection, Smith College.

West Women Meet." In it Kenyon emphasized that while in many respects Arab women lagged behind U.S. women in their thinking on women's rights, they were gradually coming to understand the importance of participation in government. Kenyon told her audience that Arab women agreed, for the most part, with the commission's program for political, educational, and economic rights, especially equal pay. But she admitted that Arab women had criticized the lack of emphasis on the home and "the problems of the wife and home-maker." The commission accepted this criticism, Kenyon noted, and agreed to discuss the subject at their next meeting.[40] In terms of her belief in the equality of all members of the world community, Kenyon thus went further than her predecessors like Mead, Andrews, and Tuttle in acknowledging that the concerns of women from other parts of the world did not always match those of elite white women from the United States and Europe. But she did not go much beyond acknowledgment. The CSW maintained its focus on individual rights, such as suffrage and equal pay, over the next several years.

Their narrow conception of women's rights was not the only thing hampering the commission's work in the late 1940s. Neither the members of the CSW, the cohort of mainstream women activists in the United States, nor

Kenyon herself could escape the increasing ideological tensions between the United States and the Soviet Union. Kenyon and her colleagues in the United States watched with alarm as what they perceived to be Soviet influence took hold of the commission. Citing the appointment of members of the Women's International Democratic Federation (WIDF), a progressive group with many communist leaders, and the efforts of the Soviet commissioner to secure consultative status for WIDF at the League of Nations, the commission's chair argued it "has now become a very lively and prize-worthy propaganda vehicle—of first class interest in the East-West contest."[41] Even Walter Kotschnig, the U.S. representative of ECOSOC, warned that "the USSR intends to use women's rights, along with other human rights, as a basis for agitation."[42] To Kenyon, however, it was increasingly clear that the Truman administration, and the State Department in particular, paid little mind to the CSW. They did not seem to care, she wrote to commission chair Bodil Begtrup, that the Soviet delegate was distorting their communication with ECOSOC and making it look like all the commission's achievements were thanks to her.[43] In other words, few at the State Department cared that the Cold War had infiltrated the CSW. And Kenyon herself soon had more pressing concerns.

Internationalist U.S. women were very active in the early years of the UN. Following Gildersleeve's lead, members of mainstream organizations wanted to make sure women were fully involved at all levels but particularly in areas related to their "special concerns," like the humanitarian work of ECOSOC. Most mainstream women were social feminists, and they successfully maneuvered to get Kenyon on the CSW and make sure it focused in this period on women's legal and political status. They all, but Kenyon in particular, felt an obligation to do this work. Kenyon was concerned not just for lasting peace but also for the status of women around the world. She saw it as U.S. women's responsibility to uplift oppressed women, and she saw the commission as the best venue for doing that. She was not able to make as much progress as she might have hoped by the time her term ended in late 1949, but she was a strong presence on the commission in its early years.

The Cold War

The bilateral tensions between the United States and the Soviet Union in the late 1940s severely weakened the United Nations, and the U.S. decision to pursue a unilateralist course, rather than taking advantage of international mechanisms to combat the threat of communism, undermined the UN even further.[44] Those tensions increasingly hampered the work of the CSW as well as the ability of organizations like the League of Women Voters to voice unequivocal support for the UN. For Kenyon and her contemporaries, the onset of the Cold War and the growth of anticommunist paranoia in the United States restricted not only women's world citizenship activities but also their willingness to talk about themselves as world citizens at all.

Rather than a site for negotiation and compromise—as envisioned by its charter—the UN became first a battleground and then a pawn in the early Cold War struggles between the United States and the Soviet Union. At the first meeting of the UN Security Council, tensions flared over the delayed withdrawal of Soviet troops from Iran, which had been jointly occupied during the war. In June 1946, Bernard Baruch, the U.S. representative to the newly formed UN Atomic Energy Commission, proposed in the General Assembly a plan that would establish international control of raw materials for nuclear weapons and regular inspections of nuclear development programs. The Soviets angrily rejected the plan. With the announcement of the Truman Doctrine in March 1947, Truman made clear the United States' willingness to circumvent the international machinery of the United Nations and to coopt the ideals of the charter into his Cold War rhetoric. He posited the United States, not the UN, as the only hope for a free world, even as he continued to use the UN as a symbol of that free world standing against communism.[45]

For some U.S. women, particularly those in such mainstream organizations as the League of Women Voters who had put so much faith in the potential of the United Nations to establish a peaceful world, these developments were troubling. They did not want the UN to become a pawn in the Cold War; they wanted it to remain a neutral site for negotiation and compromise. At the same time, many of them were becoming increasingly concerned about the spread of global communism and the potential threats it posed to liberal democracy—even as they recognized and opposed the simultaneous growth of anticommunist paranoia. The LWV, like similar groups, walked a fine line in the late 1940s between concern for the spread of both communism and anticommunism.

In June 1947 the Truman administration launched the Marshall Plan, which provided for a massive influx of foreign aid into Western Europe to act as a bulwark against Soviet expansion. Following Secretary of State George Marshall's speech introducing the plan in June, LWV president Anna Lord Strauss wrote to President Truman to express the organization's concern.

Members very much supported the plan, she assured the president, but they were concerned about a unilateral approach that bypassed the UN. Such an approach was not only contrary to the United States' established relationship with that body, she believed. It also put the United States potentially at risk: "One of the cardinal points of the programme of the League of Women Voters is 'acceptance by the United States of its full share of responsibility for strengthening the United Nations.' We know that in . . . failing to take advantage of its existing machinery, our Government is not doing its part in firmly establishing that international cooperation on which, ultimately, our own security and that of other nations depends." Strauss knew the UN's authority was entirely in the hands of its most powerful members, especially the United States. She dreaded what might happen if the United States neglected its obligations and marginalized the UN in its foreign policy. "We know that the United Nations will never become stronger," she wrote, "and hence able to fill the role we wish it could, unless in the conduct of our foreign relations day by day we take steps to strengthen it. And we know that the United States bears an especially large portion of the responsibility for strengthening the United Nations because of our position of leadership in world affairs."[46] In pressuring Truman not to weaken the UN, Strauss drew heavily on the language of responsibility so prevalent in the postwar period.

In his response Truman assured Strauss and the LWV that he had no intention of bypassing the UN. "I can assure you," he wrote, "that neither in the suggestions of the Secretary of State nor in any other aspect of American foreign policy is there any desire or intent to lessen the role of the United Nations in matters of international concern." He and Marshall felt, however, that it was best to have the European countries who were to receive aid determine among themselves exactly what they needed rather than having a body like the UN Economic Commission for Europe make those determinations for them. But the UN was being kept continually advised on the implementation of the plan, Truman further assured Strauss.[47] In reality, Truman had every intention of bypassing the UN, determined not to leave the management of any U.S. capital to a third party. Within a few years he became even more committed to a unilateral approach and more convinced of the need for a military alliance against the Soviets.[48] In the context of the Cold War, the LWV's appeals to make use of the UN carried little weight.

The LWV's Cold War concerns were not limited to the role of the UN; it was one of the most prominent women's organizations to feel the effects of increasing anticommunist paranoia in the United States. Strauss was frequently frustrated with careless accusations that she and other prominent LWV members had communist sympathies, and over time she and other national leaders became more and more cautious about their program and their public statements. By the late 1940s, for example, the organization had largely abandoned its concern for civil liberties.[49]

But the heaviest hammer dropped on organized women in the spring of 1950 when Senator Joseph McCarthy accused both Dorothy Kenyon and Esther Brunauer of harboring communist sympathies. He later swore under oath than Kenyon was a "fellow-traveler" who had been "affiliated with at least twenty-eight Communist-front organizations." Brunauer, who in 1950 was working for the State Department as a liaison to UNESCO, he accused of "Communist-front activities sufficiently serious to question her security status."[50] Kenyon immediately called McCarthy an "unmitigated liar" and declared she had "never had anything to do with any Communist fronts." Brunauer likewise avowed that she "could not possibly be" a communist and that she was "a loyal American and a loyal officer of the State Department."[51] Many prominent men and women, inside and outside the federal government, came to the defense of both women, but the damage was done. Neither ever held a public service job again. Even though McCarthy was thoroughly discredited by the early 1950s, the havoc he and other anticommunist crusaders wreaked on women's internationalist efforts in the post–World War II period cannot be underestimated.[52]

But even as prominent women and organizations were fending off McCarthy, others grew increasingly concerned about the threat of global communism. The General Federation of Women's Clubs, for instance, dedicated itself in the late 1940s and early 1950s to reinvigorating American democracy. Through their network of local clubs across the country they mobilized women voters, organized trips to state capitals, and emphasized the central role of Christianity in American life in opposition to atheistic communism.[53] Several other organizations, including the LWV, the NFBPW, and the GFWC, adopted "national security" as a central component of their platform. In October 1950 several groups came together to form the Assembly of Women's Organizations for National Security. In her keynote address, Margaret Hickey, president of the NFBPW, told the delegates that the most important component of women's citizenship was the obligation to promote world security. The best way to do that was not on the global but the local level, through service to their communities. "The battle for a secure world," she told the attendees, "starts where you are: adequate schools, libraries, clinics, housing, the improvement of child labor laws and working conditions, solving the problems of the aged."[54] In other words, women's municipal housekeeping—expanding their domestic duties as mothers and homemakers into their communities, just as they had done in the Progressive era—was the best way they could help fight the Cold War.

In this Cold War context, a much different conception of world citizenship began to emerge. In 1946 the conservative Daughters of the American Revolution (DAR) sounded the alarm on "world citizenship" as a potential communist plot. At their annual meeting members resolved to continue their "constructive campaign of education" about the humanitarian work of the United Nations and to "prevent the confusion of this plan of world responsibility with any plan for World Government involving world citizenship, universal currency, free trade, and dominance of the United States by the peoples of other nations."[55] The DAR saw world citizenship not as a practice of civic internationalism but as a threatening, totalitarian erasure of nationality and forced cooperation in a world system, implicitly a Soviet one. Their invocation of the phrase "world citizenship" as something to be feared demonstrates the kind of political environment within which other supporters of the UN, like Kenyon and the LWV, were operating in the late 1940s.

By the early 1950s many women in organizations such as the LWV had come to see the Cold War as one that had to be fought. This perception changed the way they engaged with the world more profoundly than any development since World War I. No longer were they world citizens demanding a seat at the world government table. They became ideological Cold Warriors. When they spoke about international dimensions of their U.S. citizenship, they no longer spoke of an obligation to work for peace; they invoked only the need to fight global communism.

Kenyon was not reappointed to another term on the CSW in 1949, but for the next few years she continued to extol its work, particularly in expanding women's political rights. In November 1950, in a speech at Barnard College, she pointed out that "it is easier now to describe the suffrage map of the world by listing those countries where women do not vote rather than those where they do." Noting the countries where women had won the vote since 1945, including China, Japan, India, Korea, and Syria, she proclaimed, "A revolution has swept over the earth. As part of the battle for human rights, women along with men have been given their political freedom, they have become adult citizens the world over." Kenyon attributed these victories to increased world citizenship; women and men were demanding to participate in shaping the global polity in order to improve conditions for everyone. "This great worldwide movement for democracy," she argued, "for votes for women as well as men, is based on an impulse as simple and direct as that, the impulse to have a say in what's going on, to be able to control our environment by means of better laws, better administration, to the end that we may have a better world."[56] The work of Kenyon and other commissioners to promote that worldwide movement culminated in the passage of the Convention on the Political Rights of Women in 1952.

Kenyon and other members of mainstream women's organizations such as the LWV wanted to continue in the late 1940s the work they had done during the war to help shape the peace. They promoted the United Nations as the best means not only for securing international cooperation but also for building stronger institutional mechanisms that might evolve someday into a world government. Responsible world citizenship, they believed, demanded no less. For Kenyon, the Commission on the Status of Women offered an opportunity to shape the global polity and advance women's rights at the same time. Her sense of obligation as a world citizen extended to helping women secure greater political rights, especially in those countries where she believed they were most oppressed. But she and other U.S. women like her were increasingly frustrated by the deepening Cold War and the growth of anticommunist paranoia in the United States. Though few of them were attacked as directly as Kenyon, the threat of such attacks gradually stifled women's support for the UN and turned their attention to national security as the most pressing international issue.

While mainstream women gradually came to realize by the early 1950s that the UN was not going to be the force for peace they had hoped, there were other U.S. women who had never believed the UN capable of ensuring peace in the first place. In the immediate post–World War II years, some women found their best opportunities for world citizenship not within the UN but by actively criticizing it and working to replace it. The final chapter of this book turns to women involved in the widespread popular movement for world government that paralleled the early years of the UN.

CHAPTER 8

Edith Wynner and Popular World Government in the Atomic Era

While Dorothy Kenyon and mainstream women's organizations were doing all they could to support the United Nations, Rosika Schwimmer had a different idea. In February 1945, she and Edith Wynner issued a call for a United Peoples' Conference to be held concurrently with the San Francisco Conference. "The peoples of the world are yearning for a new world order offering justice and opportunity to the whole human family," they declared. "But they have no faith in resolutions and promises made by the governments of the Great Powers, having too often seen them cynically discarded." Schwimmer and Wynner envisioned a more representative gathering than the official conference looked at that point to be. Heeding Schwimmer and Lloyd's call for an "all-inclusive" world government, the United Peoples' Conference would incorporate "colonial peoples and those from mandated areas . . . and those who are to be outlawed from the human family—Italy, Germany, Japan." Finally, Schwimmer and Wynner announced their intention to form at the conference an "Unofficial Provisional World Government" that would continue monitoring the official proceedings before it turned to carrying out whatever program the attendees devised.[1]

It is not clear whether such a conference took place, but this call represented the rebirth in the post–World War II period of Schwimmer and Lloyd's vision for an inclusive, equitable, peaceful world. This chapter centers on Edith Wynner, who along with Lloyd's children bore the mantle of the Campaign for World Government over the next several years. After Lloyd died in 1944 and Schwimmer's health declined, William Lloyd Jr. and his sister Georgia Lloyd took over the Chicago office, while Wynner ran the New York operation out of Schwimmer's apartment. The three did not see eye to eye on

the CWG. Georgia criticized the weaknesses of the UN but felt the best way
to strengthen it was to reform the charter. She wanted to cooperate with other
world federalist organizations in the United States to push for such reforms.
Wynner, on the other hand, believed there was nothing about the UN worth
saving. The only way forward was to call for a "Peoples' World Constitutional
Convention," similar to the one envisioned by Schwimmer and Lloyd in 1937,
to launch a genuine world government.

For Wynner, world citizenship meant popular action for world government, just as it had for Schwimmer and Lloyd. Unlike Brunauer, Bethune,
and Kenyon, Wynner did not make demands on governments for opportunities to participate in the existing global polity. She saw the UN as a fruitless
endeavor, no more able to keep the peace than the League of Nations had
been. Instead, following her mentors' lead, she asserted the right of the people
of the world to shape a new polity for themselves. She wanted a system of
absolute legal equality, in which all individuals were protected and no one
was immune from international law. But while Wynner carried the banner of
Schwimmer and Lloyd's belief in popular world government, she also adapted
it to the postwar era. In particular, she recognized that the atomic bomb only
made the need for world government more pressing and that some degree of
collective force would likely be necessary to control atomic technology. The
fact that the world could be annihilated so easily made Wynner's sense of
obligation as a world citizen even more acute than Schwimmer and Lloyd's
had been. Throughout the latter half of the 1940s, Wynner pushed her idea
for a peoples' convention—her updated version of the Schwimmer-Lloyd
plan—within the world federalist movement.

A Postwar World Federalist

Wynner's personal background resembled that of Schwimmer, the woman
who became her lifelong mentor and friend. She was born Edith Weiner to
Jewish parents in Budapest in 1915, making her the youngest of the women
profiled in this book and likely the only one who had no personal memory
of World War I. Her father, Robert, was a jeweler and craftsman who, like
Schwimmer, left Hungary shortly after World War I. Her mother, Frieda Her-
skovics, was mentally unstable for most of Wynner's early years. Her parents'
marriage was not a happy one; Wynner later recalled to her older brother Al
how often they fought and noted that they divorced when Robert left Hungary

and moved to the United States. They later reconciled but lived unhappily in Chicago during the 1920s. Wynner remembered her father with mixed feelings. "He encouraged my intellectual interests and that was good," she wrote her brother in 1991. "He would have made a first-rate uncle. As a husband and father he was a disaster. I give him full credit for having destroyed our mother."[2] Although it is not clear how she got there, by the early 1930s Frieda was in an insane asylum in Levoca, in eastern Slovakia. Wynner lost track of her mother during World War II, but she later learned that when the asylum staff got word in the early 1940s to prepare all the patients for transfer to a concentration camp, they decided instead to give each patient a lethal dose of morphine. "I consider their action a mercy killing of the noblest kind," Wynner told her brother.[3]

Wynner began working as Schwimmer's secretary in 1934 at age nineteen. She had hoped to attend college but was forced by the Depression to find work instead. Thanks to her peripatetic childhood, she was fluent in Hungarian, German, English, Slovak, and French, which made her a valuable asset. She quickly became interested in Schwimmer's various causes, particularly that of world government. When Schwimmer and Lloyd launched the Campaign for World Government in 1937, Wynner served as secretary of the New York office and began what would become a lifelong relationship with Lloyd's children. In 1944 she and Georgia collaborated on *Searchlight on Peace Plans: Choose Your Road to World Government*, a compilation of theories and plans for world government ranging from the leagues of ancient Greece all the way up to the reports of the Commission to Study the Organization of Peace in 1943. The book was not a best seller, but it was timely, and it made enough of an impact in Washington that Eleanor Roosevelt invited the two to dinner at the White House in June 1944.[4] At the end of the war, Wynner was still in New York, living with and caring for Schwimmer and her sister Franciska even as she continued working and traveling on behalf of the CWG. Despite their disagreements over the UN and world government philosophies, Wynner maintained her friendship with Georgia, as she did with all the Lloyd children.

Like Schwimmer, Wynner made no gendered arguments about women's inherent suitability for peace work and international activism, and she held such beliefs in contempt. In contrast to all of the other women portrayed in this book, she was never involved to any significant extent with any women's organizations such as WILPF. She was too young to have been a suffragist, and she did not go to college, which might have connected her to a group like the AAUW; so she never moved in circles where gendered beliefs were more

Figure 10. Edith
Wynner, 1944. Photo
courtesy of the
University of New
Hampshire.

common. Nor is there any evidence she joined the National Woman's Party,
though it seems safe to assume she would have supported the Equal Rights
Amendment. Unlike Tuttle or Kenyon, Wynner held firmly that women as a
group were no more "naturally" pacifist than men, and she never argued that
she herself should be involved in any given effort or organization because she
was a woman. She supported the efforts of the White House Conference to get
women appointed to postwar planning committees but not for gendered reasons; she simply believed the most qualified people should be the ones to shape
the peace. "When women are pacifists or federalists," she proclaimed, "they are
these because they have achieved a higher ideal of human behavior and not
because they are women." Women had been "conditioned to militarism" just as
much as men, she pointed out, contending that their militarization had "nul-
lified any of the protective instinct toward the young that is associated with
motherhood." Rather than sacrificing herself to protect her sons, the typical

mother sent her sons to war to protect her. "Further," Wynner continued, "she wears with pride the medals and gold stars given by governments in recognition of her abnormality and accepts the blood-money paid her as a pension for her murdered sons. Gentle, charming creature, isn't she?"[5]

Wynner's critiques of the Dumbarton Oaks proposals in 1944 were very much informed by Schwimmer and Lloyd's plan for world government. She called for changes in the structure of representation so that all nations would be immediately invited to join, delegates would be popularly elected, and each member nation would have several representatives who would not be required to vote as a bloc. The General Assembly, she argued, should have "real *legislative* not merely *talking* authority" and the power to raise revenues from such sources as international postage, communication, and transport. The Security Council, meanwhile, should be an executive body charged with administering and enforcing laws created by the Assembly, though its power had to be appropriately restrained by the judiciary.[6] Wynner wanted the United Nations to be all-inclusive and democratic, and, most importantly, she wanted to it have real authority to make and enforce international law. She saw none of those characteristics in the Dumbarton Oaks proposals. As long as the UN remained a confederation rather than a genuine world government, it could not solve the most pressing international problems.[7]

The only aspect of Schwimmer and Lloyd's plan that Wynner did not emphasize as much as they had was its nonmilitary nature. This seemed to be as much a strategic move as a philosophical one. Wynner was a pacifist, but she believed, as she once told Mary Lloyd, William and Georgia's sister, that "pacifism without world government is merely an individual creed." In order to secure a world government, Wynner had to appeal to a broad swath of people; she did not want her plan tagged as pacifist and did not think her world government merited that label. The federation model, she pointed out, was based on the U.S. Constitutional Convention—"hardly a gathering of pacifists." What was more, she had found that "non-pacifists are just as likely—and possibly more—to understand and support the international application of this mechanism [federalism] as are pacifists."[8]

The other factor, of course, that might have made Wynner modify Schwimmer and Lloyd's absolute pacifist stance was the advent of the atomic age. Regulation of nuclear weapons demanded more than the anemic commitments to disarmament and the opposition to militarism that had characterized much of the pre-1945 peace movement. The atomic age necessitated international enforcement, Wynner frequently asserted. Even the scientists who had helped create the bomb spoke out on the need to regulate its use and warned that the United Nations was not sufficient. In October 1945 a group of atomic scientists and other public figures, including Albert Einstein and Supreme Court justice Owen Roberts, wrote in a letter to the *New York Times* that "the Charter is a tragic illusion unless we are ready to take the further steps necessary to organize peace." Because the nations of the world retained absolute sovereignty within the UN, they pointed out, the charter more closely resembled the Articles of Confederation than the U.S. Constitution. "We know that this confederation did not work," they reminded their readers. "We must aim at a Federal Constitution of the world, a working world-wide legal order, if we hope to prevent an atomic world war."[9]

Einstein expanded on his views the following month in the *Atlantic*. "The secret of the bomb should be committed to a world government," he argued, "and the United States should immediately announce its readiness to do so." He proposed that a world constitution be developed by three men, each representing the United States, Britain, and the Soviet Union. Once they had drafted it and their nations had agreed to it, other nations would be invited to sign on. This world government, in his view, would oversee all military matters and have the power to intervene anywhere a majority of people were being oppressed by a minority. He went on, "Do I fear the tyranny of a world government? Of course I do. But I fear still more the coming of another war." Much like Schwimmer and Lloyd, Einstein oversimplified the process of establishing a world government, but his point was that atomic technology had to be under the control of an international authority. That was the message of many atomic scientists who were aware of the power they had helped unleash on the world.[10]

Wynner was greatly encouraged by the public statements of the atomic scientists and the wide audiences they seemed to be commanding. "I think they have done more to put world government before the people than all the rest of us during the whole previous time," she told a colleague in December 1945. She did not necessarily agree with their approach; she tried to persuade Einstein that his plan for the "big three" to shape the world government would end at best in utter failure and at worst in global domination. But she did agree that the atomic bomb made the need for world government more pressing, and she appreciated the publicity he brought to the cause. "To postpone action in this Atomic Era," she wrote, "is to choose global suicide."[11]

In 1945, not many Americans shared this perspective. A Gallup poll on August 8 revealed that 85 percent supported the bombing of Hiroshima.[12] But as news of the devastation in Japan slowly emerged in the United States over the next year, more people felt the need for international regulation of atomic weapons. The Federation of Atomic Scientists, led by Einstein and others who had worked on the Manhattan Project, supported the U.S. government's first attempt at such a plan, although they were less enthusiastic about the subsequent version presented to the UN by Franklin Roosevelt's former economic adviser Bernard Baruch. The "Baruch plan," as it became known, proposed that the United Nations assume control of nuclear power, prohibit the future production of atomic weapons, and ensure compliance through regular inspections. Baruch also proposed some modifications of the UN structure in order to strengthen its control, including limiting the veto power.[13]

The push for atomic regulation merged with the "one world" sentiment of the mid-1940s. Popularized by Wendell Willkie, a lawyer and Republican candidate for president in 1940, the idea captured the sense of humanity's common interest in lasting peace that underlay much of the popular support for the United Nations. Willkie's *One World*, an account of his forty-nine-day world tour in 1942, advocated for world federalism and called for full American participation in a postwar world organization, though it did not advance any specific plan for one. The book was an enormous success and inspired debates across the country about the United States' role in the peace process.[14] The atomic scientists echoed the phrase in their book, *One World or None*, which called for international control of nuclear weapons. "Civilization is presented with a challenge more serious perhaps than ever before," wrote Niels Bohr, "and the fate of humanity will depend on its ability to unite in averting common dangers."[15]

The world federalist movement of the late 1940s emerged to try to harness this sentiment and channel it into action for a world government. Dozens of organizations sprang up, many of them with confusingly similar names. They were far from unified; from the outset, the movement was scattered, disorganized, and competitive. Broadly speaking, there were two axes of disagreement: whether the world government should begin with regional federations or be universal from the start, and whether it was best secured through UN reform or through immediate action to replace the UN. Clarence Streit, for example, whose *Union Now* remained a best seller and went through several editions throughout the 1940s, was a world government regionalist. He referred to the UN as a "half measure" and favored scrapping it and starting over, and he continued to promote his Atlantic Union of democracies. Wynner, by contrast, was a world government universalist who wanted all nations invited immediately to join.

In her corner Wynner had the author of perhaps the most widely read postwar world government tract. Emery Reves's *The Anatomy of Peace* was a best seller in the fall of 1945. The two world wars had proved, Reves argued, that the nation-state system should be abolished because excessive nationalism always led to industrial competition, militarism, and fascism. And the United Nations was not the answer; he characterized it as "the pitiful miscarriage of the second World War" and "the Unholy Alliance stillborn in San Francisco." The only solution was a world government. Reves called for "the integration of the scattered conflicting national sovereignties into one unified, higher sovereignty, capable of creating a legal order within which all peoples may enjoy equal security, equal obligations and equal rights under law." Like many world government theorists, Reves did not elaborate on the details or implementation of his proposal. But his castigation of nationalism and his belief that the world desperately needed a greater degree of political cooperation clearly resonated with readers across the United States.[16]

But while many advocates agreed with Reves's premise, they were not prepared to jettison the UN and start from scratch. UN reform was the far more widely accepted path to world government in the late 1940s. World Federalists and Americans United for World Government were the best-known groups with this view. World Federalists was started by a group of Streit's former followers who had grown dissatisfied with his regionalism. One was Mildred Riordan Blake, who was working as an advertising copywriter in New York in the late 1930s when she began reading the work of Salvador de Madariaga. By 1939 she was a convert to the cause. "Nations as small as Switzerland and as large as the United States use the federal principle with success," she wrote in a letter to the *New York Times*. "Why not the world?"[17] Along with her colleagues Vernon Nash and Tom Griessemer, Blake worked throughout the war to publicize the ideal of world federalism. All three had originally been members of Streit's organization but broke off and formed World Federalists in 1941. Despite their seemingly common goal, Blake and Wynner did not get along well, in part because of Blake's emphasis on the need for a world police force. She had little use for pacifists, believing a world government would never succeed if it could not enforce its dictates.[18] While Wynner did not stress antimilitarism in her own vision to the extent Schwimmer and Lloyd had, she still would not have endorsed a well-armed world police.

Americans United for World Government, meanwhile, grew out of several wartime groups, including the Committee to Defend America by Aiding the Allies. Formed in 1944, the group had supported the creation of the

United Nations but believed it did not go far enough to secure peace. Americans United was firmly committed to achieving a world government by revising the UN Charter. Its members believed that "through the present United Nations Organization there must be developed a World Federal Government with limited but definite and adequate powers to prevent war, including power to control the atomic bomb and other major weapons and to maintain world inspection and police forces."[19] One of Americans United's founders and its president through the mid-1940s was Florence Jaffray Harriman, a wealthy suffragist and reformer and the former U.S. ambassador to Norway. As a firm backer of UN reform, Harriman did not agree with Wynner's desire to pursue an immediate world government, but she did share her universalist orientation. In response to Clarence Streit's regionalism, for instance, she argued, "There are others among those who talk world government who advocate immediate union by those governments who feel free to join such a combination. Surely this is dangerous, as its effect would be that of a power coalition *against* other nations."[20]

Wynner bemoaned the fragmented nature of the world government movement, but she did not see how these separate groups could ever cooperate as long as some remained wedded to regionalism or UN reform. In her mind, the atomic bomb proved the futility of gradual measures like those. "Nuclear Energy has not created the need for world government," she wrote in early 1946. "That need was just as acute before the Atomic Bomb. But most people had accepted that [the UN] ... would be a first step, that it would be developed gradually into an effective organization and perhaps even into world government. The Atomic Bomb made it clear to most of those who accepted this theme that the time for gradual development is non-existent."[21] The answer, Wynner believed, was an updated version of Schwimmer and Lloyd's plan.

The Peoples' World Constitutional Convention

In the summer of 1945, the Campaign for World Government was tiny and divided. Lola Maverick Lloyd was dead, and Schwimmer was ill and had cut off communication with Lloyd's children. Wynner's first loyalty, as it had always been, was to Schwimmer, but she continued to work with Georgia and kept in regular touch with William. All three disagreed on the best way forward. None supported the new UN as implemented, but Georgia thought it was better than nothing and wanted to find ways to strengthen it.[22] William, on the other hand, wanted to jettison the charter and start over. "If we fail to protest a hollow shell, a fraud," he wrote his sister, "at the time everyone is interested in preventing another war and ready to listen to us, we will find later on that they will not even listen to us." In a prescient statement, he added, "Domestic economic and social questions may take the center of the stage with any major postwar depression, and when that is over, people will be too busy enjoying their cars and movies to pay much attention to amending the charter of a far-away world organization."[23]

Wynner agreed. During a lecture tour to promote *Searchlight on Peace Plans*, she became convinced that Americans were ready to consider the idea of world government, thanks in large part to the atomic scientists. The problem was what to do now. She rejected both the idea that the UN Charter was a first step toward a world government and that the UN could be effectively reformed at all. Channeling Einstein, she compared the charter to the Articles of Confederation, arguing, "The change from a confederate to a federal structure is not a minor alteration job that can be done through amendment."[24] Wynner wanted instead to revive Schwimmer and Lloyd's campaign and call immediately for a popular world constitutional convention. She spent most of 1946 laying out her plans.

The key components of Wynner's proposal were identical to Schwimmer and Lloyd's, though she articulated several of them more explicitly than had her predecessors. The convention's mandate would be to draft a constitution that vested legislative authority in a representative assembly and created an executive to carry out its laws, gave the World Court jurisdiction over international disputes, and ensured that the enforcement power of the world government would extend not just to governments but to individuals.[25] Wynner made sure to reiterate her predecessors' all-inclusive, democratic, and nonmilitary vision. "The World Government shall be a federal union," she declared, "formed on the basis of the voluntary but permanent association of the peoples of the world. It shall be set up so as to allow all nations to become members; democratic in its structure; non-military in character with enforcement authority derived from the peoples of the world through fair and adequate electoral machinery, and operating on individuals."[26] While the constitutional convention would decide the scope and nature of the powers invested in the world government, Wynner suggested several functions, including admitting nations into the union, settling boundary disputes, regulating emigration and immigration, supervising elections, supervising disarmament, regulating world trade and commerce, establishing a world banking system and a uniform currency, raising standards of living, mitigating unemployment through public projects, assisting in the solution of overpopulation, and levying taxes. There would be no international military, but there would be a world police force to deal with violators of international law. Wynner's only mention of powers retained by national governments was "autonomy over their individual development, except in case of conflict with authority transferred to world government." All international alliances and treaties would become void. National police forces would be subject to international oversight. And all tariffs and other restrictions on the free movement of goods, services, and people would have to be brought into compliance with international law.[27]

Like Schwimmer and Lloyd, Wynner also made explicit provisions for world citizenship. Among the powers delegated to the world government would be the responsibility "to provide equal world citizenship to all and to regulate the rights and duties of world citizens." In order to secure the rights of individuals, she proposed a world attorney general who would "function exclusively as the champion of the people against abuse of powers by the world, national or local governments." The attorney general's duties would include safeguarding the rights and privileges of individuals, investigating complaints and prosecuting offenders, and reporting to the world legislature.[28] It is not hard to imagine that the Holocaust, as well as Wynner's personal and family experiences during World War II, had a significant effect on her thinking about the need to protect world citizens.

Wynner's updates to Schwimmer and Lloyd's plan reflected not only her concern for atomic weapons but also her recognition of growing demands for decolonization and for human rights. Both she and Schwimmer had hoped that colonial representatives would be allowed to play a greater role at the San Francisco Conference, and they had organized their United Peoples' Conference in part as a way to give voice to those representatives. A month before the conference, Wynner wrote to novelist Pearl Buck, whose humanitarian interests had developed while living in China from 1914 to 1935, that she had long been a proponent of national self-determination. "I have been advocating for years," she told Buck, "that all colonial territories have the right to determine themselves whether they are ready for independent nationhood." If a territory decided it was not ready, Wynner continued, they should have "the impartial assistance of federal world government in order to achieve national autonomy under world government."[29] This was a small but important step forward from Schwimmer and Lloyd's plan, which made no mention

of letting colonial subjects *choose* whether their territory would be administered by the world government. A year later, as colonized populations around
the world were demanding independence, Wynner wrote her beliefs into her
plan. The world government she envisioned would "supervise, administer,
and assist non-self-governing territories until their admission as members of
the union" and would "provide temporary, impartial civilian world administration of areas . . . where civil war threatens or has broken out, with the
duty, however, of conducting a referendum within the shortest possible time
to determine the freely expressed wishes of the people of the territory concerned."[30] Taken together with her antidiscrimination language below, this
represented the most egalitarian vision of any of the women profiled in this
book except Bethune. Unlike Bethune, however, Wynner did not make connections between the oppression of colonized people abroad and that of African Americans or other people of color in the United States.

Wynner's concern for autonomy and self-determination extended to individuals. In keeping with the tenor of the post–World War II era, she envisioned a global bill of rights—an update that Schwimmer and Lloyd would
undoubtedly have approved. "The World Government shall make no laws,"
Wynner proclaimed, echoing the U.S. Constitution, "restricting the fundamental liberties of the individual, such as the inherent right to free speech,
free press, freedom of conscience and assembly; freedom from arbitrary
arrest, detention, search and seizure; freedom from arbitrary imposition of
penalties; freedom of access to information; freedom of association and organization for religious, cultural, political and economic purposes." Moreover,
not only would international law be binding on individuals, but all people of
the world would be equally protected by it: "The World Government shall
make no laws providing for discriminatory or arbitrary treatment because of
race, color, creed, national origin, political belief or sex."[31] Every single one
of these provisions appeared in the Universal Declaration of Human Rights,
which the UN adopted two years later. Wynner made little mention of the
declaration, but she certainly would have been aware of its drafting between
1945 and 1948.[32]

In many ways, Wynner's vision seemed more plausible in 1946 than
Schwimmer and Lloyd's had in 1937. The United Nations existed. The United
States was no longer the neutral nation it had proclaimed itself to be in the
1930s. Nazism and fascism were no longer immediate threats. And people
throughout the country and around the world seemed more prepared to
accept some form of world government, especially to control atomic weapons.

In late September, Wynner wrote to a colleague that prominent world government advocates supported the peoples' convention plan, including atomic scientists such as Leo Szilard.[33]

At the same time, Wynner knew the bipolar world of the Cold War had already begun to emerge. George Kennan's "Long Telegram" from Moscow, in which he detailed the imminent threats posed by Soviet expansion and called on the United States to resist it, arrived in Washington in February 1946. The Truman administration took that charge seriously. The United States may no longer have professed neutrality by that point, but neither did it profess cooperation. Even during the early stages of planning for the postwar peace, U.S. officials intended for their country to become the predominant world power, countering the Soviet threat at the same time that it expanded its own political and economic influence. There was no room in this formulation for genuine participation at the UN, let alone a stronger body.[34] "The two great obstacles to world government are the United States and [the Soviet Union]," Wynner noted in January 1946. "Each represents a huge international regional government . . . with sufficient resources to believe that in a pinch each can go it alone." In an echo of Schwimmer and Lloyd's call for unofficial popular action, Wynner argued that those two countries should not stand in others' way: "If other peoples are ready to initiate action, it should not be delayed because of the absence of official participation by one or both of these mammoths at any stage of the proceedings."[35]

Within the world government movement, where most people were dedicated to UN reform, reaction to Wynner's ideas were mixed. Blake wrote to Georgia Lloyd that World Federalists liked the idea of the convention, as long as "it were clearly recognized that they were propaganda conventions, and that the leaders had no grandiose dreams of replacing the powers-that-be in this world." Blake was concerned about the possibility of actually setting up a world government. "Such talk," she told Lloyd, "discredits the whole idea with a great many people." Wynner, however, felt that the leaders of World Federalists, including Blake, were merely disappointed that they had already come out as being opposed to a popular convention just as the idea was beginning to pick up steam.[36] Florence Harriman, for her part, worried about Wynner's strong stance against the UN. In March 1946, Harriman warned a colleague against aligning with those who talked "belligerently of setting up a rival attraction called a World Constitutional Convention." In her opinion, "the net result of destroying public confidence in the U.N.O. [United Nations Organization] at this time, will be to push the world backward into anarchy instead of forward into that government under law which we so ardently ask."[37]

Believing that world government was an international cause—and perhaps sensing her lack of support within the U.S. movement—Wynner reached out to potential collaborators in other countries, especially in Europe. In 1945 she established ties with Henry Usborne, a young Labour MP from Birmingham, England, who had been a leader in Britain's Federal Union (an organization similar in outlook to but separate from Clarence Streit's Federal Union) since 1939. He met Schwimmer and Wynner on a trip to New York in April 1945 and admired their plan for a peoples' world convention. At the end of the war he focused all his energy on persuading the Labour government to adopt the cause of world federation, and he wanted Wynner to come work as his full-time secretary. Wynner was "deeply distressed," however, by Usborne's insistence, which echoed Streit's, that a European federation had to precede a world government. If he continued pressing his European plan, she told him, she could not help him.[38] While a strong partnership between the two never materialized, they did work together sporadically over the next several years.

Wynner also focused on raising money. Anticipating that governments would not be willing to act even under heavy citizen pressure, she believed large sums of money would be needed to finance a world constitutional convention called by the peoples of the world. Up to 1945, Wynner argued, world government work had been carried out thanks to "the devotion of those . . . long on ideals and short of purse." It was time for those with means to make their fair contribution—at least as much, if not more, than they had contributed to various war efforts. Wynner referred to this as "self-taxation." For every tax dollar that went toward war, those who could ought to contribute at least as much to the world government cause.[39]

Many world government leaders felt their movement would be stronger if the disparate groups across the country were consolidated into one large umbrella organization. To that end, representatives gathered in Asheville, North Carolina, in February 1947. Over two days of meetings at the George Vanderbilt Hotel, more than two hundred attendees, including Wynner, Georgia Lloyd, Mildred Blake, and Florence Harriman, debated the platform of the new organization—in particular, whether it should advocate UN reform or the peoples' convention approach. The meeting was bifurcated from the start, however; the planning committee decided that only "membership" organizations would be eligible to join the new group. That meant bodies like the Campaign for World Government, which did not have members, were sidelined from the outset, while World Federalists and Americans United were among those represented at the principal meetings. Lloyd was especially frustrated with this arrangement and felt the membership groups had no interest in any input from other organizations. Both she and Wynner recognized that because the merging groups were dominated by people like Blake and Harriman who favored UN reform over a peoples' convention, any support for an alternate agenda would be hard to come by. Lloyd characterized the conference as nothing less than a hostile takeover of the world government movement by those advocating UN reform.[40]

Wynner agreed with Lloyd's take on the situation to a point, but overall her impression of the conference was positive. She was convinced before she got to Asheville that the conference would be "rigged" against her plan. Therefore she put her energy into trying to influence the proceedings indirectly. She kept in close touch with the handful of people in membership organizations that she knew were amenable to the peoples' convention idea and urged them to keep agitating for it. She fed them information and in some cases even helped write their public remarks. She effectively exploited those who were frustrated by the idea of pursuing only UN reform and secured several promises from elected leaders in the new group that they would continue to advocate for the peoples' convention.[41]

At a dinner attended by most of the delegates, Wynner had one chance to speak for herself. "The atomic bomb leaves us no margin for error," she proclaimed. Time was of the essence in pushing for world government, therefore all methods should be pursued simultaneously. "There ought to be room for those seeking a minimum of world federal government and those seeking a maximum," Wynner contended, referring first to UN Charter revision and then to the peoples' convention. A convention, she believed, would serve additional functions, including raising awareness, educating the public, and increasing pressure on the UN and national governments to take action. That was why all fundraising efforts should go immediately toward such a program. "Those with surplus funds," she declared, referring to wealthy Americans in general, "must be moved to buy the one insurance that can safeguard them against total loss: the insurance that only world government can provide." And if anyone needed extra persuading to donate to the cause, Wynner continued, they should be reminded that "the wealthy of Hiroshima burned just as effectively as the poor. In a world rendered largely barren after an atomic war, wealth in terms of money, of stocks and bonds and bank deposits will have about as much meaning as a diamond belt on a life-raft in mid-Pacific."[42]

Wynner believed her speech had been a tremendous success. "It had a magical effect," she told Henry Usborne, "insofar as all those who had hostile and closed minds to the Peoples' Convention idea turned at least into a friendly listening position." Thanks to her, she continued, several official delegates at the conference introduced the idea of the convention in the merger sessions, though they failed to win much support. On the train back to New York, Wynner talked with several "Americans United men and women," most of whom "had the attitude of being willing to be convinced even though they weren't yet." She also reported that many members of the new organization were dissatisfied with its platform and would therefore be open to cooperation.[43]

The platform of the United World Federalists, the new organization formed in Asheville, undercut Wynner's estimation of her success by declaring the group's commitment to UN reform. Its statement of purpose read, "While endorsing the efforts of the United Nations to bring about a world community favorable to peace, we will work primarily to strengthen the United Nations into a world government of limited power adequate to prevent war and having direct jurisdiction over the individual within its area of competence." Asserting that the American people were frustrated by the "impotence" of the UN, especially after the failure of the Baruch Plan for atomic control and the declaration of the Truman Doctrine, United World Federalists promised to a plan to strengthen the UN and secure for it more influence over the growing tensions between the United States and the Soviet Union.[44]

Though disappointed by the platform of the federalists, Wynner left Asheville still enthusiastic about her plan for a peoples' convention and encouraged by the support she felt she had found. Over the next year, she directed most of her attention toward Europe, determined to bolster her idea among world government supporters in England and throughout the continent. To that end she spent the spring and summer of 1947 abroad and attended meetings of various world government organizations in France, Luxembourg, and other countries. Her travels only hardened her conviction that a peoples' convention was the best path to world government. Neither individual nation-states nor the UN had seriously attempted to devise a global system strong enough to guarantee peace and nuclear security; therefore it was time for the ordinary women and men of the world to band together and demand one. When Wynner returned to the United States, she launched her last major effort on behalf of her plan—raising enough money to implement it.

Funding World Government

Popular action for world government did not come cheap. Schwimmer had been exploring ways to secure funding for a world constitutional convention since the late 1930s. In 1947 Wynner estimated she would need at least a quarter of a million dollars to start the effort properly. Her budget included salaries for herself and a handful of other key workers; travel to and from Europe to further international cooperation; and speaking tours, literature, and publicity campaigns across the United States and Europe. She envisioned four offices in the United States, each staffed by a team of five people, that would develop publicity campaigns and a process for identifying potential delegates to the world constitutional convention. With all that in place, she hoped a convention could be held as early as 1950.[45]

Wynner's primary target lived in Chicago, where Schwimmer and Lola Maverick Lloyd had first launched their campaign. Anita McCormick Blaine was the daughter of Cyrus McCormick and an heir to the McCormick reaper fortune. Born in 1866, she had been a philanthropist from a young age, funding settlement houses, kindergartens, and education initiatives in Chicago as early as the 1880s. In 1889 she married Emmons Blaine, a railroad executive and son of presidential candidate James G. Blaine, but he died three years later following a brief illness. The couple's only child, Emmons Blaine Jr., died of influenza in 1918. Anita Blaine was a staunch admirer of Woodrow Wilson and advocated for U.S. membership in the League of Nations throughout the 1920s (though she was never a member of Tuttle's organization). In 1939 she organized the short-lived World Citizens Association in Chicago, which compiled study packets on international cooperation to educate Americans about the need for a postwar organization. Blaine supported the creation of the United Nations just as strongly as she had the League of Nations; like Blake and Harriman she hoped it would be the germ of a genuine world government. She gave regular but comparatively small donations throughout the mid-1940s to various organizations such as the United World Federalists. By 1948 she had become a champion and financial backer of Henry Wallace, former vice president and Progressive Party candidate for president. Blaine's close association with Wallace made some federalists wary, however, because he had already become a target of anticommunists.[46]

While she was in Europe, Wynner began encouraging various colleagues to approach Blaine about a large donation, but she was frustrated with their efforts. When Henry Usborne began planning a speaking tour in the United States in late 1947, Wynner was determined to put him together with Blaine, convinced his charm could elicit a large donation. But Usborne proved a disappointment. "When Mrs. B. asked him how much would be needed to crystalize an organization," Wynner reported to Georgia and Mary Lloyd, "the dope told her three thousand!" Wynner had been hoping for an initial contribution of tens of thousands, if not much more.[47] From the outset she was territorial about any potential donation, wanting to make sure it went to her peoples' convention plan rather than to the general study of world government or to UN reform. She was frustrated, for instance, that Blaine had pledged a thousand dollars a month to a rival organization, money Wynner accused them of "frittering away" while she worked tirelessly and without pay or reimbursement for materials and mailing costs.[48]

Throughout the first seven months of 1948, Wynner and several others schemed and competed for a donation from Blaine, which everyone came to assume would total one million dollars. Wynner's focus was on working out a definite plan and budget for a peoples' convention in 1950 that she could sell to Blaine. She joined forces with new partners, including Harris Wofford, a young and charismatic leader in the movement who later became a distinguished Democratic politician in Pennsylvania, and Stringfellow Barr, who by that time had been a leader in Streit's Federal Union, the United World Federalists, and the Committee to Frame a World Constitution, a study group convened at the University of Chicago in 1945. Barr was an eloquent spokesman for a peoples' convention and enjoyed a personal relationship with Blaine through mutual connections in Chicago. In June 1948, Wynner, Wofford, and Barr collaborated on a strategy to convince Blaine to make the donation. Over the next month, Barr communicated with her regularly, winning her trust and finally securing the money in early August. On August 3—the same day Rosika Schwimmer died—Blaine presented Barr with a check for one million dollars to support the cause of world government.[49] The money was designated for a new Foundation for World Government devoted to educating the public for a "new and higher level of world citizenship" and building support for the "establishment of a world government representing all mankind." Barr, who was named the foundation's first director, assured Wynner that the peoples' convention would be a high priority.[50]

The foundation ran into trouble almost immediately, however, when word leaked out that Blaine intended Henry Wallace to be one of the trustees. Press reports in early September claimed Blaine had only given the money to establish the foundation so that it could become a platform for Wallace to spread communism in the United States. "Henry A. Wallace has a made-to-order cause to occupy him after the election," the *New York World-Telegram* reported on its front page on September 14. "It will provide him a million-dollar kitty to work with and a worldwide sounding board." World government groups were in an "uproar," the article claimed. "It was their instant and almost unanimous opinion that Mr. Wallace, surrounded as he is by Communists and partial to the Soviet Union, would put the kiss of death on the entire world government movement." Ely Culbertson, a prominent world government advocate and president of the Citizens Committee for United Nations Reform, declared in *Newsweek* that "as far as our organization is concerned, anything Wallace is associated with is a red herring—double and redoubled." And in an article titled "$1,000,000 Nobody Wants," the *Manchester Guardian* reported that Wallace's association with the foundation had made it an anathema: "World federalists are as jealous of their doctrinal differences as bridge players on modern French governments. But they are united in their fear of being mistaken for laborers in the vineyard of Henry Wallace's One World."[51] None of the articles, however, named the source of these accusations.

That source, it turned out, was Edith Wynner. Just weeks after Blaine's donation—for which she had worked for almost two years—Wynner torpedoed the entire endeavor. In an interview in 1980 she claimed it was because she wanted "to keep the money out of Communist hands." This was very likely true, not because Wynner was anticommunist herself but because she understood that world government proposals were susceptible to anticommunist attacks from what she called "the patrioteer crowd."[52] But she also felt deeply betrayed by her colleagues, especially Barr and Wofford. Wynner felt the three had a clear understanding that Blaine's money would be used to finance the peoples' convention. But it quickly became clear that the named leaders of the foundation, including Barr, had no such intentions. "The Foundation thought it ought to concentrate on essential research and support of the World Government Movement," one of Barr's colleagues told Mary Lloyd vaguely. Barr, Wofford, and a small group of others began meeting as foundation trustees in October and actively maneuvered to keep Wynner out of the way. Barr, in his first official report as president of the foundation in January 1949, wrote Wynner out of its history entirely, declaring that the whole idea of the peoples' convention had emerged "from a group within United World Federalists"—the same organization that had shunned the idea in Asheville—and that when the foundation was established "its objective was wisely generalized into a 'Public Educational Campaign in the Principles of World Government.'"[53]

To say Wynner was frustrated would be an understatement, as her efforts to discredit the foundation show. She nursed this grudge for the rest of her life. The episode with Blaine was "just the last straw in being misused by federalists," she told Mary Lloyd. "From now on anybody in federalist circles trying to push me around is going to get slugged so promptly that they will carry an indelible mark to commemorate the event."[54] Over the next few years, she sporadically attended world government meetings and conferences in the United States, and she continued to correspond frequently with the Lloyds and other colleagues in the movement. When the Korean War broke out in the fall of 1950, Wynner feared it portended the start of World War III. "The present development tends in the direction of world unity," she acknowledged, but that unity would be based only on the "overwhelming power of a single state," whether the United States or the Soviet Union. Korea did not mark the success of the UN, as some contemporaries proclaimed, because the Soviet Union had not participated in the decision to intervene. Federalists like herself, Wynner pointed out, had predicted that as soon as the five-power structure of the Security Council broke down, war was inevitable.[55]

As it had for Schwimmer and Lloyd, world citizenship for Edith Wynner meant popular action for world government, specifically the convening of a world constitutional convention to design a genuine world federation. She envisioned a global system based on the principles of democracy, equality, and inclusiveness that would safeguard not only nuclear security but also the human rights of all women and men. Like her predecessors, however, Wynner could neither rouse sufficient support nor raise sufficient funds for her proposed endeavor.

In 1954 Wynner published *World Federal Government: Why? What? How? In Maximum Terms*. In it she reiterated her arguments for a world federation and also argued that a world constitutional convention was still the best way to achieve it. She offered an imaginative and rather florid vision of the future, in which historians would look back on the mid-twentieth century as the era that inaugurated lasting peace:

If we are luckier than we are wise, perhaps the chronicler of the distant future will be able to say of this period: "A peculiar characteristic of the first half of the twentieth century was the tendency of the peoples to honor mass-murderers and to assassinate spiritually or physically their greatest peace-makers. But in the later part of this era, due to conditions not yet clear to us, a complete change of social values took place. World Government was finally negotiated, the military caste was abolished, repression and violence were made crimes against society and the present era of human happiness began. No record of the person or persons who worked this miracle remains. Perhaps even in those barbaric times people realized that the achievement was too great for conventional honors. Some of our scholars even lean to the theory that no human agency was responsible. They give credit for this fundamental revolution in human behavior to an invasion of benevolent bacteria which paralyzed man's aggressive instinct."[56]

Wynner was the only woman spotlighted in this book who lived into the twenty-first century. By the time she died in 2003, she would have known this history was far from being written. But it shows her sense of what was at stake and how revolutionary she believed world government could be, especially in the midst of the nuclear threats and Cold War paranoia of the 1950s. As a citizen of the world, Wynner felt in the years following World War II a strong obligation to work for world government and to demand for ordinary women and men the right to secure it for themselves. Despite the opposition she faced both inside and outside the movement, she persevered in these years, driven by her "inner conviction that this cause is right for mankind's highest welfare."[57]

Conclusion

The closest the U.S. government ever got to seriously considering the idea of world government was a pair of subcommittee hearings in the House and Senate in late 1949 and early 1950. They centered on a resolution introduced in both chambers: "Resolved ... That it is the sense of the Congress that it should be a fundamental objective of the foreign policy of the United States to support and strengthen the United Nations and to seek its development into a world federation open to all nations with defined and limited powers adequate to preserve peace and prevent aggression through the enactment, interpretation, and enforcement of world law."[1] More than one hundred witnesses testified at the two hearings, including most of the male leaders of such organizations as the United World Federalists. Proponents of world government, however, were countered by an equal number of opponents, including representatives of the U.S. State Department and other members of Congress.

Only a handful of women spoke at the hearings, some for and others against the resolution. Dorothea Buck, president of the General Federation of Women's Clubs, testified that her organization endorsed it and called upon the U.S. government "to initiate the procedure necessary to transform the United Nations ... into a world lawmaking body with power to prevent war and to enforce justice upon individuals."[2] Jane Hayford, national director of the World Organization of Mothers for All Nations, a short-lived group founded by journalist Dorothy Thompson, also spoke in favor. "We, the mothers," she declared, "demand the kind of United Nations in which peace cannot be vetoed by international gangsters, where specific and concrete measures for the elimination of the atomic and armament race are enforced by an international police force, under the authority of a world court."[3] The League of Women Voters, meanwhile, did not go so far as to endorse the resolution, but it did support a "limited program of action" to strengthen the power of the UN, for instance, by bolstering its power to collect revenues.[4]

As they had throughout the late 1940s, the Daughters of the American Revolution led women's opposition to world government. Their representative,

Madalen Dingley Leetch, was the only woman to testify before the House sub-committee; she also spoke in the Senate. "In the name of peace," she warned, "skillful intellectuals are selling internationalism in the place of Americanism. Unmasked, it is communism, merciless, militant, and un-Christian. . . . 'One world' is not possible with Communist Russia, except on her terms. When America is submerged in world socialism, bankrupt and disarmed, the world's richest prize will lie prostrate before the advancing hordes of atheistic communism."[5] With this statement Leetch captured the decline—by that point nearly complete—of world citizenship as a concept centered on international cooperation and work for long-term peace. A different image of world citizenship, one that signified Soviet domination and American subjugation, had taken its place. In Leetch's view, the need for national security trumped any need or desire for cooperation.

Neither Edith Wynner nor any of the other women profiled in this book spoke at the hearings—Mead, Andrews, Tuttle, Lloyd, and Schwimmer had all died or were near death by the time the hearings convened—but it is worth taking a moment to consider how each might have responded to such a resolution. The idea of developing an existing world body into a stronger one centered on world law would have appealed strongly to Mead, given that it echoed many of the points she had laid out in her practical program in 1904, and given that after World War I she continued writing and speaking on behalf of the causes she had championed all her life: international organization (she favored U.S. membership in the League of Nations and the World Court), disarmament, and the peaceful settlement of disputes. She died in 1936 at the age of eighty, a week after sustaining a head injury when she was caught in a crowd while boarding a subway car in Boston.[6] Less than two months before her death she made a plea for greater international understanding in the pages of the *New York Times*. "The world is trembling and chaotic because of lack of plan, lack of psychology and lack of consecrated effort," she wrote, as the Spanish Civil War raged and Hitler expanded the German military. "But it is not yet too late to turn the tide toward rationality."[7]

Though a more conservative internationalist than some of her contemporaries, as a proponent of world government and of the UN, Andrews likewise would have supported the resolutions. She was less involved in promoting the League of Nations than either Mead or Tuttle, but her interest in internationalism continued even after the American School Citizenship League dissolved. In 1923 Andrews earned a PhD in international relations from

Harvard and went on to study the League of Nations mandate system in the Middle East. She died in January 1950 of arteriosclerosis at the age of eighty-two, after having lived long enough to see her work for education manifested in UNESCO. She described in her autobiography her reaction to hearing President Truman announce in 1946 that the United States would join that body: "I am sure my readers can well understand that I could not but feel some sense of personal triumph."[8]

Tuttle undoubtedly would have supported the resolution, given her arguments throughout the 1920s and early 1930s that the world needed stronger mechanisms for international cooperation and the regulation of armaments. In her last years she wrote an autobiography, never published, in which she reflected on her many years of work for the League of Nations. Looking back from the perspective of the post–World War II atomic era, she noted that the world situation had only become more dire, the choices more stark: "It is one world or chaos," she wrote, evoking Wendell Willkie's phrase, "civilization or annihilation. The atomic bomb is the real killer." But she also remained hopeful. She believed the truth of "one world" would prevail, and she took comfort in the idea that her grandchildren would find a way to do good in the world, as she felt she had. "In my last years," she wrote, "I am still upholding the torch."[9] She died in 1951 at age eighty-three.

It is more difficult to guess what Lloyd might have thought. She recognized the weaknesses of the UN, but like her youngest daughter, Georgia, she might have been optimistic after the war about the chances for reforming it into a world federation. Schwimmer, who was opposed to the UN from the start, would not have endorsed the resolution, but she would have approved the idea of the world federation being "open to all nations." Lloyd died at the age of sixty-eight in July 1944 after a short battle with pancreatic cancer. After her death, relations between Schwimmer and the Lloyd children grew increasingly fraught, due in large part to the former's difficult personality. Despite insisting she had retired from the Campaign for World Government in order to write her memoir, Schwimmer continued to voice her displeasure with William Lloyd Jr. and Georgia's work for world government. Her own health steadily worsened, however, greatly taxing Wynner, who now lived with Schwimmer and her sister Franciska and worked as their secretary and informal nurse. Schwimmer died in August 1948 at the age of seventy, after being severely ill for several months with bronchial pneumonia and complications from diabetes. Emily Greene Balch, a longtime WILPF leader and the recipient of the 1946 Nobel Peace Prize, eulogized her in the *New York Times*:

"Her will was like a powerfully running current which never paused or slackened night or day. Such a will is a great power and, joined with her keen and original intelligence, her energy and her gift of unstinted devotion, it made Rosika Schwimmer the powerful person that she was."[10]

Brunauer, Bethune, Kenyon, and Wynner were all still alive at the time of the House and Senate hearings, though only Wynner left a record of her reactions to them. Given her belief in collective security, Brunauer likely would have supported the language in the resolution about enforcing world law. At the same time, given her personal familiarity with anticommunism, she likely would not have endorsed open membership, fearing such a stance would be interpreted as Soviet sympathy. Brunauer supported the work of the UN through the late 1940s from her position within the U.S. State Department. In 1947 she represented the United States on the Preparatory Commission of UNESCO at the rank of minister—one of only three women to hold that title at that time. But she was fired from the State Department in 1952 in the wake of Joseph McCarthy's accusation that she associated with communists, despite the fact that a Senate subcommittee dismissed the accusation as "a fraud and a hoax." That year she and her husband left Washington and moved to Evanston, Illinois, where she worked as a textbook editor for Rand-McNally until her death in 1959 at the age of fifty-seven.[11]

One can only imagine Bethune would have supported any measure promising to strengthen the UN, even though she knew well its weaknesses. In her weekly column for the *Chicago Defender* she praised the UN in October 1949, calling on her readers to "'affirm our faith' in the ability of this council of nations of the world as 'a living force for solving the major problems' of its people." That same year she resigned as president of the National Council of Negro Women and retired to her home in Daytona Beach. She remained active for the rest of her life, traveling to the Bahamas, Haiti, Canada, and Switzerland as a member of the international movement for "moral re-armament," promoting human unity and human rights. In 1952 she journeyed to Liberia as a U.S. representative to the second inauguration of President William Tubman. She continued writing for the *Chicago Defender* until her death. "The privilege of having this column to chat with my thousands of friends across the nations is a marvelous one," she wrote in 1953. "It helps me to be the world citizen that I am in my mind and thought." She died in May 1955 and was buried on the campus of Bethune-Cookman College. The *Defender* eulogized her as "one of the most eloquent advocates of first-class citizenship and one of the wisest interpreters of American democracy."[12]

Like Bethune, Kenyon was well aware of the limits of the UN's authority by 1949, and like Brunauer, she may have been wary of endorsing universal membership in a world federation. One could imagine her dismissing the congressional resolution as weak and irrelevant. After being replaced on the Commission on the Status of Women, Kenyon turned her attention to progressive causes within the United States. Thanks to McCarthy, she never again held a public post, but she continued to serve on the board of the American Civil Liberties Union and contribute her legal expertise to briefs both for the ACLU and the NAACP Legal Defense Fund. She also continued her activism on behalf of workers and women, and she opposed U.S. involvement in the Vietnam War. Though she was a longtime advocate for protective labor legislation, she eventually came to support the Equal Rights Amendment as a necessary measure to advance women's equality. Kenyon died of cancer at the age of eighty-three in 1972, just three years before the first United Nations Conference on Women in Mexico City. She did witness myriad achievements of the CSW in the intervening years, including the adoption by the General Assembly of the Declaration on the Elimination of Discrimination Against Women in 1967.[13]

Wynner is the only one who left a record of her reaction to the hearings. She acknowledged the weakness of the House and Senate resolution, but she was pleased by the attention they garnered. "World government is increasingly in the public eye here in the USA," she wrote to Henry Usborne in late October 1949. "Hardly any of the State Department and U.S. UN delegates open their mouths without making some reference to it and there have been House Hearings on the various . . . resolutions. It shows that even with the inefficient and weak activity that has been put forth, events are increasing interest in it."[14] But she knew the resolution was limited. It did not call for strengthening the UN into a world federation; it merely proposed that such an end become a "fundamental objective" of U.S. foreign policy.

Even that weak language proved too strong for Congress's taste. The concurrent resolution never progressed beyond the House and Senate subcommittees. In the end, members were swayed by the testimony of Dean Rusk, who appeared as a representative of the U.S. State Department and later became a key Cold Warrior. The problem of the postwar world, Rusk argued, was not the weakness of the UN but the aggressive nature of "Soviet conduct." The answer to that problem, likewise, was not a stronger UN but the combined force of the North Atlantic Treaty Organization.[15] In the final report of the Senate subcommittee, chairman Elbert Thomas reiterated Rusk's bipolar view. "The fundamental issue of the day," Thomas declared, "is the East-West conflict, not the question of the nature and extent of international organization." In Thomas's view, not even the UN—much less a world government—could solve the problems of the Cold War. He refused to vote the resolution out of his subcommittee.[16]

Wynner, dispirited and disillusioned after being sidelined in 1948, continued to advocate for world government in the early 1950s, though she gradually became less active in the movement. By the end of the decade she had retreated to the confines of the New York Public Library, where she installed herself as a volunteer archivist. With the financial support of the Lloyd family and the tacit approval of the library staff, she took charge of organizing the library's massive Schwimmer-Lloyd collection and adding to its catalogue every world government tract she could get her hands on. Her mission was to write the definitive biography of Schwimmer. For the next forty years until her death in 2003, she pored over old letters, made notes, and corresponded with Schwimmer's and her own former colleagues. She also jealously guarded her territory, often making it difficult for visiting researchers and graduate students to access the Schwimmer-Lloyd collection. But she never finished the book.[17]

The years between 1945 and 1950 proved to be the heyday of the world government movement. After 1950 the idea did not gain traction again until the fall of the Soviet Union, when a unified world once more seemed possible to some. But when it did reemerge, the concept was fundamentally different in many ways. Most notably, global governance had replaced world government. Non-state entities now conduct and coordinate international work for conflict resolution, humanitarian relief, and environmental protection as much as do the UN, the World Bank, and other intergovernmental agencies. Many of these entities have extensive reach and resources, but all of them lack strong mechanisms to enforce compliance. In the minds of the women profiled here, that was precisely the problem world government would have solved. Though they did not agree on the form such a government should take, they all agreed the world needed some sort of central body capable of creating and enforcing world law. They may have endorsed twenty-first-century forms of global governance, but they would not have considered them sufficient to secure peace.

The concept of world citizenship has also changed—though less, I would argue, than world government. Like the women in this book, today's global citizens demand to participate in shaping the global polity. Many of them feel an urgent sense of responsibility, not only to secure peace but also to slow climate change and to improve the quality of life for people everywhere. And many believe in the equal worth of all human beings, even to a greater extent than the women I have profiled here. Three developments are worth noting. First, the ways in which people can express demands and participate in the global polity have expanded, thanks to advances in technology that make travel and especially communication easier and accessible to a wider range of people. Second, discourses of global citizenship now center much more on human rights, including women's rights, than they did before World War II. And third, world citizenship and world government no longer go hand in hand. Global citizenship today is often disconnected from any kind of government, whether national or international, real or imagined.

Would the women in this book have celebrated these changes? In many ways, I think so. They would have bemoaned the absence of world government, of course. But Schwimmer and Lloyd were already promoting human rights and urging popular, nongovernmental action in the 1930s. They also believed their plan would find popular support once it was more widely publicized; they would have loved the internet. Bethune would have lauded human rights efforts and economic programs in underdeveloped regions, especially Africa. I am less certain that someone like Andrews would have welcomed the democratization of global citizenship. It is possible she would have subscribed to what writer Teju Cole has called the "white-savior industrial complex"—the modern-day version of the Anglo-Saxon civilizing mission.[18] But again, the primary thing all these women had in common was that they saw the world as an integrated whole and saw themselves as equal members of the world community. That perspective would resonate, I imagine, with most of today's global citizens.

Despite its increased visibility in scholarship and popular culture in the last thirty years, global citizenship did not begin in the 1990s. The concept is thousands of years old; these women were among many who promoted it in the early to mid-twentieth century, at a time when the concomitant call for some form of international government was frequently heard from many Americans. But for these women, the notion of citizenship was more fraught than it was for their male counterparts, given that they were not full citizens of their own country. They had to assert their world citizenship in ways men did not. They demanded to participate in shaping the global polity because they knew such opportunities would not be automatically granted to them. They proclaimed their obligations to the world community, sometimes in gendered ways. And they believed in the egalitarian nature of citizenship, even though many of them did not apply it fully to people of color.

Long before better-known advocates like Clarence Streit, Wendell Willkie, and Albert Einstein drew attention to world government in the late 1930s and 1940s, the women in this book and others like them sought a politically unified world and promoted systems to govern it. Mead referred to the world as one "organism" in 1904; Andrews asserted the importance of "world community" in 1911. Schwimmer and Lloyd rarely got the credit they deserved for their plan for a popular world government, and when they did, it was only because Wynner was there to remind people that it was their idea. Even in the 1940s, as women's groups banded together to demand seats at the postwar planning tables, Brunauer, Bethune, and Kenyon were marginalized in discussions on the form and function of the UN, even though they were all experts in their respective fields.

Tuttle captured this state of affairs near the end of her life. Looking back on the 1920s and 1930s from the perspective of the post–World War II atomic era, she noted that she and others dedicated many years to the idea of "one world" that many Americans seemed to have discovered only recently. "For twenty years," she wrote, "our American organization, the League of Nations Association, worked to establish One World before magnetic Wendell Willkie thought he coined the phrase. I myself wrote, spoke, and . . . [tried] to inform public opinion that we live in 'one world.' It was like trying to push a snowball uphill. Two wars and countless losses of human lives were necessary before one world would become even partially accepted."[19] Tuttle did not say it, but it is also clear that the notion did not command widespread public attention until it was promoted by men. It is time she and other women world citizens get their due.

NOTES

Introduction

1. Lucia Ames Mead, "Organize the World," *Club Worker* 5, no. 5 (March 1904): 95; Florence Guertin Tuttle, *Alternatives to War* (New York: Harper & Brothers, 1931), 22; and Mary McLeod Bethune, "Our Stake in Tomorrow's World," *Aframerican Woman's Journal* (June 1945): 2.

2. Derek Heater, *World Citizenship and Government: Cosmopolitan Ideas in the History of Western Political Thought* (New York: St. Martin's, 1996), x.

3. In addition to Heater, *World Citizenship and Government*, see Darren J. O'Byrne, *The Dimensions of Global Citizenship: Political Identity Beyond the Nation-State* (London: Frank Cass, 2003), 51–74; and April Carter, *The Political Theory of Global Citizenship* (London: Routledge, 2001), 11–71.

4. See, for example, Richard Falk, "The Making of Global Citizenship," in *The Condition of Citizenship*, ed. Bart Van Steenbergen (London: Sage, 1994), 127–40; Nigel Dower, "The Idea of Global Citizenship," *Global Society* 14, no. 4 (2000): 553–67; Nigel Dower and John Williams, eds., *Global Citizenship: A Critical Introduction* (New York: Routledge, 2002); Hans Schattle, *The Practices of Global Citizenship* (Lanham, MD: Rowman & Littlefield, 2008); Luis Cabrera, *The Practice of Global Citizenship* (New York: Cambridge University Press, 2010); and Engin F. Isin, *Citizens Without Frontiers* (London: Bloomsbury Academic, 2012).

5. Cabrera, *Practice of Global Citizenship*, 3–4; Falk, "Making of Global Citizenship," 132; and Isin, *Citizens Without Frontiers*.

6. Schattle, *Practices of Global Citizenship*.

7. Kimberly Hutchings, "Feminism and Global Citizenship," in Dower and Williams, *Global Citizenship*, 53–63. See also Hutchings, "Feminist Politics and Cosmopolitan Citizenship," in *Cosmopolitan Citizenship*, ed. Kimberly Hutchings and Roland Dannreuther (New York: St. Martin's, 1999), 120–42.

8. Some of the key works that have influenced my thinking on citizenship include Linda K. Kerber, "The Meanings of Citizenship," *Journal of American History* 84, no. 3 (December 1997): 833–54; Andrew Linklater, "Cosmopolitan Citizenship," *Citizenship Studies* 2, no. 1 (February 1998): 23–41; Linda Bosniak, "Citizenship Denationalized," *Indiana Journal of Global Legal Studies* 7, no. 2 (2000): 447–509; and David Thelen, "How Natural Are National and Transnational Citizenship? A Historical Perspective," *Indiana Journal of Global Legal Studies* 7, no. 2 (April 2000): 549–65.

9. Bosniak, "Citizenship Denationalized," 489.

10. Linklater, "Cosmopolitan Citizenship," 34, 25.

11. The phrase comes from Ursula Vogel, "Is Citizenship Gender-Specific?" in *The Frontiers of Citizenship*, ed. Ursula Vogel and Michael Moran (New York: St. Martin's, 1991), 58.

12. Mary G. Dietz, "Context Is All: Feminism and Theories of Citizenship," *Daedalus* 116, no. 4 (1987): 2, 5. See also Ruth Lister, *Citizenship: Feminist Perspectives* (New York: New York University Press, 2003); and Marilyn Friedman, ed., *Women and Citizenship* (New York: Oxford University Press, 2005).

13. Kathleen Canning and Sonya O. Rose, "Gender, Citizenship and Subjectivity: Some Historical and Theoretical Considerations," *Gender & History* 13, no. 3 (November 2001): 431–32.

14. See especially Jane Addams, *Democracy and Social Ethics* (New York: Macmillan, 1902); Louise W. Knight, *Citizen: Jane Addams and the Struggle for Democracy* (Chicago: University of Chicago Press, 2005); and Marilyn Fischer, Carol Nackenoff, and Wendy E. Chmielewski, eds., *Jane Addams and the Practice of Democracy* (Urbana: University of Illinois Press, 2009).

15. Candice Lewis Bredbenner, *A Nationality of Her Own: Women, Marriage, and the Law of Citizenship* (Berkeley: University of California Press, 1998), 47. On the gendered nature of U.S. citizenship, see also Linda K. Kerber, *No Constitutional Right to Be Ladies: Women and the Obligations of Citizenship* (New York: Hill and Wang, 1998); Alice Kessler-Harris, *In Pursuit of Equity: Women, Men, and the Quest for Economic Citizenship in 20th Century America* (New York: Oxford University Press, 2001); Martha Gardner, *The Qualities of a Citizen: Women, Immigration, and Citizenship, 1870–1965* (Princeton: Princeton University Press, 2005); Evelyn Nakano Glenn, *Unequal Freedom: How Race and Gender Shaped American Citizenship and Labor* (Cambridge, MA: Harvard University Press, 2002); Nancy F. Cott, *Public Vows: A History of Marriage and the Nation* (Cambridge, MA: Harvard University Press, 2000); and Barbara Young Welke, *Law and the Borders of Belonging in the Long Nineteenth Century United States* (New York: Cambridge University Press, 2010).

16. Kunal M. Parker, *Making Foreigners: Immigration and Citizenship Law in America, 1600–2000* (New York: Cambridge University Press, 2015), 130–31. See also Welke, *Law and the Borders of Belonging*; Glenn, *Unequal Freedom*; Lauren L. Basson, *White Enough to Be American? Race Mixing, Indigenous People, and the Boundaries of State and Nation* (Chapel Hill: University of North Carolina Press, 2008); Doug Coulson, *Race, Nation, and Refuge: The Rhetoric of Race in Asian American Citizenship Cases* (Albany: State University of New York Press, 2017); Hoang Gia Phan, *Bonds of Citizenship: Law and the Labors of Emancipation* (New York: New York University Press, 2013); and Mark Stuart Weiner, *Americans Without Law: The Racial Boundaries of Citizenship* (New York: New York University Press, 2006).

17. Sam Erman, *Almost Citizens: Puerto Rico, the U.S. Constitution, and Empire* (Cambridge: Cambridge University Press, 2019), 3. See also Paul A. Kramer, *The Blood of Government: Race, Empire, the United States, and the Philippines* (Chapel Hill: University of North Carolina Press, 2006).

18. Proceedings of the fourth annual meeting of the American Equal Rights Association, New York City, May 1869, in *History of Woman Suffrage*, ed. Elizabeth Cady Stanton et al., vol. 2 (New York: Fowler and Wells, 1882), 391; "Declaration of Principles," in *Proceedings of the Thirty-Sixth Annual Convention of the National American Woman Suffrage Association* (NAWSA, 1904), 20. On racialized attitudes of suffragists, Progressives, and other white reformers, see especially Louise Michele Newman, *White Women's Rights: The Racial Origins of Feminism in the United States* (New York: Oxford University Press, 1999); Marilyn Lake, *Progressive New World: How Settler Colonialism and Transpacific Exchange Shaped American Reform* (Cambridge, MA: Harvard University Press, 2019); Alan Dawley, *Changing the World: American Progressives in War and Revolution* (Princeton: Princeton University Press, 2003); and Gail Bederman, *Manliness*

and Civilization: A Cultural History of Gender and Race in the United States, 1880–1917 (Chicago: University of Chicago Press, 1995).

19. Edith Wynner and Georgia Lloyd, *Searchlight on Peace Plans: Choose Your Road to World Government* (New York: E. P. Dutton, 1944), 4–6.

20. Thomas G. Weiss, "What Happened to the Idea of World Government?" *International Studies Quarterly* 53, no. 2 (2009): 257, 262. See also Thomas G. Weiss, *Global Governance: Why? What? Whither?* (Malden, MA: Polity, 2013).

21. Dante Alighieri, *De Monarchia*, Book 1, Chapter 4, in *Monarchy and Three Political Letters*, trans. Donald Nicholl (New York: Noonday, 1954), 9; and Immanuel Kant, *Toward Perpetual Peace and Other Writings on Politics, Peace, and History*, ed. Pauline Kleingeld (New Haven: Yale University Press, 2006). For more on the history of world government, see Wynner and Lloyd, *Searchlight on Peace Plans*; Heater, *World Citizenship and Government*; Mark Mazower, *Governing the World: The History of an Idea* (New York: Penguin, 2012); Strobe Talbott, *The Great Experiment: The Story of Ancient Empires, Modern States, and the Quest for a Global Nation* (New York: Simon & Schuster, 2008); James A. Yunker, *The Idea of World Government: From Ancient Times to the Twenty-First Century* (Abingdon, UK: Routledge, 2011); and Mary Ann Glendon, *The Forum and the Tower: How Scholars and Politicians Have Imagined the World, from Plato to Eleanor Roosevelt* (New York: Oxford University Press, 2011).

22. Warren F. Kuehl, *Seeking World Order: The United States and International Organization to 1920* (Nashville: Vanderbilt University Press, 1969), 125–35. See also Kuehl, "The World-Federation League: A Neglected Chapter in the History of a Movement," *World Affairs Quarterly* 31, no. 4 (January 1960): 349–64; David S. Patterson, *Toward a Warless World: The Travail of the American Peace Movement, 1887–1914* (Bloomington: Indiana University Press, 1976); Francis Anthony Boyle, *Foundations of World Order: The Legalist Approach to International Relations (1898–1922)* (Durham, NC: Duke University Press, 1999); Arthur N. Holcombe, "Edwin Ginn's Commitment to World Government," *International Organization* 20, no. 3 (Summer 1966): 419–29; and Daniel Hucker, "'Our Expectations Were Perhaps Too High': Disarmament, Citizen Activism, and the 1907 Hague Peace Conference," *Peace & Change* 44, no. 1 (January 2019): 5–32.

23. Warren F. Kuehl and Lynne Dunn, *Keeping the Covenant: American Internationalists and the League of Nations, 1920–1939* (Kent, OH: Kent State University Press, 1997); Charles DeBenedetti, *Origins of the Modern American Peace Movement, 1915–1929* (Millwood, NY: KTO, 1978); Harriet Hyman Alonso, *The Women's Peace Union and the Outlawry of War, 1921–1942* (Knoxville: University of Tennessee Press, 1989); Charles Chatfield, *For Peace and Justice: Pacifism in America, 1914–1941* (Knoxville: University of Tennessee Press, 1971); Thomas Richard Davies, *The Possibilities of Transnational Activism: The Campaign for Disarmament Between the Two World Wars* (Leiden: Martinus Nijhoff, 2007); Michael Dunne, *The United States and the World Court, 1920–1935* (New York: St. Martin's, 1988); Daniel Gorman, *The Emergence of International Society in the 1920s* (Cambridge: Cambridge University Press, 2012); Andrew Johnstone, *Against Immediate Evil: American Internationalists and the Four Freedoms on the Eve of World War II* (Ithaca, NY: Cornell University Press, 2014); Samuel Zipp, *The Idealist: Wendell Willkie's Wartime Quest to Build One World* (Cambridge, MA: Harvard University Press, 2020); Or Rosenboim, *The Emergence of Globalism: Visions of World Order in Britain and the United States, 1939–1950* (Princeton: Princeton University Press, 2017); Dorothy B. Robins, *Experiment in Democracy: The Story of U.S. Citizen Organizations in Forging the Charter of the United Nations* (New York: Parkside, 1971); and Andrew Johnstone, *Dilemmas of Internationalism: The*

American Association for the United Nations and US Foreign Policy, 1941–1948 (Farnham, UK: Ashgate, 2009).

24. Johnstone, *Dilemmas of Internationalism*; Robert D. Accinelli, "Pro-U.N. Internationalists and the Early Cold War: The American Association for the United Nations and U.S. Foreign Policy, 1947–52," *Diplomatic History* 9, no. 4 (1985): 347–62; Joseph Preston Baratta, *The Politics of World Federation: From World Federation to Global Governance* (Westport, CT: Praeger, 2004); Fritz Bartel, "Surviving the Years of Grace: The Atomic Bomb and the Specter of World Government, 1945–1950," *Diplomatic History* 39, no. 2 (April 2015): 275–302; and Wesley T. Wooley, "Finding a Usable Past: The Success of American World Federalism in the 1940s," *Peace & Change* 24, no. 3 (July 1999): 329–39.

25. Examples include Johnstone, *Dilemmas of Internationalism*; Johnstone, *Against Immediate Evil*; Bartel, "Surviving the Years of Grace"; and Zipp, *Idealist*.

26. See, for instance, Mazower, *Governing the World*; Rosenboim, *Emergence of Globalism*; Oona Anne Hathaway and Scott Shapiro, *The Internationalists: How a Radical Plan to Outlaw War Remade the World* (New York: Simon & Schuster, 2017); and Adam Tooze, *The Deluge: The Great War, America and the Remaking of the Global Order, 1916–1931* (New York: Penguin, 2014). For a similar critique, see Glenda Sluga, "'Add Women and Stir': Gender and the History of International Politics," *Humanities Australia* 5 (2014): 65–72.

27. Harriet Hyman Alonso, *Peace as a Women's Issue: A History of the U.S. Movement for World Peace and Women's Rights* (Syracuse, NY: Syracuse University Press, 1993); Bonnie S. Anderson, *Joyous Greetings: The First International Women's Movement, 1830–1860* (Oxford: Oxford University Press, 2000); Ian Tyrrell, *Woman's World/Woman's Empire: The Woman's Christian Temperance Union in International Perspective, 1880–1930* (Chapel Hill: University of North Carolina Press, 1991); Leila J. Rupp, *Worlds of Women: The Making of an International Women's Movement* (Princeton: Princeton University Press, 1997); Megan Threlkeld, *Pan American Women: U.S. Internationalists and Revolutionary Mexico* (Philadelphia: University of Pennsylvania Press, 2014); Karen Garner, *Shaping a Global Women's Agenda: Women's NGOs and Global Governance, 1925–85* (Manchester: Manchester University Press, 2010); and Helen Laville, *Cold War Women: The International Activities of American Women's Organisations* (Manchester: Manchester University Press, 2002). For more on this historiography, see Megan Threlkeld, "Twenty Years of *Worlds of Women*: Leila Rupp's Impact on the History of U.S. Women's Internationalism," *History Compass* 15, no. 6 (June 2017): https://doi.org/10.1111/hic3.12381.

28. Patricia Owens and Katharina Rietzler, eds., *Women's International Thought: A New History* (Cambridge: Cambridge University Press, 2021); and Robert Vitalis, *White World Order, Black Power Politics: The Birth of American International Relations* (Ithaca, NY: Cornell University Press, 2015). On the emergence of U.S. military supremacy, see Stephen Wertheim, *Tomorrow, the World: The Birth of U.S. Global Supremacy* (Cambridge, MA: Harvard University Press, 2020).

29. Glenda Sluga and Patricia Clavin, "Rethinking the History of Internationalism," in *Internationalisms: A Twentieth-Century History*, ed. Sluga and Clavin (Cambridge: Cambridge University Press, 2017), 7–8.

30. Schwimmer was not born in the United States and was barred from becoming a citizen, but historians have granted her a kind of honorary citizenship by including her in *Notable American Women* and *American National Biography*. Beth S. Wenger, "Radical Politics in a Reactionary Age: The Unmaking of Rosika Schwimmer, 1914–1930," *Journal of Women's History* 2, no. 2 (1990): 91.

31. Joyce Ann Hanson, *Mary McLeod Bethune and Black Women's Political Activism* (Columbia: University of Missouri Press, 2003), 95–96. The best work on these varied conceptions of feminism is still Nancy Cott, *The Grounding of Modern Feminism* (New Haven: Yale University Press, 1987).

32. Lake, *Progressive New World*, 14. See also Dawley, *Changing the World*, 261–62.

33. Hanson, *Mary McLeod Bethune*, 168.

34. Fannie Fern Andrews to William Andrew, 13 December 1919, Box 10, Folder 93, Fannie Fern Andrews Papers, Schlesinger Library, Radcliffe Institute, Cambridge, MA.

Chapter 1

1. Warren F. Kuehl, *Seeking World Order: The United States and International Organization to 1920* (Nashville: Vanderbilt University Press, 1969); Cecilie Reid, "Peace and Law: Peace Activism and International Arbitration, 1895–1907," *Peace & Change* 29, no. 3-4 (2004): 527–48; Daniel Gorman, *International Cooperation in the Early Twentieth Century* (London: Bloomsbury Academic, 2017), 78–79; and C. F. Howlett, "Women Pacifists of America: Women's Views at the Lake Mohonk Conferences for International Arbitration, 1895–1916," *Peace Research* 21, no. 1 (1989): 27–74.

2. Lucia Ames Mead, "The International Peace Conference," *Advance*, September 29, 1904.

3. John M. Craig, *Lucia Ames Mead (1856–1936) and the American Peace Movement* (Lewiston, NY: Edwin Mellen, 1990); and Warren F. Kuehl, "Mead, Lucia True Ames," in *Notable American Women, 1607–1950*, ed. Edward T. James and Janet Wilson James, vol. 2 (Cambridge, MA: Harvard University Press, 1971), 522–24. She changed her name to "Lucia True" sometime before 1870. Craig, *Lucia Ames Mead*, 4. Lucia Ames, *Memoirs of a Millionaire* (Boston: Houghton, 1889).

4. Craig, *Lucia Ames Mead*, 23–35.

5. Mead, *To Whom Much Is Given* (New York: T. Y. Crowell, 1899), 9, 27.

6. Mead, "The Woman Who Reads," *Journal of Education* 53, no. 13 (March 1901): 199.

7. Mead, "The Evils and Obstacles to Be Overcome," in *Report of the Eighth Annual Meeting of the Lake Mohonk Conference on International Arbitration* (1902), 64.

8. Mead, *To Whom Much Is Given*, 30. Emphasis in original.

9. Mead, "Evils and Obstacles," 64.

10. Frances Willard, *Annual Address: A Retrospect and a Forecast* (Chicago: Woman's Temperance Publishing Association, 1894), 117. See also Ian R. Tyrrell, *Woman's World/Woman's Empire: The Woman's Christian Temperance Union in International Perspective, 1880–1930* (Chapel Hill: University of North Carolina Press, 1991), 174.

11. "Public Meeting on International Arbitration," in *The International Congress of Women of 1899* (London: T. F. Unwin, 1900), 237.

12. Mead, "Peace and Arbitration," in *The Woman Citizen's Library: A Systematic Course of Reading in Preparation for the Larger Citizenship*, ed. Shailer Mathews, vol. 11 (Chicago: Civics Society, 1914), 2734; Mead, *What Women Might Do with the Ballot: The Abolition of the War System* (New York: National American Woman Suffrage Association, 1909), 4; and Mead, *Swords and Ploughshares: Or, the Supplanting of the System of War by the System of Law* (New York: G. P. Putnam's Sons, 1912), 43.

13. "Arbitration Conference," *Woman's Tribune*, May 2, 1896.

14. May Wright Sewall, "The Universal Demonstration of Women in Behalf of Arbitration and Peace," in *Report of the Ninth Annual Meeting of the Lake Mohonk Conference on International Arbitration* (1903), 79.

15. Mead, *Patriotism and the New Internationalism* (Boston: Ginn, 1906), 5–6.

16. Mead, address, in *Report of the Third Annual Meeting of the Lake Mohonk Conference on International Arbitration* (1897), 95.

17. Benjamin Franklin Trueblood, *The Federation of the World* (Boston: Houghton, Mifflin, 1899), 7, 124.

18. Raymond L. Bridgman, *World Organization* (Boston: Ginn, 1905), 43.

19. Mead, "What Are We to Do?" *Advocate of Peace* 65, no. 8 (1903): 142–44.

20. Mead, "The Practical Program for World Organization," in Mead, *A Primer of the Peace Movement* (Boston: American Peace Society, 1904).

21. Mead, *Swords and Ploughshares*, 6–7; and Immanuel Kant, *Toward Perpetual Peace and Other Writings on Politics, Peace, and History*, ed. Pauline Kleingeld (New Haven: Yale University Press, 2006), 74–78.

22. Mead, "The Next Step: A World Congress," *Union Signal*, August 11, 1904, 5.

23. Mead, "What Are We to Do?" 143.

24. David S. Patterson, *Toward a Warless World: The Travail of the American Peace Movement, 1887–1914* (Bloomington: Indiana University Press, 1976), 108–9; and Benjamin Allen Coates, *Legalist Empire: International Law and American Foreign Relations in the Early Twentieth Century* (New York: Oxford University Press, 2016), 77.

25. Mead, "Woman's Work for Peace," *Woman's Journal* 35, no. 12 (March 19, 1904): 93; and Mead, *What Women Might Do with the Ballot*, 11.

26. Mead, "A Stated International Congress," in *Primer of the Peace Movement*; Mead, "What Are We to Do?" 143; and Mead, "Organize the World," *Club Worker* 5, no. 5 (March 1904): 97.

27. Mead, "Organize the World," 96; and Mead, remarks, *Official Report of the Thirteenth Universal Peace Congress* (Boston: Peace Congress Committee, 1904), 122.

28. Mead, "Organize the World," 97; and Mead, "What Are We to Do?" 142.

29. "Convention Between Chile and the Argentine Republic Respecting the Limitation of Naval Armaments, Signed May 28, 1902," *American Journal of International Law* 1 Supp. (1907): 294–95.

30. Mead, "International Police," *Outlook* 74 (July 18, 1903): 705–6.

31. "Seventy-Seventh Annual Report of the Directors of the American Peace Society," *Advocate of Peace* 67 (1905): 121; "Concerning Women," *Woman's Journal* 35, no. 47 (November 19, 1904): 369; *Official Report of the Thirteenth Universal Peace Congress* (Boston: Peace Congress Committee, 1904), 214; and Robert Erskine Ely to Woodrow Wilson, March 25, 1907, in *The Papers of Woodrow Wilson*, vol. 17, ed. Arthur Link et al. (Princeton: Princeton University Press, 1974), 92–93. See also Craig, *Lucia Ames Mead*, 86.

32. Kuehl, *Seeking World Order*, 53–74.

33. "A Constitution of the World," *Independent* 62 (April 11, 1907): 826; Hayne Davis, "The Final Outcome of the Declaration of Independence," *Independent* 55 (July 2, 1903): 1545; and Bridgman, *World Organization*, 63–70.

34. Andrew Carnegie, "Introduction," in *Among the World's Peacemakers*, ed. Hayne Davis (New York: Progressive, 1907), xii; and Kuehl, *Seeking World Order*, 55, 90–91.

35. Daniel Hucker, "'Our Expectations Were Perhaps Too High': Disarmament, Citizen Activism, and the 1907 Hague Peace Conference," *Peace & Change* 44, no. 1 (January 2019): 7.

36. Bridgman, *World Organization*, 145; Richard Bartholdt, "The Interparliamentary Union and the Arbitration Group in Congress," in *Report of the Tenth Lake Mohonk Conference on International Arbitration* (1904), 122; Hayne Davis, "A World's Congress," *Independent* 57

(July 7, 1904): 15; "Constitution of the World," 826; and Hucker, "'Our Expectations Were Perhaps Too High,'" 14.

37. Mead, "International Police," 706.

38. Mead, "Next Step: World Congress," 6.

39. Craig, *Lucia Ames Mead*, 84.

40. Mead, "Organize the World," 95.

41. Mead, "Teaching Patriotism in the Public Schools," *Journal of Education* 59, no. 6 (1904): 83; and Mead, *Patriotism and Peace: How to Teach Them in Schools* (Boston: International School of Peace, 1910), 21–23.

42. Mead, "Woman's Work for Peace"; Mead, *Patriotism and the New Internationalism*, 57; Mead, address, in *Report of the Third Annual Meeting*, 97; and Patterson, *Toward a Warless World*, 133–36.

43. Fannie Fern Andrews, "The Relation of Teachers to the Cause of Peace," *Journal of Social Science* 45 (September 1907): 153–54.

44. Fannie Fern Andrews, "Interdependence of Nations," in *A Course in Citizenship*, ed. Ella Lyman Cabot (Boston: Houghton Mifflin, 1914), 344.

45. Hannah J. Bailey, address, *Report of the First Annual Meeting of the Lake Mohonk Conference on International Arbitration* (1895), 67; and Bailey, "Internationalism," August 20, 1902, Box 1, Folder 3, Hannah Johnston Bailey Papers, Swarthmore College Peace Collection, Swarthmore, PA.

46. Paul A. Kramer, *The Blood of Government: Race, Empire, the United States, and the Philippines* (Chapel Hill: University of North Carolina Press, 2006); Paul A. Kramer, "Power and Connection: Imperial Histories of the United States in the World," *American Historical Review* 116, no. 5 (2011): 1381; Christopher Capozzola, *Bound By War: How the United States and the Philippines Built America's First Pacific Century* (New York: Basic, 2020); Emily S. Rosenberg, *Financial Missionaries to the World: The Politics and Culture of Dollar Diplomacy, 1900–1930* (Cambridge, MA: Harvard University Press, 1999); Mary A. Renda, *Taking Haiti: Military Occupation and the Culture of U.S. Imperialism, 1915–1940* (Chapel Hill: University of North Carolina Press, 2001); Laura Briggs, *Reproducing Empire: Race, Sex, Science, and U.S. Imperialism in Puerto Rico* (Berkeley: University of California Press, 2002); and Michel Gobat, *Confronting the American Dream: Nicaragua Under U.S. Imperial Rule* (Durham, NC: Duke University Press, 2005).

47. Mead, *Patriotism and the New Internationalism*, 44–45.

48. Mead, *Patriotism and the New Internationalism*, 41.

49. Mead, *A Primer of the Peace Movement*, 6th ed. (Boston: American Peace Society, 1915): 4–5.

Chapter 2

1. Twentieth Century Association, *Lucia Ames Mead Memorial Meeting* (Boston: Privately printed by T. Todd, 1937). Portions of this chapter were previously published as Megan Threlkeld, "Education for Pax Americana: The Limits of Internationalism in Progressive Era Peace Education," *History of Education Quarterly* 57 (November 2017): 515–41, © Cambridge University Press. Reprinted with permission.

2. Fannie Fern Andrews, *Memory Pages of My Life* (Boston: Talisman, 1948), 1–21; and Warren F. Kuehl, "Andrews, Fannie Fern Phillips," in *Notable American Women, 1607–1950*, ed. Edward T. James and Janet Wilson James (Cambridge, MA: Harvard University Press, 1971), 1:92–94.

3. Andrews, *Memory Pages of My Life*, 32–34.

4. Andrews, "The Relation of Teachers to the Cause of Peace," *Journal of Social Science* 45 (September 1907): 144.

5. "General Statement," in *First Annual Report of the American School Peace League* (Boston: American School Peace League, 1909), 11.

6. Charles DeBenedetti, *The Peace Reform in American History* (Bloomington: Indiana University Press, 1980), 79–93; and Benjamin Allen Coates, *Legalist Empire: International Law and American Foreign Relations in the Early Twentieth Century* (New York: Oxford University Press, 2016), 86–88.

7. Susan Zeiger, "The Schoolhouse vs. the Armory: U.S. Teachers and the Campaign Against Militarism in the Schools, 1914–1918," *Journal of Women's History* 15, no. 2 (Summer 2003): 152; and Christy Jo Snider, "Peace and Politics: Fannie Fern Andrews, Professional Politics, and the American Peace Movement, 1900–1941," *Mid-America: An Historical Review* 79, no. 1 (Winter 1997): 71–95.

8. Zeiger, "Schoolhouse vs. Armory," 154.

9. Edwin Ginn to Andrews, February 20, 1909, Box 12, Folder 105, Fannie Fern Andrews Papers, Schlesinger Library, Radcliffe Institute, Cambridge, MA (hereafter Andrews Papers); and Arthur N. Holcombe, "Edwin Ginn's Commitment to World Government," *International Organization* 20, no. 3 (Summer 1966): 419–29.

10. Andrews, "How Can We Be of Service in the World Family," in *A Course in Citizenship*, ed. Ella Lyman Cabot et al. (Boston: Houghton Mifflin, 1914), 374; Threlkeld, "Education for Pax Americana"; and Susan Zeiger, "Teaching Peace: Lessons from a Peace Studies Curriculum of the Progressive Era," *Peace & Change* 25, no. 1 (January 2000): 52–69.

11. Andrews, "World Conferences Leading to World Federation," in Cabot et al., *A Course in Citizenship*, 372.

12. David S. Patterson, *Toward a Warless World: The Travail of the American Peace Movement, 1887–1914* (Bloomington: Indiana University Press, 1976), 103; and Warren F. Kuehl, *Seeking World Order: The United States and International Organization to 1920* (Nashville: Vanderbilt University Press, 1969), 68, 127.

13. Andrews, "The United States and World Brotherhood," in Cabot et al., *A Course in Citizenship*, 319–20.

14. Cabot et al., *A Course in Citizenship*, 27, 360–61, 171, 196.

15. Andrews, "The New Internationalism and its Relation to Teaching," in *Second Annual Report of the American School Peace League* (Boston: American School Peace League, 1910), 11.

16. "Future Work in the Philippines," *New York Times*, February 7, 1899, 6.

17. Andrews, "How Can We Be of Service," 375.

18. Andrews to Philander Claxton, September 2, 1914, Box 18, Folder 256, Andrews Papers.

19. Andrews to Katherine Devereaux Blake, September 23, 1914, Box 79, Andrews Papers.

20. David S. Patterson, *The Search for Negotiated Peace: Women's Activism and Citizen Diplomacy in World War I* (New York: Routledge, 2008); and Michael Kazin, *War Against War: The American Fight for Peace, 1914–1918* (New York: Simon & Schuster, 2017).

21. Madeleine Z. Doty, *The Central Organization for a Durable Peace (1915–1919): Its History, Work and Ideas* (Geneva, 1945), 29–31.

22. Doty, *Central Organization*.

23. Andrews, "World Plan for Durable Peace," *Independent* 86 (June 12, 1916): 446.

24. Kuehl, *Seeking World Order*, 219–24.

25. Andrews, "World Plan for Durable Peace," 446.

26. Andrews to David Starr Jordan, May 4, 1916, Box 52, Andrews Papers.

27. Andrews, "The Central Organization for a Durable Peace," *Annals of the American Academy of Political and Social Science* 66 (July 1, 1916): 18, 20.

28. Alan Dawley, *Changing the World: American Progressives in War and Revolution* (Princeton: Princeton University Press, 2003); and Tony Smith, *Why Wilson Matters: The Origin of American Liberal Internationalism and Its Crisis Today* (Princeton: Princeton University Press, 2017).

29. Andrews, "The United States," in Ella Lyman Cabot et al., *A Course in Citizenship and Patriotism*, rev. ed. (Boston: Houghton Mifflin, 1918), 284.

30. League to Enforce Peace, "Warrant from History," quoted in Ruhl Jacob Bartlett, *The League to Enforce Peace* (Chapel Hill: University of North Carolina Press, 1944), 40.

31. Thomas J. Knock, *To End All Wars: Woodrow Wilson and the Quest for a New World Order* (New York: Oxford University Press, 1992), 56–62.

32. "Woman's Peace Party: Preamble and Platform Adopted at Washington, January 10, 1915," Box 1, Records of the Women's International League for Peace and Freedom, U.S. Section, Swarthmore College Peace Collection, Swarthmore, PA (hereafter WILPF Records).

33. Harriet Hyman Alonso, *Peace as a Women's Issue: A History of the U.S. Movement for World Peace and Women's Rights* (Syracuse, NY: Syracuse University Press, 1993), 65.

34. Jane Addams, Emily Greene Balch, and Alice Hamilton, *Women at the Hague: The International Congress of Women and Its Results* (New York: Macmillan, 1915), 152–54.

35. Addams et al., *Women at the Hague*, 154–55.

36. *Report of the International Congress of Women, Zurich, May 12 to 17, 1919* (Geneva: WILPF, 1919), 282.

37. Addams et al, *Women at the Hague*, 157. Emphasis added.

38. Andrews to Henry Cabot Lodge, October 30, 1918, Box 58, Andrews Papers.

39. Erez Manela, *The Wilsonian Moment: Self-Determination and the International Origins of Anticolonial Nationalism* (New York: Oxford University Press, 2007), 39–40; and Knock, *To End All Wars*, 142–47.

40. Woodrow Wilson, "Address of the President of the United States Delivered at a Joint Session of the Two Houses of Congress, January 8, 1918," in *Papers Relating to the Foreign Relations of the United States*, 1918, Supplement 1, *The World War*, vol. 1, ed. Joseph V. Fuller (Washington, DC: Government Printing Office, 1933), Document 5, https://history.state.gov/historicaldocuments/frus1918Supp01v01/d5 (accessed April 26, 2021).

41. Andrews, "American Rights and Interests in the Mandatory System," *Annals of the American Academy of Political and Social Science* 96 (July 1921): 95; and Andrews, *Memory Pages of My Life*, 114.

42. Andrews, "Women and the Peace Conference," Box 18, Folder 260, Andrews Papers.

43. "Text of the Proposed Constitution of the League of Nations," *New York Times*, February 15, 1919, 2.

44. Kuehl, *Seeking World Order*, 299.

45. Kuehl, *Seeking World Order*, 301–8; and John Milton Cooper, *Breaking the Heart of the World: Woodrow Wilson and the Fight for the League of Nations* (Cambridge: Cambridge University Press, 2001), 91.

46. Andrews to Marian C. Nichols, June 25, 1919, Box 31, Folder 368, Andrews Papers.

47. *Proceedings of the Conferences of Delegates of Allied Societies for a League of Nations* (New York: League to Enforce Peace, 1919), 24–27; and Kuehl, *Seeking World Order*, 267–69.

48. Andrews, "Women and the Peace Conference"; and Mona L. Siegel, *Peace on Our Terms: The Global Battle for Women's Rights After the First World War* (New York: Columbia University Press, 2020).

49. "International Council of Women and Conference of Women Suffragists," Box 18, Folder 263, Andrews Papers.

50. "The Covenant of the League of Nations," in *Papers Relating to the Foreign Relations of the United States: The Paris Peace Conference, 1919*, vol. 13, ed. Joseph V. Fuller (Washington, DC: Government Printing Office, 1947), https://history.state.gov/historicaldocuments /frus1919Parisv13/ch10subch1 (accessed April 26, 2021).

51. Andrews, "Women and the Peace Conference."

52. "Resolutions and Proposals," in *Report of the International Congress of Women*, 242–43.

53. *Report of the International Congress of Women*, 60–62, 220; and Siegel, *Peace on Our Terms*, 147.

54. "Resolutions and Proposals," 246–48.

55. Andrews to Marian C. Nichols, June 25, 1919, Box 31, Folder 368, Andrews Papers.

56. Florence Guertin Tuttle, "An Omission of Diplomacy," Box 3, Folder 7, Florence Guertin Tuttle Papers, Sophia Smith Collection, Smith College, Northampton, MA.

57. Lola Maverick Lloyd, "A Chance for Democratic Control of Foreign Policy," October 27, 1918, Box 45, Folder 2, Lola Maverick Lloyd Papers, Archives and Manuscripts Division, New York Public Library, New York, NY.

58. Jessie Wallace Hughan, "The Paris Draft of the World League," Box 3, Folder 6, Jessie Wallace Hughan Papers, Swarthmore College Peace Collection, Swarthmore, PA.

59. Andrews, "American Rights and Interests," 95.

60. Susan Pedersen, *The Guardians: The League of Nations and the Crisis of Empire* (Oxford: Oxford University Press, 2015), 272.

61. Manela, *Wilsonian Moment*.

62. Glenda Sluga, *The Nation, Psychology, and International Politics, 1870–1919* (New York: Palgrave Macmillan, 2006), 126.

63. Andrews, "Mr. Root's Reservations," *League of Nations Magazine* 5, no. 7 (July 1919): 430.

64. Andrews to Dr. B. de Jong van Beek en Donk, July 17, 1919, Box 112, Andrews Papers.

65. Andrews, *Memory Pages of My Life*, 32; and Andrews to William Andrew, 13 June 1919, Box 10, Folder 93, Andrews Papers.

66. Andrews, "The Mandates," *American Scholar* 1, no. 3 (May 1932): 307.

Chapter 3

1. Florence Guertin Tuttle, "Voting Women and Internationalism," Box 3, Folder 7, Florence Guertin Tuttle Papers, Sophia Smith Collection, Smith College, Northampton, MA (hereafter Tuttle Papers).

2. "Tuttle, Florence Guertin," in *The Biographical Cyclopaedia of American Women*, ed. Erma Conkling Lee and Henry C. Wiley, vol. 3 (New York: Williams-Wiley, 1928), 225–28; and Tuttle, "I Travelled Hopefully," unpublished autobiography, Box 1, Folder 4, Tuttle Papers.

3. Tuttle, *Give My Love to Maria* (New York: Abingdon, 1917), 13–16.

4. Tuttle, *The Awakening of Woman: Suggestions from the Psychic Side of Feminism* (New York: Abingdon, 1915), 48, 26–27.

5. Tuttle, "I Travelled Hopefully," 16.

6. Tuttle, *Awakening of Woman*, 83–84, 145. See also Wendy Kline, *Building a Better Race: Gender, Sexuality, and Eugenics from the Turn of the Century to the Baby Boom* (Berkeley: University of California Press, 2001); and Thomas C. Leonard, *Illiberal Reformers: Race, Eugenics, and American Economics in the Progressive Era* (Princeton: Princeton University Press, 2016).

7. Kimberly A. Hamlin, *From Eve to Evolution: Darwin, Science, and Women's Rights in Gilded Age America* (Chicago: University of Chicago Press, 2014), 15–22; and Beryl Satter, *Each Mind a Kingdom: American Women, Sexual Purity, and the New Thought Movement, 1875–1920* (Berkeley: University of California Press, 1999), 36–37.

8. Charlotte Perkins Gilman, "Nursery-Mindedness," *Forerunner* 1, no. 6 (April 1910): 10; Cynthia J. Davis, *Charlotte Perkins Gilman: A Biography* (Stanford: Stanford University Press, 2010), 300; and Gilman, *Women and Economics: A Study of the Economic Relation Between Men and Women as a Factor in Social Evolution* (Boston: Small, Maynard, 1898). See also Judith A. Allen, *The Feminism of Charlotte Perkins Gilman: Sexualities, Histories, Progressivism* (Chicago: University of Chicago Press, 2009).

9. Tuttle, "I Travelled Hopefully," 18.

10. Hamlin, *From Eve to Evolution*, 161–62.

11. Margaret Sanger, *Woman and the New Race* (New York: Brentano's, 1920), 45–46.

12. "'Women Will Vote,' Says Mrs. Catt," *New York Times*, February 14, 1915, 2.

13. Quoted in "Tuttle, Florence Guertin," 226.

14. Tuttle, "A Call to Arms," *Four Lights*, May 19, 1917, 1.

15. Tuttle, open letter to Woodrow Wilson, August 18, 1917, Box 4, Folder 9, Tuttle Papers.

16. Tuttle, "Voting Women and Internationalism," Box 3, Folder 7, Tuttle Papers.

17. Tuttle, "Voting Women and Internationalism"; and Megan Threlkeld, *Pan American Women: U.S. Internationalists and Revolutionary Mexico* (Philadelphia: University of Pennsylvania Press, 2014), 48.

18. Tuttle, *Women and World Federation* (New York: R. M. McBride, 1919), 228–29, 242, 238–39.

19. Tuttle, *Women and World Federation*, 66, 72, 83.

20. Tuttle, *Women and World Federation*, 10–11, xiii–xiv.

21. Tuttle, *Women and World Federation*, 17–18, 14–15.

22. Tuttle, *Women and World Federation*, 85, 106–7.

23. Mark Pittenger, *American Socialists and Evolutionary Thought, 1870–1920* (Madison: University of Wisconsin Press, 1993); James T. Kloppenberg, *Uncertain Victory: Social Democracy and Progressivism in European and American Thought, 1870–1920* (New York: Oxford University Press, 1986); and Peter Beilharz and Chris Nyland, eds., *The Webbs, Fabianism, and Feminism* (Aldershot, UK: Ashgate, 1998).

24. Tuttle, *Women and World Federation*, 97; *Labour and the New Social Order: A Report on Reconstruction* (London: Labour Party, 1918).

25. Tuttle, *Women and World Federation*, 231–32, 235.

26. Lara Vapnek, "The 1919 International Congress of Working Women: Transnational Debates on the 'Woman Worker,'" *Journal of Women's History* 26, no. 1 (March 2014): 160–84; Dorothy Sue Cobble, "A Higher 'Standard of Life' for the World: U.S. Labor Women's Reform Internationalism and the Legacies of 1919," *Journal of American History* 100, no. 4 (March 2014): 1052–85; and Eileen Boris, *Making the Woman Worker: Precarious Labor and the Fight for Global Standards, 1919–2019* (New York: Oxford University Press, 2019), 19–20.

27. Tuttle, *Women and World Federation*, 169, 180.

28. Brooke L. Blower, "From Isolationism to Neutrality: A New Framework for Understanding American Political Culture, 1919–1941," *Diplomatic History* 38, no. 2 (April 2014): 345–76.

29. Tuttle, "An American Woman's Visit to the League of Nations," *Birth Control Review* 5, no. 5 (May 1921): 14.

30. Tuttle, "The Woman's Pro-League Council," Box 6, Folder 8, Tuttle Papers.

31. Tuttle to members, May 26, 1921, Box 6, Folder 8, Tuttle Papers; and Portia Willis to Tuttle, n.d., Box 2, Folder 5, Tuttle Papers.

32. Carrie A. Foster, *The Women and the Warriors: The U.S. Section of the Women's International League for Peace and Freedom, 1915–1946* (Syracuse, NY: Syracuse University Press, 1995), 36–109.

33. Beatrice McKenzie, "The Power of International Positioning: The National Woman's Party, International Law and Diplomacy, 1928–34," *Gender & History* 23, no. 1 (April 2011): 130–46; Ellen Carol DuBois, "Internationalizing Married Women's Nationality: The Hague Campaign of 1930," in *Globalizing Feminisms, 1789–1945*, ed. Karen Offen (London: Routledge, 2010), 204–16; and Jaci Leigh Eisenberg, "American Women and International Geneva, 1919–1939" (PhD diss., Graduate Institute of Geneva, 2014).

34. Warren F. Kuehl, *Seeking World Order: The United States and International Organization to 1920* (Nashville, TN: Vanderbilt University Press, 1969), 330; Republican platform quoted in John Milton Cooper, *Breaking the Heart of the World: Woodrow Wilson and the Fight for the League of Nations* (Cambridge: Cambridge University Press, 2001), 383; Warren F. Kuehl and Lynne Dunn, *Keeping the Covenant: American Internationalists and the League of Nations, 1920–1939* (Kent, OH: Kent State University Press, 1997), 28–29; and Warren I. Cohen, *Empire Without Tears: America's Foreign Relations, 1921–1933* (Philadelphia: Temple University Press, 1987), 46–47.

35. Mrs. Robert Nelson to Warren Harding, August 18, 1921, Box 2, Folder 19, Tuttle Papers; WPLC Minutes, August 19, 1921, Box 6, Folder 8, Tuttle Papers; and Harriet Laidlaw to members, October 17, 1921, Folder 1, Woman's Pro-League Council Records, Swarthmore College Peace Collection, Swarthmore College, Swarthmore, PA (hereafter Peace Collection).

36. Laidlaw to members, October 17, 1921, Folder 1, Peace Collection.

37. Tuttle, "Peace on Earth, Good Will to Men: American Women and the Washington Conference" *Owlet* 1, no. 13–14 (December 6–20, 1921): 1, 5.

38. Tuttle to members, June 8, 1922, Box 6, Folder 7, Tuttle Papers; Portia Willis, "Report of the Political Committee Chairman," Box 2, Folder 5, Tuttle Papers; and Tuttle to Warren Harding, November 14, 1922, Box 6, Folder 7, Tuttle Papers.

39. Tuttle, "World Policies Women Want," *Our World* (December 1922): 43–44.

40. Tuttle, "World Policies Women Want," 48.

41. Tuttle, "What the American Woman Thinks," *Woman Citizen* 7, no. 20 (February 24, 1923): 16–17.

42. Kuehl and Dunn, *Keeping the Covenant*, 40.

43. Minutes of the League of Nations Non-Partisan Association, January 25, 1924, Container 23, Clark Eichelberger Papers, Manuscripts and Archives Division, New York Public Library, New York, NY; Tuttle to Mabel Keep, August 1, 1924, Box 6, Folder 3, Tuttle Papers; Tuttle to Arthur Bullard, Box 6, Folder 1, Tuttle Papers; and WPLC minutes, March 3, 1925, Box 6, Folder 8, Tuttle Papers.

44. Tuttle to Charles Bauer, January 10, 1923, Box 6, Folder 7, Tuttle Papers.

45. "Kellogg-Briand Pact of 1928," *Avalon Project*, Yale Law School, Lillian Goldman Law Library, https://avalon.law.yale.edu/20th_century/kbpact.asp (accessed April 26, 2021); and Oona Anne Hathaway and Scott Shapiro, *The Internationalists: How a Radical Plan to Outlaw War Remade the World* (New York: Simon & Schuster, 2017), 109–30.

46. Michael Dunne, *The United States and the World Court, 1920-1935* (New York: St. Martin's, 1988).

47. Elinor Byrns, statement, *Constitutional Amendment Making War Legally Impossible: Hearing Before a Subcommittee of the Committee on the Judiciary of the United States Senate* (Washington, DC: Government Printing Office, 1927), 2.

48. Florence Brewer Boeckel, "Women in International Affairs," *Annals of the American Academy of Political and Social Science* 143 (May 1929): 245.

49. Harriet Hyman Alonso, *Peace as a Women's Issue: A History of the U.S. Movement for World Peace and Women's Rights* (Syracuse, NY: Syracuse University Press, 1993), 121–22.

50. Virginia Gildersleeve, "Women's Part in World Peace," Box 62, Virginia Gildersleeve Papers, Butler Library, Columbia University, New York, NY.

51. *Report of the Conference on the Cause and Cure of War* (Washington, DC: n.p., 1925), 22.

52. Mary Woolley, "Women's Part and Power in the Peace Movement," Box 35, Folder 23, Mary Woolley Papers, Archives and Special Collections, Mount Holyoke College, South Hadley, MA.

53. Tuttle, *Alternatives to War* (New York: Harper, 1931), 21–22.

54. Tuttle, *Alternatives to War*, x, 262.

55. Tuttle, "An American Woman's Reaction to the Disarmament Conference," Box 5, Folder 3, Tuttle Papers.

56. Thomas Richard Davies, *The Possibilities of Transnational Activism: The Campaign for Disarmament Between the Two World Wars* (Leiden: Martinus Nijhoff, 2007); and Karen Garner, *Shaping a Global Women's Agenda: Women's NGOs and Global Governance, 1925–85* (Manchester: Manchester University Press, 2010).

57. Tuttle, "Journey to Geneva," Box 1, Folder 3, Tuttle Papers.

Chapter 4

1. Rosika Schwimmer, "Mankind's Greatest Adventure: The Birth of a New World Order" Box 45, Folder 6, Lola Maverick Lloyd Papers, Manuscripts and Archives Division, New York Public Library, New York, NY (hereafter Lloyd Papers). Portions of this chapter have been published as Megan Threlkeld, "'Chaos, War, or a New World Order?' A Radical Plan for Peace and World Government in the 1930s," *Peace & Change* 43 (October 2018): 473–97.

2. Lola Maverick Lloyd and Schwimmer, "Chaos, War, or a New World Order?" [1937] Box 3, Folder 1, Mary Ware Dennett Papers, Schlesinger Library, Radcliffe Institute, Cambridge, MA. Schwimmer and Lloyd later published their plan as *Chaos, War, or a New World Order? What We Must Do to Establish the All-Inclusive, Non-Military, Democratic Federation of Nations* (Chicago: Campaign for World Government, 1942).

3. Martin David Dubin, "Schwimmer, Rosika," in *Notable American Women, 1607–1950*, vol. 3, ed. Barbara Sicherman and Carol Hurd Green (Cambridge, MA: Harvard University Press, 1971), 249–52. See also Dagmar Wernitznig, "Out of Her Time? Rosika Schwimmer's Transnational Activism After the First World War," *Women's History Review* 26, no. 2 (2017): 262–79; Wernitznig, "Living Peace, Thinking Equality: Rosika Schwimmer's (1877–1948) War

on War," in *Living War, Thinking Peace (1914–1924): Women's Experiences, Feminist Thought, and International Relations*, ed. Bruna Bianchi and Geraldine Ludbrook (Newcastle upon Tyne: Cambridge Scholars, 2016), 123–38; Wernitznig, "Between Front Lines: The Militant Pacifist Rosika Schwimmer (1877–1948) and Her Total Peace Effort," in *Reconsidering Peace and Patriotism During the First World War*, ed. Justin Quinn Olmstead (New York: Palgrave Macmillan, 2017), 91–114; Beth S. Wenger, "Radical Politics in a Reactionary Age: The Unmaking of Rosika Schwimmer, 1914–1930," *Journal of Women's History* 2, no. 2 (1990): 66–99; and Margaret H. McFadden, "Borders, Boundaries, and the Necessity of Reflexivity: International Women Activists, Rosika Schwimmer (1877–1948), and the Shadow Narrative," *Women's History Review* 20, no. 4 (September 2011): 533–42. The best source on Lloyd is Melanie Susan Gustafson, "Lola Maverick Lloyd: 'Truly a Live Wire and a Brick and Everything Else That Goes to Make Up a Militant Pacifist'" (MA thesis, Sarah Lawrence College, 1983). See also Janet Stevenson, "Lola Maverick Lloyd: 'I Must Do Something for Peace!'" *Chicago History* 9, no. 1 (April 1, 1980): 47–57.

4. David S. Patterson, *The Search for Negotiated Peace: Women's Activism and Citizen Diplomacy in World War I* (New York: Routledge, 2008), 80–81.

5. The phrase is Patterson's; on Schwimmer's involvements with Henry Ford and the failed "Peace Ship," see Barbara S. Kraft, *The Peace Ship: Henry Ford's Pacifist Adventure in the First World War* (New York: Macmillan, 1978); and Burnet Hershey, *The Odyssey of Henry Ford and the Great Peace Ship* (New York: Taplinger, 1967).

6. Lloyd, "For a People's Peace," October 6, 1917, Box 8, Folder 6, Campaign for World Government, Records of the New York Office, Manuscripts and Archives Division, New York Public Library (hereafter CWG NY Records).

7. Lloyd, "A New Application of Democracy," May 1, 1918, Box 8, Folder 6, CWG NY Records.

8. Lloyd, "A Chance for Democratic Control of Foreign Policy," October 27, 1918, Box 45, Folder 2, Lloyd Papers.

9. Warren F. Kuehl and Lynne Dunn, *Keeping the Covenant: American Internationalists and the League of Nations, 1920–1939* (Kent, OH: Kent State University Press, 1997), 53–54.

10. "How to Achieve World Peace: Outline of a Plan," Box 18, Folder 2, CWG NY Records.

11. Schwimmer and Lloyd to Bertrand Russell, June 24, 1924, Box 31, Folder 4, CWG NY Records.

12. *Transcript of Record, United States v. Schwimmer*, 279 U.S. 644 (1929), 6–7. Emphasis added.

13. *Transcript of Record*, 11.

14. *United States v. Schwimmer*, 648, 650.

15. Megan Threlkeld, "Citizenship, Gender, and Conscience: *United States v. Schwimmer*," *Journal of Supreme Court History* 40, no. 2 (July 2015): 154–71.

16. Schwimmer, "The German Crisis and World Citizenship: The Problem of Exile Grows More Acute the World Over," *Polity* 2, no. 12 (September 1934): 207–8; and Laura Barnett, "Global Governance and the Evolution of the International Refugee," *International Journal of Refugee Law* 14, no. 2 and 3 (2002): 242–43.

17. Edith Wynner, remarks to the Third Annual Conference of the American Committee for the Protection of the Foreign-Born, February 25, 1939, vol. 2073, *American Civil Liberties Union Records, Subgroup 1*, Department of Special Collections, Princeton University Library, Princeton, NJ.

18. Salvador de Madariaga, "World Government: Dream or Necessity," *Century* 120 (April 1930): 204; Nicholas Murray Butler, "The Federal Principle," *World Unity Magazine* 15 (January 1935): 231–32; Oscar Newfang, "World Federation Manifesto," *World Unity Magazine* 15 (February 1935): 352–53; and Clarence K. Streit, *Union Now: A Proposal for a Federal Union of the Democracies of the North Atlantic* (New York: Harper & Brothers, 1939).

19. Lloyd and Schwimmer, *Chaos, War?* 2.

20. Lloyd and Schwimmer, *Chaos, War?* 3.

21. Lloyd and Schwimmer, *Chaos, War?* 3, 6.

22. Lloyd to William Allan Neilson, January 19, 1940, Box 22, Folder 3, Lloyd Papers.

23. Lloyd, "An International Magna Charta for Women," *Equal Rights* 23, no. 10 (1937): 75–76.

24. Salvador de Madariaga, "Citizens of the World," *Forum & Century* 98 (September 1937): 123. He was referring to Italy.

25. John Herman Randall, *A World Community: The Supreme Task of the Twentieth Century* (New York: Frederick A. Stokes, 1930), 58, 61.

26. "Common Sense and Colonies," *World Federation—Now* 1, no. 2 (June 1939): 3.

27. Lloyd and Schwimmer, *Chaos, War?* 5.

28. Florence Guertin Tuttle, *Women and World Federation* (New York: R. M. McBride, 1919), 133.

29. Jessie Wallace Hughan, *A Study of International Government* (New York: T. Y. Crowell, 1923), 241. See also Melinda Plastas, *A Band of Noble Women: Racial Politics in the Women's Peace Movement* (Syracuse, NY: Syracuse University Press, 2011); Joyce Blackwell, *No Peace Without Freedom: Race and the Women's International League for Peace and Freedom, 1915–1975* (Carbondale: Southern Illinois University Press, 2004); and Leila J. Rupp, "Challenging Imperialism in International Women's Organizations, 1888–1945," *NWSA Journal* 8, no. 1 (1996): 8–27.

30. J. A. Hobson, *Towards International Government* (London: George Allen & Unwin, 1915), 161; Toynbee quoted in Richard J. Mayne, John Pinder, and John C. de V. Roberts, *Federal Union: The Pioneers: A History of Federal Union* (Basingstoke, UK: Macmillan, 1990), 14; and Streit, *Union Now*, 245.

31. Lloyd and Schwimmer, *Chaos, War?* 5–6.

32. Michael R. Marrus, *The Unwanted: European Refugees in the Twentieth Century* (New York: Oxford University Press, 1985), 122–45.

33. Candice Lewis Bredbenner, *A Nationality of Her Own: Women, Marriage, and the Law of Citizenship* (Berkeley: University of California Press, 1998); and Helen Irving, *Citizenship, Alienage and the Modern Constitutional State: A Gendered History* (Cambridge: Cambridge University Press, 2016).

34. Madariaga, "World Government"; and Madariaga, "Citizens of the World."

35. Streit, *Union Now*, 245.

36. Carrie Chapman Catt to Lloyd, December 15, 1937, Box 8, Folder 5, Records of the Campaign for World Government, Chicago Office, New York Public Library (hereafter CWG Chicago Records).

37. Elinor Byrns to Lloyd, February 14, 1938, Box 8, Folder 4, CWG Chicago Records; and Alice Thacher Post to Schwimmer, February 16, 1938, Box 1, Folder 2, CWG NY Records.

38. Lloyd to Schwimmer, March 9, 1938, Box 6, Folder 5, CWG NY Records.

39. Caroline Lexow Babcock to Chairman, Platform Committee, Republican State Convention, Saratoga Springs, NY, September 29, 1938, Box 2, Folder 2, CWG NY Records. See also

Babcock to Mrs. Stephen Foster Hunt, September 9, 1938, Box 2, Folder 2, CWG NY Records; and Schwimmer to Lloyd, August 30, 1938, Box 2, Folder 1, CWG NY Records.

40. Babcock and William Lloyd Jr. to Franklin Delano Roosevelt, September 29, 1938, Box 6, Folder 5, CWG NY Records.

41. Justus D. Doenecke and John Edward Wilz, *From Isolation to War, 1931–1941*, 4th ed. (Malden, MA: John Wiley & Sons, 2015); Doenecke, *Storm on the Horizon: The Challenge to American Intervention, 1939–1941* (Lanham, MD: Rowman & Littlefield, 2000); Nancy Beck Young, *Why We Fight: Congress and the Politics of World War II* (Lawrence: University Press of Kansas, 2013); and David F. Schmitz, *The Triumph of Internationalism: Franklin D. Roosevelt and a World in Crisis, 1933–1941* (Washington, DC: Potomac, 2007).

42. Quoted in "Congress Gets World Federation Resolution," *World Federation—Now* 1, no. 2 (June 1939): 1.

43. Lloyd Jr. to Jerry Voorhis, August 31, 1939, Box 3, Folder 3, CWG NY Records.

44. Schmitz, *Triumph of Internationalism*, 63–84; Harold Josephson, *James T. Shotwell and the Rise of Internationalism in America* (Rutherford, NJ: Fairleigh Dickinson University Press, 1974), 236–45; Doenecke and Wilz, *From Isolation to War*, 131–37; and Charles Chatfield, *For Peace and Justice: Pacifism in America, 1914–1941* (Knoxville: University of Tennessee Press, 1971), 311–28.

45. Quoted in Carrie A. Foster, *The Women and the Warriors: The U.S. Section of the Women's International League for Peace and Freedom, 1915–1946* (Syracuse, NY: Syracuse University Press, 1995), 136.

46. Lloyd, "World Government: A Democratic Start," *Fellowship* (October 1938): 11–12, Box 8, Folder 6, CWG NY Records.

47. "Minutes of the Post-Convention Meeting of the National WIL Board," May 2, 1938, Box 5, Folder 4, Series A2, Women's International League for Peace and Freedom Records, Swarthmore College Peace Collection, Swarthmore, PA (hereafter WILPF Records); "Resolutions Adopted by the National Board of the WILPF," January 19–20, 1939, Box 3, Folder 1, CWG NY Records; "Annual Meeting, 1939," Box 9, Folder 3, Series A2, WILPF Records; and Executive Committee minutes, June 6, 1939, Box 9, Folder 2, Series A2, WILPF Records.

48. "From WIL National Board Minutes," January 20–21, 1940, Box 91, Folder 2, CWG Chicago Records; and Lloyd to Dorothy Detzer, September 7, 1940, Box 23, Folder 4, Lloyd Papers.

49. Detzer to Lloyd, September 12, 1940, Box 23, Folder 4, Lloyd Papers; Detzer to Lloyd, July 31, 1940, Box 23, Folder 2, Lloyd Papers; and Dorothy Medders Robinson to Lloyd, July 9, 1942, Box 25, Folder 5, Lloyd Papers.

50. Edith Wynner to Schwimmer, October 5, 1938, Box 2, Folder 1, Edith Wynner Papers, Manuscripts and Archives Division, New York Public Library (hereafter Wynner Papers); Schwimmer to Lloyd, October 12, 1938, Box 2, Folder 3, CWG NY Records; "Proposal Approved at Meeting of United Pacifist Committee," October 14, 1938, Box 31, Folder 9, CWG NY Records; and Wynner to Schwimmer, October, 18, 1938, Box 2, Folder 3, CWG NY Records. See also Leilah Danielson, *American Gandhi: A. J. Muste and the History of Radicalism in the Twentieth Century* (Philadelphia: University of Pennsylvania Press, 2014), 218.

51. Schwimmer to Streit, March 5, 1939, Box 3, Folder 1, CWG NY Records; and Streit to Eva Ingersoll Wakefield, February 25, 1939, Box 19, Folder 7, CWG NY Records.

52. Schwimmer to Lloyd Jr., March 13, 1939, Box 3, Folder 1, CWG NY Records; and Schwimmer, *Union Now, for Peace or War? The Danger in the Plan of Clarence Streit* (New York: published by the author, 1939), 2.

53. Lloyd Jr. to Wynner, February 10, 1940, Box 90, Folder 3, Mary Maverick Lloyd Papers, Manuscripts and Archives Division, New York Public Library (hereafter Mary Maverick Lloyd Papers); and Schwimmer to Lloyd, May 30, 1940, Box 22, Folder 7, Lloyd Papers.

54. Schwimmer to Albert Einstein, September 4, 1939, Box 3, Folder 3, CWG NY Records; and Einstein to Schwimmer, September 6, 1939, Box 3, Folder 3, CWG NY Records.

55. Schwimmer to Lloyd, October 14, 1939, Box 133, Folder 1, Wynner Papers.

56. Lloyd Jr. to Tracy Mygatt, December 10, 1941, Box 91, Folder 3, Mary Maverick Lloyd Papers.

57. Schwimmer to Lloyd, March 12, 1942, Box 7, Folder 7, CWG NY Records.

Chapter 5

1. Esther Caukin Brunauer, "Notes on My Experiences in Germany in 1933," Reel 1, Folder 17, *American Association of University Women Archives, 1881–1976* (Sanford, NC: Microfilming Corporation of America, 1980) (hereafter AAUW Archives); and Brunauer, *Germany, the National Socialist State: A Study Course* (Washington, DC: American Association of University Women, 1934).

2. Brunauer, "Notes on My Experiences in Germany"; and Christine von Oertzen, *Science, Gender, and Internationalism: Women's Academic Networks, 1917–1955* (New York: Palgrave Macmillan, 2012), 145–49.

3. Pierre Van Paassen and James Waterman Wise, eds., *Nazism: An Assault on Civilization* (New York: H. Smith and R. Haas, 1934); and Michaela Hönicke Moore, *Know Your Enemy: The American Debate on Nazism, 1933–1945* (New York: Cambridge University Press, 2010).

4. Betty Miller Unterberger, "Brunauer, Esther Delia Caukin," in *Notable American Women: The Modern Period*, ed. Barbara Sicherman and Carol Hurd Green, vol. 1 (Cambridge, MA: Harvard University Press, 1980), 114; Jonathan M. Schoenwald, "Brunauer, Esther (1901–1959)," International Affairs Specialist and State Department Official," *American National Biography* (New York: Oxford University Press, 1999); and "Lewis Brunauer," *Journal of the American Association of University Women* 31, no. 3 (April 1938): 174.

5. Brunauer to Florence Kitchelt, June 21, 1943, Box 5, Folder 122, Florence Ledyard Cross Kitchelt Papers, Schlesinger Library, Radcliffe Institute, Cambridge, MA; and Susan Levine, *Degrees of Equality: The American Association of University Women and the Challenge of Twentieth-Century Feminism* (Philadelphia: Temple University Press, 1995), 39–41.

6. Levine, *Degrees of Equality*, 107–14.

7. David F. Schmitz, *The Triumph of Internationalism: Franklin D. Roosevelt and a World in Crisis, 1933–1941* (Washington, DC: Potomac, 2007), 22. See also Justus D. Doenecke and John Edward Wilz, *From Isolation to War, 1931–1941*, 4th ed. (Malden, MA: John Wiley & Sons, 2015); and Robert Dallek, *Franklin D. Roosevelt and American Foreign Policy, 1932–1945* (New York: Oxford University Press, 1995).

8. Brunauer, review of *Review of the Study of International Relations in the United States*, by Edith E. Ware, *Pacific Affairs* 8, no. 4 (1935): 530.

9. Brunauer, "Unity of Purpose; Diversity of Method," *Journal of Educational Sociology* 10, no. 6 (1937): 333.

10. *Delegate's Worksheet, Fourteenth Conference on the Cause and Cure of War*, No. 2 (Washington, DC: National Committee on the Cause and Cure of War, 1939), 2. Emphasis in original.

11. Brunauer, ed., *National Defense: Institutions, Concepts, Policies* (New York: Womans Press, 1937), 50.

12. *Delegate's Worksheet, Thirteenth Conference on the Cause and Cure of War*, No. 4 (Washington, DC: National Committee on the Cause and Cure of War, 1938), 2.

13. Mary Woolley, "The College Woman in the World Community," February 20, 1935, Box 37, Folder 1, Mary Emma Woolley Papers, Archives and Special Collections, Mount Holyoke College, South Hadley, MA (hereafter Woolley Papers).

14. Mary Woolley, "The Intelligent Citizen in the Twentieth Century," January 10, 1936, Box 37, Folder 26, Woolley Papers. Emphasis in original.

15. Minutes of AAUW International Relations Committee, May 4, 1938, Box 69, Folder 5, Records of the National Committee on the Cause and Cure of War, Schlesinger Library, Radcliffe Institute (hereafter NCCCW Records); and minutes of AAUW International Relations Committee, September 30, 1938, Box 69, Folder 5, NCCCW Records.

16. Levine, *Degrees of Equality*, 57.

17. "Meeting of the Board of Directors, National League of Women Voters," November 11–15, 1935, Part I, Reel 6, *Papers of the League of Women Voters, 1918–1974* (Frederick, MD: University Publications of America, 1985); and Louise M. Young, *In the Public Interest: The League of Women Voters, 1920–1970* (New York: Greenwood, 1989), 128–29.

18. Marguerite Wells to Louise Leonard Wright, October 31, 1938, Box 3, Folder 91, Louise Leonard Wright Papers, Schlesinger Library, Radcliffe Institute (hereafter Wright Papers).

19. Louise Leonard Wright, *Toward a Collective Peace System* (Washington, DC: National League of Women Voters, 1937), 42.

20. "Dr. Emily Hickman Dies in Auto Crash," *New York Times*, June 13, 1947.

21. Minutes of the YWCA International Relations Committee, January 7, 1936, Box 394, Folder 12, YWCA of the U.S.A. Records, Sophia Smith Collection, Smith College, Northampton, MA (hereafter YWCA Records).

22. Emily Hickman, "Special Peace Program" Report, June 1938, Box 39, Folder 17, YWCA Records.

23. Emily Hickman, "The World Community and War," April 25, [1938], Box 39, Folder 17, YWCA Records.

24. Josephine Schain, "A Short Review of the Activities of the Conference on the Cause and Cure of War," *Delegate's Worksheet, Twelfth Conference on the Cause and Cure of War*, No. 1 (Washington, DC: National Committee on the Cause and Cure of War, 1937), 2.

25. Eleanor Roosevelt, "Monday Evening Session," *Delegate's Worksheet, Fourteenth Conference*, No. 3, 2.

26. Emily Hickman, "Wednesday Afternoon Session," *Delegate's Worksheet, Fourteenth Conference*, No. 4, 4.

27. "Program for 1937," *Delegate's Worksheet, Twelfth Conference*, No. 4, 22.

28. Brunauer, "NCCCW Suggested Statement," Box 15, Folder 9, NCCCW Records. Emphasis in original.

29. Emily Hickman, "Outline of Summary," *Delegate's Worksheet, Thirteenth Conference*, No. 4, 8.

30. Andrew Johnstone, *Against Immediate Evil: American Internationalists and the Four Freedoms on the Eve of World War II* (Ithaca, NY: Cornell University Press, 2014), 36.

31. *American Neutrality Policy: Hearings Before the Committee on Foreign Affairs, House of Representatives, 67th Congress, 1st Session, on Present Neutrality Law (Public Res. No. 27)* (Washington, DC: Government Printing Office, 1939), 379–85.

32. Johnstone, *Against Immediate Evil*, 11; and Stephen Wertheim, "Instrumental Internationalism: The American Origins of the United Nations, 1940–3," *Journal of Contemporary History* 54, no. 2 (April 2019): 266.

33. Commission to Study the Organization of Peace, ed., *Building Peace: Reports of the Commission to Study the Organization of Peace, 1939–1972* (Metuchen, NJ: Scarecrow, 1973), xi.

34. Commission to Study the Organization of Peace, *Third Report: The United Nations and the Organization of Peace* (New York: Carnegie Endowment for International Peace, 1943); and Stephen Wertheim, "Tomorrow, the World: The Birth of U.S. Global Supremacy in World War II" (PhD diss., Columbia University, 2015), 96.

35. *Delegate's Worksheet, Fourteenth Conference*, No. 4, 1.

36. Commission on a Permanent World Society (CPWS), "Study Outline: Inter-American Cooperation," Box 28, Folder 6, NCCCW Records.

37. CPWS, "Conclusions of the Commission," August 1, 1940, Box 66, Folder 5, NCCCW Records.

38. CPWS, "Conclusions of the Commission"; and "Conclusions of the CPWS," June 17, 1940, Box 66, Folder 5, NCCCW Records.

39. CPWS Minutes, May 8, 1940, Box 28, Folder 7, NCCCW Records.

40. CPWS Minutes, June 17, 1940, Box 28, Folder 7, NCCCW Records.

41. Brunauer, *Building the New World Order* (New York: League of Nations Association, 1939), 11, 43–44, 34.

42. CPWS Minutes, June 5, 1939, Box 29, Folder 5, NCCCW Records.

43. Brunauer, *Building the New World Order*, 26.

44. Brunauer, "Power Politics and Democracy," *Annals of the American Academy of Political and Social Science* 216 (July 1941): 111–16.

45. "Preliminary Report of the Commission on World Peace Through World Organization," Woman's Centennial Congress, November 25–27, 1940, Box 21, Folder 3, Carrie Chapman Catt Papers, Manuscript Division, Library of Congress.

46. "Preliminary Report."

47. "Preliminary Report."

48. Elizabeth Borgwardt, *A New Deal for the World: America's Vision for Human Rights* (Cambridge, MA: Harvard University Press, 2005), 61–69.

49. "Preliminary Report."

50. "Preliminary Report."

51. Mary Woolley, "The Crisis and Our Responsibility," November 9, 1939, Box 39, Folder 28, Woolley Papers.

52. Brunauer, *Building the New World Order*, 33.

53. Stephen Wertheim, *Tomorrow, the World: The Birth of U.S. Global Supremacy* (Cambridge, MA: Harvard University Press, 2020). For other perspectives on official planning efforts, see Or Rosenboim, *The Emergence of Globalism: Visions of World Order in Britain and the United States, 1939–1950* (Princeton: Princeton University Press, 2017); Patrick J. Hearden, *Architects of Globalism: Building a New World Order During World War II* (Fayetteville: University of Arkansas Press, 2002); and Stephen C. Schlesinger, *Act of Creation: The Founding of the United Nations: A Story of Superpowers, Secret Agents, Wartime Allies and Enemies, and Their Quest for a Peaceful World* (Boulder, CO: Westview, 2003).

54. Brunauer, "Women on the Ramparts," *Vital Issues* 1, no. 2 (July 1941): 20.

Chapter 6

1. "Letter from Mary McLeod Bethune to Franklin Delano Roosevelt, 1940," in *Mary McLeod Bethune: Building a Better World: Essays and Selected Documents*, ed. Audrey Thomas McCluskey and Elaine M. Smith (Bloomington: Indiana University Press, 1999), 173–74.

2. Joyce Ann Hanson, *Mary McLeod Bethune and Black Women's Political Activism* (Columbia: University of Missouri Press, 2003), 182.

3. Mary McLeod Bethune, "A Philosophy of Education for Negro Girls," in McCluskey and Smith, *Mary McLeod Bethune*, 84–85. See also Hanson, *Mary McLeod Bethune*, 11–55; Elaine M. Smith, "Bethune, Mary McLeod," in *Notable American Women: The Modern Period* (Cambridge, MA: Harvard University Press, 1980); Darlene Clark Hine, "Bethune, Mary Jane McLeod (1875–1955)," in *American National Biography* (New York: Oxford University Press, 2000); and Paula Giddings, *When and Where I Enter: The Impact of Black Women on Race and Sex in America* (New York: William Morrow, 1984), 199–230.

4. Rebecca Tuuri, *Strategic Sisterhood: The National Council of Negro Women in the Black Freedom Struggle* (Chapel Hill: University of North Carolina Press, 2018), 17. On the Black Cabinet, see Jill Watts, *The Black Cabinet: The Untold Story of African Americans and Politics During the Age of Roosevelt* (New York: Grove, 2020).

5. Penny M. Von Eschen, *Race Against Empire: Black Americans and Anticolonialism, 1937–1957* (Ithaca, NY: Cornell University Press, 1997), 19, 60; and Tuuri, *Strategic Sisterhood*, 11–17. The quote is from Bettye Collier-Thomas, *N.C.N.W., 1935–1980* (Washington, DC: National Council of Negro Women, 1981), 4.

6. "Women Must Lead the Way," Community Workshop for Citizenship Training Manual, Series 13, Folder 83, National Council of Negro Women Records, National Archives for Black Women's History, Landover, MD (hereafter NCNW Records).

7. Hanson, *Mary McLeod Bethune*, 177–81.

8. Michelle Rief, "Thinking Locally, Acting Globally: The International Agenda of African American Clubwomen, 1880–1940," *Journal of African American History* 89, no. 3 (Summer 2004): 215–18; and Bethune, "President's Monthly Message," in McCluskey and Smith, *Mary McLeod Bethune*, 163.

9. Addie W. Dickinson, "The Political Scene of 1940: A Symposium," *Aframerican Woman's Journal* 1, no. 1 (Spring 1940): 9.

10. Audley Moore, "Conference Impressions," *Aframerican Woman's Journal* 2, no. 1/2 (Summer/Fall 1941): 16. On Moore's early internationalism and later Pan-Africanism, see Ashley D. Farmer, "Mothers of Pan-Africanism: Audley Moore and Dara Abubakari," *Women, Gender, and Families of Color* 4, no. 2 (2016): 274–95.

11. Bethune, "The President's Message," *Aframerican Woman's Journal* 2, no. 3 (Winter 1941–1942): 1.

12. "Report of the Commission on Findings of the NCNW," *Aframerican Woman's Journal* 2, no. 3 (Winter 1941–1942): 8.

13. Bethune, "Annual Report to the Council," *Aframerican Woman's Journal* 3, no. 3 (1943): 2.

14. Keisha N. Blain, *Set the World on Fire: Black Nationalist Women and the Global Struggle for Freedom* (Philadelphia: University of Pennsylvania Press, 2018), esp. 133–65.

15. Bethune, "Annual Report to the Council," 8.

16. Clark M. Eichelberger, *Organizing for Peace: A Personal History of the Founding of the United Nations* (New York: Harper & Row, 1977), 195–204; Andrew Johnstone, *Dilemmas of Internationalism: The American Association for the United Nations and US Foreign Policy,*

1941–1948 (Farnham, UK: Ashgate, 2009), 53–55; Christopher D. O'Sullivan, *Sumner Welles, Postwar Planning, and the Quest for a New World Order, 1937–1943* (New York: Columbia University Press, 2008); and Stephen Wertheim, *Tomorrow, the World: The Birth of U.S. Global Supremacy* (Cambridge, MA: Harvard University Press, 2020).

17. Vera Micheles Dean, *The Struggle for World Order* (New York: Foreign Policy Association, 1942). See also Andrew Jewett, "Collective Security for Common Men and Women: Vera Micheles Dean and US Foreign Relations," in *Women's International Thought: A New History*, ed. Patricia Owens and Katharina Riestzler (Cambridge: Cambridge University Press, 2021), 306–26.

18. Lena Madesin Phillips to "Sir," February 17, 1942, Box 5, Folder 151, Lena Madesin Philipps Papers, Schlesinger Library, Radcliffe Institute, Cambridge, MA (hereafter Philipps Papers).

19. P[ierre] Waelbroeck to Phillips, February 26, 1942, Box 5, Folder 151, Philipps Papers.

20. "Report of the Chairman of the Interim Planning Committee," April 8, 1943, Box 50, Folder 9, National Committee on the Cause and Cure of War Records, Schlesinger Library, Radcliffe Institute (hereafter NCCCW Records).

21. "Summary of Motions," March 17, 1943, Box 13, Folder 7, NCCCW Records.

22. "Minutes of Conference," September 15, 1942, Box 16, Folder 4, Mary Woolley Papers, Archives and Special Collections, Mount Holyoke College, South Hadley, MA (hereafter Woolley Papers).

23. "Round Table of Representatives of Women's Organizations," October 28, 1942, Box 16, Folder 4, Woolley Papers.

24. "Meeting of the Committee for the Membership of Women in Policy-Shaping Agencies in the Present and Postwar World," February 19, 1943, Box 16, Folder 9, Woolley Papers.

25. Inabel Burns Lindsay, "The Postwar Planning Committee of the NCNW, Inc.," May 31, 1943, Series 5, Folder 415, NCNW Records.

26. Patrick D. Reagan, *Designing New America: The Origins of New Deal Planning, 1890–1943* (Amherst: University of Massachusetts Press, 1999), 216–22.

27. Lindsay, "Postwar Planning Committee."

28. "The Report of the Committee on Findings, the Council Workshop Convention," *Aframerican Woman's Journal* 3, no. 3 (1943): 11.

29. Bethune, "Certain Unalienable Rights," in *What the Negro Wants*, ed. Rayford W. Logan (Chapel Hill: University of North Carolina Press, 1944): 249–50, 258. For similar arguments from African Americans see Von Eschen, *Race Against Empire*; Carol Anderson, *Eyes off the Prize: The United Nations and the African American Struggle for Human Rights, 1944–1955* (New York: Cambridge University Press, 2003); Anderson, *Bourgeois Radicals: The NAACP and the Struggle for Colonial Liberation, 1941–1960* (New York: Cambridge University Press, 2015); and Brenda Gayle Plummer, *Rising Wind: Black Americans and U.S. Foreign Affairs, 1935–1960* (Chapel Hill: University of North Carolina Press, 1996).

30. Stephen C. Schlesinger, *Act of Creation: The Founding of the United Nations—A Story of Superpowers, Secret Agents, Wartime Allies and Enemies, and Their Quest for a Peaceful World* (Boulder, CO: Westview, 2003), 38–47. See also Wertheim, *Tomorrow, the World*; O'Sullivan, *Sumner Welles*; and Patrick J. Hearden, *Architects of Globalism: Building a New World Order During World War II* (Fayetteville: University of Arkansas Press, 2002).

31. Dorothy B. Robins, *Experiment in Democracy: The Story of U.S. Citizen Organizations in Forging the Charter of the United Nations* (New York: Parkside, 1971), 32.

32. "A Message to the Republican and Democratic Conventions from the Negroes of America," *Aframerican Woman's Journal* 4, no. 2 (Summer 1944): 9–10.

33. "A Summary Statement of the Conference," June 14, 1944, Box 8, Folder 1, Charl Williams Papers, Manuscript Division, Library of Congress (hereafter Williams Papers).

34. "Roster of Qualified Women," January 3, 1945, Box 8, Folder 7, Williams Papers.

35. United States State Department, *Questions and Answers on the Dumbarton Oaks Proposals*, Department of State Publication 2218 (Washington, DC: Government Printing Office, 1944), 4.

36. Robert C. Hilderbrand, *Dumbarton Oaks: The Origins of the United Nations and the Search for Postwar Security* (Chapel Hill: University of North Carolina Press, 1990); Hearden, *Architects of Globalism*; Richard Crowder, *Aftermath: The Makers of the Postwar World* (London: I. B. Tauris, 2015); and Georg Schild, *Bretton Woods and Dumbarton Oaks: American Economic and Political Postwar Planning in the Summer of 1944* (New York: St. Martin's, 1995).

37. Andrew Johnstone, "The Perils of Perfectionism: American Reaction to the Dumbarton Oaks Proposals," *Journal of Contemporary History* 54, no. 2 (April 2019): 295; League of Women Voters, *The Story of Dumbarton Oaks by the League of Women Voters* (Washington, DC: National League of Women Voters, 1945); and Robins, *Experiment in Democracy*, 41–43, 179–81.

38. Paul Gordon Lauren, *The Evolution of International Human Rights: Visions Seen* (Philadelphia: University of Pennsylvania Press, 2011), 165–72; Jessie Wallace Hughan, *New Leagues for Old: Blueprints or Foundations?* (New York: Plowshare, 1945), 3; Dorothy Detzer, "Memorandum on Conversation with the Secretary of State," November 30, 1944, Box 41, Folder 33, Women's International League for Peace and Freedom Records, Swarthmore College Peace Collection, Swarthmore, PA; and Edith Wynner, "Searchlight on Dumbarton Oaks," *Common Sense*, December 1944, 422.

39. "Colonial Question Ignored at Dumbarton Oaks Peace Session," *Pittsburgh Courier*, October 28, 1994, 4; and Anderson, *Eyes off the Prize*, 38.

40. "The Annual Workshop: Council Holds Historic Meeting," *Aframerican Woman's Journal* 4, no. 3 (Fall 1944): 11.

41. "Annual Workshop," 11–12.

42. Edward Stettinius, opening remarks, October 16, 1944, Box 169, Harley Notter Files, National Archives and Records Administration II, College Park, MD.

43. "Conferences Attended and Participated in by the NCNW," *Aframerican Woman's Journal* 4, no. 3 (Fall 1944): 12–13.

44. Grace V. Leslie, "'United, We Build a Free World': The Internationalism of Mary McLeod Bethune and the National Council of Negro Women," in *To Turn the Whole World Over: Black Women and Internationalism*, ed. Keisha N. Blain and Tiffany M. Gill (Urbana: University of Illinois Press, 2019), 199–200.

45. "One Point of View," *Aframerican Woman's Journal* (March 1945): 1–2.

46. "Memorandum to the Committee on Administration," April 18, 1945, Box II:A:639, Folder 4, National Association for the Advancement of Colored People Records, Manuscript Division, Library of Congress (hereafter NAACP Records).

47. Bethune to friends, May 10, 1945, Series 5, Folder 497, NCNW Records; and Bethune, "Our Stake in Tomorrow's World," *Aframerican Woman's Journal* (June 1945): 2.

48. Alison M. Parker, *Unceasing Militant: The Life of Mary Church Terrell* (Chapel Hill: University of North Carolina Press, 2020), 148, 284; and Mona L. Siegel, *Peace on Our Terms: The*

Global Battle for Women's Rights After the First World War (New York: Columbia University Press, 2020), 75–83.

49. Acting Secretary of State to Williams, January 31, 1945, Box 8, Folder 7, Williams Papers.

50. Williams to Eleanor Roosevelt, March 1, 1945, Box 7, Folder 2, Williams Papers.

51. Virginia Crocheron Gildersleeve, *Many a Good Crusade: Memoirs* (New York: Macmillan, 1954), 330; and Christy Jo Snider, "Planning for Peace: Virginia Gildersleeve at the United Nations Conference on International Organization," *Peace & Change* 32, no. 2 (April 2007): 179–80.

52. Virginia Gildersleeve, "Woman's Part in the Peace That Is to Come," in *Women's Share in Implementing the Peace* (San Francisco: United Women's Conference, 1945), 60. On republican motherhood, see Linda K. Kerber, *Women of the Republic: Intellect and Ideology in Revolutionary America* (Chapel Hill: University of North Carolina Press, 1980).

53. Quoted in Katherine M. Marino, *Feminism for the Americas: The Making of an International Human Rights Movement* (Chapel Hill: University of North Carolina Press, 2019), 214. On women's roles in San Francisco, see also Glenda Sluga, "'Spectacular Feminism': The International History of Women, World Citizenship and Human Rights," in *Women's Activism: Global Perspectives from the 1890s to the Present*, ed. Francisca de Haan et al. (London: Routledge, 2012), 44–58.

54. Marino, *Feminism for the Americas*, 210–11.

55. NAACP resolution, April 9, 1945, Box II:A:639, Folder 5, NAACP Records. See also Plummer, *Rising Wind*, 132; and "Statement on Behalf of NAACP Delegation to the San Francisco Conference," April 19, 1945, Box II:A:639, Folder 5, NAACP Records.

56. Article 1, Chapter 1, Charter of the United Nations, https://www.un.org/en/about-us/un-charter/chapter-1 (accessed April 26, 2021); Anderson, *Eyes off the Prize*, 43–44; Plummer, *Rising Wind*, 138–39; and Von Eschen, *Race Against Empire*, 78–83.

57. Sue Bailey Thurman, "Behind the Scenes in San Francisco," *Aframerican Woman's Journal* (June 1945): 4.

58. "Unofficial Observers Plead for Equality," *Pittsburgh Courier*, May 5, 1945.

59. Quoted in Plummer, *Rising Wind*, 136.

60. D. G. Gibson, "Berkeley, California," *Chicago Defender*, May 19, 1945, 9; and Leslie, "'United, We Build a Free World,'" 203–4.

61. Bethune to Lyman White, March 21, 1947, Series 5, Folder 497, NCNW Records; and Julie A. Gallagher, "The National Council of Negro Women, Human Rights, and the Cold War," in *Breaking the Wave: Women, Their Organizations, and Feminism, 1945–1985*, ed. Kathleen A. Laughlin and Jacqueline L. Castledine (New York: Routledge, 2011), 85.

62. Sue Bailey Thurman, "Feminine Personalities Brighten Frisco Parley," *Chicago Defender*, June 2, 1945, 18; and *Women's Share in Implementing the Peace*.

63. "Afternoon Session," in *Women's Share in Implementing the Peace*, 55.

64. Gibson, "Berkeley, California."

65. "Statement of Mrs. Mary McLeod Bethune," June 23, 1945, Box 3, Folder 17, Mary McLeod Bethune Papers, Amistad Research Center, Tulane University, New Orleans, LA. Emphasis in original. See also Anderson, *Eyes off the Prize*, 57.

66. Gallagher, "National Council of Negro Women"; and Helen Laville, "Spokeswomen for Democracy: The International Work of the National Council of Negro Women in the Cold War," in *CrossRoutes: The Meanings of "Race" for the 21st Century*, ed. Paola Boi and Sabine Broeck

(Piscataway, NJ: Transaction, 2003), 125–37. On the limits of Bethune's internationalism see Leslie, "'United, We Build a Free World,'" 207–9.

Chapter 7

1. Dorothy Kenyon, "Crossing New Frontiers," June 19, 1949, Box 21, Folder 3, Dorothy Kenyon Papers, Sophia Smith Collection, Smith College, Northampton, MA (hereafter Kenyon Papers).

2. Kenyon, "Crossing New Frontiers."

3. Article I, Chapter 1, Charter of the United Nations, https://www.un.org/en/about-us/un-charter/chapter-1 (accessed April 26, 2021).

4. Kenyon, "Cooperation and World Order," Box 21, Folder 1, Kenyon Papers.

5. "Judge Dorothy Kenyon Is Dead," *New York Times*, February 14, 1972, 32; Susan M. Hartmann, "Kenyon, Dorothy," in *Notable American Women: The Modern Period* (Cambridge, MA: Harvard University Press, 1980), 432–34; and "Transcript of Interview with Dorothy Kenyon," August 18, 1971, Box 4, Folder 7, Kenyon Papers.

6. "Transcript of Interview with Dorothy Kenyon," 8.

7. Kenyon, "The New World Comes of Age," Box 20, Folder 3, Kenyon Papers.

8. Kenyon, "New World Comes of Age."

9. Carol Susan Linskey, "Invisible Politics: Dorothy Kenyon and Women's Internationalism, 1930–1950" (PhD diss., State University of New York, Binghamton, 2013), 139–40. See also Jaci Eisenberg, "The Status of Women: A Bridge from the League of Nations to the United Nations," *Journal of International Organizations Studies* 4, no. 2 (Fall 2013): 8–24; Regula Ludi, "Setting New Standards: International Feminism and the League of Nations' Inquiry into the Status of Women," *Journal of Women's History* 31, no. 1 (March 2019): 12–36; and Carol Miller, "'Geneva—the Key to Equality': Inter-War Feminists and the League of Nations," *Women's History Review* 3, no. 2 (June 1, 1994): 219–45.

10. Quoted in Helen Laville, *Cold War Women: The International Activities of American Women's Organisations* (Manchester: Manchester University Press, 2002), 96.

11. "The Charter," *New York Times*, July 30, 1945, 18.

12. Chapter IX, Article 55, Charter of the United Nations, https://www.un.org/en/about-us/un-charter/chapter-9 (accessed April 26, 2021).

13. Patricia Clavin, *Securing the World Economy: The Reinvention of the League of Nations, 1920–1946* (New York: Oxford University Press, 2013), 307.

14. Virginia Gildersleeve, "Report on San Francisco," July 30, 1945, Box 26, Virginia Crocheron Gildersleeve Papers, Rare Book and Manuscript Library, Columbia University, New York, NY (hereafter Gildersleeve Papers).

15. Virginia Gildersleeve, "Women Must Help Stop Wars," *Woman's Home Companion* 72 (May 1945): 32.

16. Virginia Gildersleeve, "Through the Golden Gate," March 22, 1945, Box 62, Gildersleeve Papers.

17. "Report of Conference on the United Nations and the Special Interests of Women," September 19, 1945, Box II:483, Folder 10, Papers of the League of Women's Voters, Manuscript Division, Library of Congress (hereafter LWV Papers); and "Minutes of Conference on the United Nations and the Special Interests of Women, Wednesday, September 19, 1945, Interdepartmental Auditorium, Washington D.C.," Box 8, Folder C-G-1-1, *Records of the Women's Bureau of the U.S. Department of Labor, 1918–1965*, Part I (Frederick, MD: University Publications of America, 1986).

18. Helen Laville, "A New Era in International Women's Rights? American Women's Associations and the Establishment of the UN Commission on the Status of Women," *Journal of Women's History* 20, no. 4 (2008): 34–56; Karen Garner, *Shaping a Global Women's Agenda: Women's NGOs and Global Governance, 1925–85* (Manchester: Manchester University Press, 2010); and Jo Ella Butterfield, "Gendering 'Universal' Human Rights: International Women's Activism, Gender Politics and the Early Cold War, 1928–1952" (PhD diss., University of Iowa, 2012).

19. "Report of Conference on the United Nations."

20. "Report of Conference on the United Nations"; and "Minutes of Conference on the United Nations."

21. "History of Committee on Legal Status of Women," Series 5, Box 34, Folder 9, National Council of Negro Women Records, National Archives for Black Women's History, Landover, MD (hereafter NCNW Records).

22. "Report of Conference on the United Nations."

23. Kenyon, "The Awakening of Women," Box 21, Folder 2a, Kenyon Papers.

24. "Global Housekeeping" *Backlog for Action*, June 1946.

25. Kenyon, untitled speech, Box 20, Folder 11, Kenyon Papers.

26. "An Act for the Development and Control of Atomic Energy," Pub. L. No. 79–585, 60 Stat. 755 (August 1, 1946).

27. Women's Action Committee, statement, Box 50, Folder 6, Records of the National Committee on the Cause and Cure of War, Schlesinger Library, Radcliffe Institute, Cambridge, MA (hereafter NCCCW Records).

28. Kenyon, "Duties of Citizenship," Box 21, Folder 3, Kenyon Papers.

29. Katherine M. Marino, *Feminism for the Americas: The Making of an International Human Rights Movement* (Chapel Hill: University of North Carolina Press, 2019), esp. 198–224; Helen Laville, "Protecting Difference or Promoting Equality? US Government Approaches to Women's Rights and the UN Commission on the Status of Women, 1945–50," *Comparative American Studies* 5, no. 3 (September 2007): 291–305; and Butterfield, "Gendering 'Universal' Human Rights," 176–228.

30. *The United Nations and the Advancement of Women, 1945–1996*, rev. ed. (New York: United Nations Department of Public Information, 1996), 3.

31. Garner, *Shaping a Global Women's Agenda*, 179.

32. Eisenberg, "Status of Women," 15.

33. Kenyon, "We and the United Nations," *Pioneer Woman*, March 1948, Box 21, Folder 1, Kenyon Papers; "Convention on the Political Rights of Women, Adopted by the General Assembly on 20 December 1952," in *United Nations and the Advancement of Women*, 164; and Devaki Jain, *Women, Development, and the UN: A Sixty-Year Quest for Equality and Justice* (Bloomington: Indiana University Press, 2005), 23.

34. Kenyon, "Awakening of Women."

35. Kenyon, "The United Nations: The Hope of the World," Box 21, Folder 1, Kenyon Papers.

36. Louise Michele Newman, *White Women's Rights: The Racial Origins of Feminism in the United States* (New York: Oxford University Press, 1999); and Antoinette M. Burton, *Burdens of History: British Feminists, Indian Women, and Imperial Culture, 1865–1915* (Chapel Hill: University of North Carolina Press, 1994).

37. Jain, *Women, Development, and the UN*, 25.

38. Nova Robinson, "Arab Internationalism and Gender: Perspectives from the Third Session of the United Nations Commission on the Status of Women, 1949," *International Journal of Middle East Studies* 48, no. 3 (August 2016): 578–83.

39. Kenyon to Mme. Khaddoura, June 3, 1949, Box 57, Folder 11, Kenyon Papers.

40. Dorothy Kenyon, "Beirut: East and West Women Meet," *Women Lawyers Journal* 36, no. 1 (1950): 4–5.

41. Quoted in Laville, *Cold War Women*, 114. On the WIDF, see Francisca de Haan, "The Women's International Democratic Federation (WIDF): History, Main Agenda and Contributions, 1945–1991," in *Women and Social Movements International, 1840 to Present*, ed. Thomas Dublin and Kathryn Kish Sklar (Alexandria, VA: Alexander Street Press, 2012).

42. Quoted in Laville, *Cold War Women*, 115.

43. Kenyon to Bodil Begtrup, April 1, 1948, Box 57, Folder 1, Kenyon Papers.

44. Harold Josephson, "The Search for Lasting Peace: Internationalism and Foreign Policy, 1920–1950," in *Peace Movements and Political Cultures*, ed. Charles Chatfield and Peter van den Dungen (Knoxville: University of Tennessee Press, 1988), 205.

45. Walter LaFeber, *America, Russia, and the Cold War, 1945–2006*, 10th ed. (Boston: McGraw-Hill, 2008), 48; and Anthony Gaglione, *The United Nations Under Trygve Lie, 1945–1953* (Lanham, MD: Scarecrow, 2001), 35.

46. "American News: League of Women Voters and the President," *International Women's News* 42, no. 2 (1947): 27.

47. "American News: League of Women Voters and the President."

48. Gaglione, *United Nations Under Trygve Lie*, 90–91.

49. Laville, *Cold War Women*, 105–7.

50. McCarthy quoted in William S. White, "McCarthy Says Miss Kenyon Helped 28 Red Front Groups," *New York Times*, March 9, 1950, 1; and White, "McCarthy Accuses Point Four Official," *New York Times*, March 14, 1950, 4.

51. Kenyon quoted in White, "McCarthy Says Miss Kenyon Helped 28 Red Front Groups"; and Brunauer quoted in White, "McCarthy Accuses Point Four Official."

52. Landon R. Y. Storrs, *The Second Red Scare and the Unmaking of the New Deal Left* (Princeton: Princeton University Press, 2013); Kate Weigand, *Red Feminism: American Communism and the Making of Women's Liberation* (Baltimore: Johns Hopkins University Press, 2001); Laura McEnaney, *Civil Defense Begins at Home: Militarization Meets Everyday Life in the Fifties* (Princeton: Princeton University Press, 2000); and Laville, *Cold War Women*.

53. Paige Meltzer, "'The Pulse and Conscience of America': The General Federation and Women's Citizenship, 1945–1960," *Frontiers: A Journal of Women Studies* 30, no. 3 (September 2009): 59.

54. "Women's Organizations: Mobilize," transcript, October 6, 1950, Box 7, Folder 146, Lucy Somerville Howorth Papers, Schlesinger Library, Radcliffe Institute.

55. Quoted in Margaret Nunnelley Olsen, "One Nation, One World: American Clubwomen and the Politics of Internationalism, 1945–1961" (PhD diss., Rice University, 2008), 69.

56. Kenyon, "What Women Have Done," November 14, 1950, Box 21, Folder 6, Kenyon Papers.

Chapter 8

1. Rosika Schwimmer and Edith Wynner, "Memorandum on Immediate Action for World Government," February 19, 1945, Box 6, Folder 1, Campaign for World Government, Records of

the New York Office, Manuscripts and Archives Division, New York Public Library, New York, NY (hereafter CWG NY Records).

2. Wynner to Al Wynner, July 9, 1991, Box 9, Folder 4, Edith Wynner Papers, Manuscripts and Archives Division, New York Public Library (hereafter Wynner Papers).

3. Wynner to Al Wynner, January 8, 1991, Box 9, Folder 4, Wynner Papers.

4. Edith Wynner and Georgia Lloyd, *Searchlight on Peace Plans: Choose Your Road to World Government* (New York: E. P. Dutton, 1944); and Malvina Lindsay, "Girls Present Peace Plans in Capsules," *Washington Post*, June 17, 1944.

5. Wynner to Gerry Krauss, December 7, 1949, Box AA7, Folder 1, Rosika Schwimmer–Lola Maverick Lloyd Papers, Manuscripts and Archives Division, New York Public Library (hereafter Lloyd Papers).

6. Wynner, "Timid Angels," 1944, Box 49, Folder 8, Wynner Papers. Emphasis in original.

7. Wynner, "The People, the Charter, and the Atomic Bomb," *News from World Citizens*, May 1945, 5; and Wynner, "Memo II on a Peoples' World Constitutional Convention," September 25, 1946, Box 8, Folder 4, CWG NY Records.

8. Wynner to Jessie Wallace Hughan, April 23, 1945, Box 4, Folder 3, Wynner Papers.

9. "Letters to the *Times*: Peace by Law Our One Hope," *New York Times*, October 10, 1945, 20.

10. "Einstein on the Atomic Bomb," *Atlantic* 176 (November 1945): 44; Lawrence Wittner, *One World or None: A History of the World Nuclear Disarmament Movement Through 1953*, vol. 1 of *The Struggle Against the Bomb* (Stanford: Stanford University Press, 1993), 59–66; and Joseph Preston Baratta, *The Politics of World Federation*, vol. 1, *United Nations, UN Reform, Atomic Control* (Westport, CT: Praeger, 2004), 127–39.

11. Wynner to Fyke Farmer, December 6, 1945, Box 14, Folder 5, CWG NY Records; Wynner to John L. Balderston Jr., June 18, 1946, Box 6, Folder 1, CWG NY Records; Albert Einstein to Wynner [translated by Wynner], September 27, 1954, Box 40, Folder 2, Georgia Lloyd Papers, Manuscripts and Archives Division, New York Public Library; and Wynner, "People, Charter, and Atomic Bomb," 6.

12. Wittner, *One World or None*, 55.

13. Baratta, *Politics of World Federation*, vol. 1, 177–98.

14. Wendell L. Willkie, *One World* (New York: Simon and Schuster, 1943); Samuel Zipp, *The Idealist: Wendell Willkie's Wartime Quest to Build One World* (Cambridge, MA: Harvard University Press, 2020); and David Levering Lewis, *The Improbable Wendell Willkie: The Businessman Who Saved the Republican Party and His Country, and Conceived a New World Order* (New York: Liveright, 2018).

15. Niels Bohr, "Science and Civilization," in *One World or None*, ed. Dexter Masters and Katharine Way (New York: Whittlesey House, 1946), ix. For a more global perspective on the internationalism of the immediate postwar period, see Glenda Sluga, *Internationalism in the Age of Nationalism* (Philadelphia: University of Pennsylvania Press, 2013), 79–87.

16. Emery Reves, *The Anatomy of Peace*, 2d ed. (New York: Harper, 1945), 274, 125; and Fritz Bartel, "Surviving the Years of Grace: The Atomic Bomb and the Specter of World Government, 1945–1950," *Diplomatic History* 39, no. 2 (April 2015): 284.

17. Mildred Blake, Letter to the Editor, *New York Times*, February 12, 1939, 81.

18. "Reminiscences of Mildred Riordan Blake," Columbia Center for Oral History, Butler Library, Columbia University, New York, NY.

19. Americans United for World Government, undated resolution, Box 13, Folder 6, Florence Jaffray Harriman Papers, Manuscript Division, Library of Congress (hereafter Harriman Papers).

20. Harriman to Raymond Gram Swing, March 2, 1946, Box 13, Folder 6, Harriman Papers. Emphasis in original.

21. Wynner, "Memorandum on an Action Program to Secure Federal World Government," January 31, 1946, Box 6, Folder 1, CWG NY Records.

22. Press release, May 24, 1945, Box 95, Folder 1, Campaign for World Government, Records of the Chicago Office, New York Public Library (hereafter CWG Chicago Records).

23. Lloyd Jr. to Georgia Lloyd, July 2, 1945, Box 56, Folder 5, Georgia Lloyd Papers.

24. Wynner, "Memorandum on an Action Program."

25. Wynner, "Memorandum on an Action Program."

26. Wynner, "Memorandum II on Action to End War and Organize a Peoples' World Constitutional Convention," September 25, 1946, Box 8, Folder 4, CWG NY Records.

27. Wynner, "Memorandum II on Action to End War."

28. Wynner, "Outline of a World Constitution," August 12, 1946, Box 15, Folder 7, CWG NY Records.

29. Wynner to Pearl Buck, March 25, 1945, Box 4, Folder 2, Wynner Papers.

30. Wynner, "Memorandum II on Action to End War."

31. Wynner, "Memorandum II on Action to End War."

32. United Nations, "Universal Declaration of Human Rights," December 10, 1948, https://www.un.org/en/about-us/universal-declaration-of-human-rights (accessed April 26, 2021). On its drafting, see Paul Gordon Lauren, *The Evolution of International Human Rights: Visions Seen*, 3rd ed. (Philadelphia: University of Pennsylvania Press, 2011); Mary Ann Glendon, *A World Made New: Eleanor Roosevelt and the Universal Declaration of Human Rights* (New York: Random House, 2001); and Johannes Morsink, *The Universal Declaration of Human Rights: Origins, Drafting, and Intent* (Philadelphia: University of Pennsylvania Press, 1999).

33. Wynner to Henry Usborne, September 29, 1946, Box 14, Folder 7, CWG NY Records.

34. Stephen Wertheim, *Tomorrow, the World: The Birth of U.S. Global Supremacy* (Cambridge, MA: Harvard University Press, 2020), 115–44.

35. Wynner, "Memorandum on an Action Program."

36. Mildred Riordan Blake to Georgia Lloyd, September 11, 1946, Box 26, Folder 4, CWG Chicago Records; and Wynner to Usborne, November 12, 1946, Box 14, Folder 8, CWG NY Records.

37. Harriman to Raymond Gram Swing, March 2, 1946, Box 13, Folder 6, Harriman Papers.

38. Usborne to Wynner and Schwimmer, August 29, 1945, Box 14, Folder 5, CWG NY Records; Usborne to Wynner, October 1, 1945, Box 4, Folder 3, Wynner Papers; Usborne to Wynner, November 11, 1945, Box 14, Folder 5, CWG NY Records; and Wynner to Usborne, December 6, 1945, Box 14, Folder 5, CWG NY Records.

39. Wynner, "People, Charter, and Atomic Bomb," 6.

40. Georgia Lloyd, "Federalists Meet in Asheville," Box 59, Folder 9, Georgia Lloyd Papers; and "Minutes of World Government Congress," February 21–23, 1947, Box 22, Folder 1, Harriman Papers. See also Baratta, *Politics of World Federation*, vol. 1, 215–34.

41. Wynner to Georgia Lloyd, January 28, 1947, Box 37, Folder 7, Georgia Lloyd Papers; and Wynner to Usborne, February 25, 1947, Box 24, Folder 2, CWG NY Records.

42. Wynner, excerpt of dinner speech, February 22, 1947, Box 24, Folder 2, CWG NY Records.

43. Wynner to Usborne, February 25, 1947, and Wynner to Farmer, February 27, 1947, Box 24, Folder 2, CWG NY Records.

44. "The Crisis of 1947," Box 21, Folder 2, Harriman Papers.

45. Wynner to Usborne, December 8, 1947, Box 14, Folder 9, CWG NY Records.

46. Gilbert A. Harrison, *A Timeless Affair: The Life of Anita McCormick Blaine* (Chicago: University of Chicago Press, 1979); James C. Schneider, "Blaine, Anita Eugenie McCormick," in *Biographical Dictionary of Internationalists*, ed. Warren F. Kuehl (Westport, CT: Greenwood, 1983), 78–80; and "Mrs. Anita Blaine Is Dead in Chicago," *New York Times*, February 13, 1954, 13.

47. Wynner to Mary and Georgia Lloyd, October 27, 1947, Box 29, Folder 6, CWG Chicago Papers.

48. Wynner to Farmer, July 12, 1947, Box 5, Folder 4, Wynner Papers.

49. Wynner to Patrick Armstrong, July 1, 1948, Box 454, Folder 5, Rosika Schwimmer Papers, Manuscripts and Archives Division, New York Public Library (hereafter Schwimmer Papers); and Mary Lloyd to Wynner, July 5, 1948, Box 40, Folder 4, Georgia Lloyd Papers.

50. Quoted in Baratta, *Politics of World Federation*, vol. 2, *From World Federation to Global Governance* (Westport, CT: Praeger, 2004), 392; and "Minutes of Pocono Pines Coordinating Committee," August 10, 1948, Box 15, Folder 10, CWG NY Records.

51. "Angel's Millions Gives Wallace Post-Vote Job," *New York World-Telegram*, September 14, 1948, 1; "For Wallace's World," *Newsweek*, September 20, 1948, 35; and "$1,000,000 Nobody Wants," *Manchester Guardian*, September 17, 1948, Box 1, Folder 2, Frieda Langer Lazarus Papers, Manuscripts and Archives Division, New York Public Library.

52. Quoted in Baratta, *Politics of World Federation*, vol. 2, 393; and Wynner to Lloyds, February 27, 1950, Box 38, Folder 1, Georgia Lloyd Papers.

53. Mary Lloyd to Wynner, August 16, 1948, Box 455, Folder 6, Schwimmer Papers; and Juanita Lutz to Wynner, October 13, 1948, Box 15, Folder 10, CWG NY Records. Quoted in "Estate of Anita McCormick Blaine, deceased . . . v. Commissioner of Internal Revenue," Tax Court of the United States, September 20, 1954, Box 16, Folder 4, CWG NY Records.

54. Wynner to Mary Lloyd, November 19, 1949, Box 15, Folder 2, CWG NY Records.

55. Wynner, "Observations on Federalist Policy and the Korean War," August 11, 1950, Box 146, Folder 1, Jessie Lloyd O'Connor Papers, Sophia Smith Collection, Smith College, Northampton, MA.

56. Edith Wynner, *World Federal Government: Why? What? How? In Maximum Terms—Proposals for United Nations Charter Revision* (Afton, NY: Fedonat, 1954), 81.

57. Wynner to Norton Gerber, June 19, 1950, Box AA9, Folder 8, Schwimmer-Lloyd Collection, Manuscripts and Archives Division, New York Public Library.

Conclusion

1. H. Con. Res. 64, 81st Cong., 1st Sess. (1949).

2. *Revision of the United Nations Charter: Hearings Before a Subcommittee of the Committee on Foreign Relations, United States Senate* (Washington, DC: Government Printing Office, 1950), 675.

3. *Revision of the United Nations Charter*, 562.

4. *Revision of the United Nations Charter*, 374.

5. *To Seek Development of the United Nations into a World Federation: Hearings Before the Committee on Foreign Affairs, House of Representatives*, 81st Congress, 1st Session (Washington, DC: Government Printing Office, 1949), 262.

6. "Mrs. Edwin Mead, 80, Peace Worker, Dead," *New York Times*, November 2, 1936, 21.

7. Lucia Ames Mead, "Averting Strife," Letter to the Editor, *New York Times*, August 23, 1936, E9.

8. Warren F. Kuehl, "Andrews, Fannie Fern Phillips," in *Notable American Women, 1607–1950*, ed. Edward T. James and Janet Wilson James, vol. 1 (Cambridge, MA: Harvard University Press, 1971), 92–94; and Fannie Fern Andrews, *Memory Pages of My Life* (Boston: Talisman, 1948), 188.

9. Florence Guertin Tuttle, "I Travelled Hopefully," unpublished autobiography, Box 1, Folder 4, Florence Guertin Tuttle Papers, Sophia Smith Collection, Smith College, Northampton, MA.

10. Emily Greene Balch, Letter to the Editor, *New York Times*, August 13, 1948, 14.

11. "Esther C. Brunauer," *Washington Post*, June 28, 1959; and "Mrs. Esther Brunauer, 57, Dead," *New York Times*, June 27, 1959, 23.

12. Mary McLeod Bethune, "United Nations Day Is Renewal of Our Faith in Peaceful World," *Chicago Defender*, October 8, 1949, 6; Bethune, "Mrs. Bethune's Home Town in Florida Becoming Big Little World," *Chicago Defender*, March 28, 1953, 11; Elaine M. Smith, "Bethune, Mary McLeod," in *Notable American Women: The Modern Period* (Cambridge, MA: Harvard University Press, 1980); Joyce Ann Hanson, *Mary McLeod Bethune and Black Women's Political Activism* (Columbia: University of Missouri Press, 2003), 202–3; and "Our Opinions: Mrs. Mary McLeod Bethune," *Chicago Defender*, May 28, 1955, 9.

13. Susan M. Hartmann, "Kenyon, Dorothy," in *Notable American Women: The Modern Period* (Cambridge, MA: Harvard University Press, 1980), 433.

14. Wynner to Henry Usborne, October 17, 1949, Box 24, Folder 7, Campaign for World Government, Records of the New York Office, New York Public Library, New York, NY.

15. *Revision of the United Nations Charter*, 400–2.

16. "Report of the Senate Committee on Foreign Relations on Revision of the United Nations Charter," in *Review of the United Nations Charter: A Collection of Documents* (Washington, DC: Government Printing Office, 1954), 866.

17. J. T. Murray to Wynner, December 22, 1976, Box 40, Folder 7, Georgia Lloyd Papers, Manuscripts and Archives Division, New York Public Library. For an example of Wynner's territoriality, see her correspondence with Joseph Baratta, Box 6, Folder 9, Edith Wynner Papers, Manuscripts and Archives Division, New York Public Library.

18. Teju Cole, "The White-Savior Industrial Complex," *Atlantic*, March 21, 2012, https://www.theatlantic.com/international/archive/2012/03/the-white-savior-industrial-complex/254843/ (accessed April 20, 2021).

19. Tuttle, "I Travelled Hopefully," III, 8.

INDEX

ACKNOWLEDGMENTS

The first thing I did when I decided to investigate the phrase "citizen of the world" was to search for it on *Women and Social Movements, International* (Alexander Street). Had that resource not existed, I'm not sure I would have realized there was a book to be written on the concept. Thank you to Thomas Dublin, Kathryn Kish Sklar, and their team for the hard work that went into the database.

Research for this book would not have been possible without the assistance of librarians and archivists across the country. First and foremost, thank you to the wonderful staff at the Denison Library, including Amy Elliott, Earl Griffiths, Kent Huffman, Rachel Krak, Pam Magelaner, Carol Miller, and interlibrary loan specialist extraordinaire Susan Rice. They make it possible to do intensive research at a small college in a small town—even during a pandemic. Thank you also to Thomas Lannon and the staff of the New York Public Library Manuscripts and Archives Division; Sarah Hutcheon, Amanda Strauss, and everyone at the Schlesinger Library; Wendy Chmielewski and others at the Swarthmore College Peace Collection; Mary Biddle and the staff at the Sophia Smith Collection; Micha Broadnax at the Mount Holyoke Archives and Special Collections; and Kenneth Chandler at the National Archives for Black Women's History. Much of this research was supported by an R. C. Good Fellowship from Denison University, by grants from the Denison University Research Foundation, and by a short-term fellowship from the New York Public Library. Several Denison students also provided valuable assistance, including Anne Finn, Nikki Hurley, Kaitlyn Specht, and Ellie Thien.

Critical feedback on various parts of this book made the end result much stronger. In particular I want to thank Brooke Blower, Mark Bradley, Katherine Marino, Julie Mujic, Andrew Preston, Amy Sayward, Bonnie Smith, David Steigerwald, Sandra VanBurkleo, and Sharon Wood. There are others whose names I don't know; I'm grateful to all the anonymous peer reviewers over the last eight years who read and commented on fellowship proposals, article submissions, and my promotion dossier. At Penn, thank you to Bob Lockhart, Jennifer Mittelstadt, Christopher Dietrich, and especially Eileen Boris and the other manuscript reviewer. Members of the Denison history department have provided not just feedback but also support and collegiality; my thanks to Lauren Araiza, Adam Davis, Leslie Hempson, Trey Proctor, Mitchell Snay, Karen Spierling, Jo Tague, Shao-yun Yang, and Adrian Young, and extra thanks to Hoda Yousef for organizing our summer writing groups. Other fellow historians bolstered this book and its author at key moments, in ways both large and small. For their help and encouragement, I want to acknowledge Eileen Boris, Jo Butterfield, Ellen DuBois, Kristin Hoganson, Kimberly Jensen, Linda Kerber, Paul Kramer, Michael McGandy, Katherine Sibley, and Glenda Sluga.

Finally, my network of friends and family continues to sustain me. Thanks to Marlaine Browning, Courtney Gerber, Sarah Hunt, Hannah Miller, Julie Mujic, and Adam, Heather, Mabel, and Penny Rhodes. I'm especially grateful for Brian Threlkeld, Taylor Proctor, and my husband, Trey Proctor. This book is dedicated to my mom, Laurisa Sellers; my dad, Mark Threlkeld; and my stepdad, Arnie Shore. I couldn't ask for three more loving, supportive parents.

CPSIA information can be obtained
at www.ICGtesting.com
Printed in the USA
LVHW110854290322
714353LV00007B/5/J